A NEW QUEST
OF THE
HISTORICAL JESUS
And Other Essays

JAMES M. ROBINSON

FORTRESS PRESS   PHILADELPHIA

Foreword © 1983 by Fortress Press

A New Quest of the Historical Jesus was first published by SCM Press, Ltd., London, 1959.

"The Formal Structure of Jesus' Message" was first published in *Current Issues in New Testament Interpretation: Essays in Honor of Otto A. Piper,* edited by William Klassen and Graydon F. Snyder (New York: Harper & Row, 1962), pp. 91–110, 273–84, and is reprinted by permission.

"The Recent Debate on the 'New Quest'" was first published in *The Journal of Bible and Religion* 30 (1962): 198–208, and is reprinted by permission.

"Albert Schweitzer's *Quest of the Historical Jesus* Today" was first published as an introduction to Schweitzer's book in German, *Die Geschichte der Leben-Jesu-Forschung* (Taschenbuch-Ausgabe; Munich and Hamburg: Siebenstern Taschenbuch, 1966), pp. 7–24, and in English, *The Quest of the Historical Jesus* (New York: Macmillan Co., 1968), pp. xi–xxxiii.

"Jesus' Parables as God Happening," by James M. Robinson, reprinted from *Jesus and the Historian: Written in Honor of Ernest Cadman Colwell.* Copyright © MCMLXVIII The Westminster Press. Reprinted by permission.

Biblical quotations, unless otherwise noted, are from the Revised Standard Version of the Bible, copyright 1946, 1952, © 1971, 1973 by the Division of Christian Education of the National Council of the Churches of Christ in the U.S.A. and are used by permission.

First Fortress Press Edition 1983

Library of Congress Cataloging in Publication Data

Robinson, James McConkey, 1924–
    A new quest of the historical Jesus and other essays.

    Includes bibliographical references and indexes.
        1. Jesus Christ—Historicity—Addresses, essays,
    lectures.   2. Demythologization—Addresses, essays,
    lectures.   3. Bultmann, Rudolf Karl, 1884–1976—
    Addresses, essays, lectures.   4. Jesus Christ—Teachings
    —Addresses, essays, lectures.   5. Jesus Christ—Parables
    —Addresses, essays, lectures.   I. Title.
    BT303.2.R63 1983   232.9'08   82–48586
    ISBN 0–8006–1698–7

9768182   Printed in the United States of America   1–1698

CONTENTS

LIST OF ABBREVIATIONS

BEvT	Beiträge to *Evangelische Theologie*
BHT	Beiträge zur historischen Theologie
BZ, n.F.	*Biblische Zeitschrift*, neue Folge
BZNW	Beihefte to *Zeitschrift für die neutestamentliche Wissenschaft*
ChrW	*Die Christliche Welt*
ET	English Translation
EVB	Ernst Käsemann, *Evangelische Versuche und Besinnungen*
EvTh	*Evangelische Theologie*
ExpT	*The Expository Times*
FRLANT	Forschungen zur Religion und Literatur des Alten und Neuen Testaments
GuV	Rudolf Bultmann, *Glauben und Verstehen*
HTR	*Harvard Theological Review*
JBR	*The Journal of Bible and Religion*
JBL	*Journal of Biblical Literature*
JTS, n.s.	*Journal of Theological Studies*, new series
KD	Karl Barth, *Kirchliche Dogmatik*, 1932 ff.
KuD	*Kerygma und Dogma*
KuM	*Kerygma und Mythos*, ed. H. W. Bartsch, 1948–55
RGG	*Die Religion in Geschichte und Gegenwart*
SBT	Studies in Biblical Theology
SgV	*Sammlung gemeinverständlicher Vorträge*
SThU	*Schweizerische theologische Umschau*
STK	*Svensk Teologisk Kvartalskrift*
TB	*Theologische Blätter*
TF	*Theologische Forschung*
TLZ	*Theologische Literaturzeitung*
TR, n.F.	*Theologische Rundschau*, neue Folge
TZ	*Theologische Zeitschrift*
TDNT	*Theological Dictionary of the New Testament*
TWNT	*Theologisches Worterbüch zum Neuen Testament*
USQR	*Union Seminary Quarterly Review*
Vuf	*Verkündigung und Forschung*
ZNW	*Zeitschrift für die neutestamentliche Wissenschaft*
ZTK	*Zeitschrift für Theologie und Kirche*

FOREWORD

A New Quest of the Historical Jesus was first published in 1959 by SCM Press in Great Britain and by Alec R. Allenson in the United States; it underwent a seventh impression by Lewis Reprints Ltd. in 1971, and was reprinted by Scholars Press in 1979. Since it is here again reprinted in its original form, it may be useful to sketch not only its origin but also its subsequent evolution in other publications.

A New Quest of the Historical Jesus grew out of a paper entitled "The Kerygma and the Quest of the Historical Jesus" presented in September 1957 at the Congress on "The Four Gospels in 1957" at Christ Church, Oxford. The original address was published in *Theology Today* 15 (1958): 183–197 as "The Quest of the Historical Jesus Today," with but minor editing and an assimilation of its title to that of the journal. Furthermore a representative of SCM Press who heard the presentation at Oxford arranged a meeting with the publisher in London at the conclusion of the Congress. He suggested that the quantity of German jargon could be reduced, beginning with the title, and proposed that the text be enlarged to the format of the Studies in Biblical Theology series.

The title finally agreed upon for the book, *A New Quest of the Historical Jesus,* was thus in a sense an afterthought. It was not intended to suggest the presumption latent in the current short title *"the* new quest." Nor was it intended to ignore Rudolf Bultmann's *Jesus and the Word,* first published in 1926, as a valid precursor. Rather the book argues that the kind of quest there exemplified, though not carried forward by Bultmann himself, was a possible and legitimate development of the Bultmannian position. It was in this sense that the term "post-Bultmannian" was coined (see page 19 below). Hence the main American critique of the book,

5

Van A. Harvey and Schubert M. Ogden's essay "How New Is the 'New Quest of the Historical Jesus'?" in *The Historical Jesus and the Kerygmatic Christ: Essays on the New Quest of the Historical Jesus,* edited by Carl E. Braaten and Roy A. Harrisville in 1964, pp. 197–242, has seemed in this regard an uncalled-for misreading, and hence hardly the basis for an ongoing debate of much substance.

When *A New Quest of the Historical Jesus* was on the brink of publication I used the manuscript as the basis for a lecture course in the summer semester of 1959 at the University of Göttingen. My German assistant Heinz-Dieter Knigge translated the English manuscript into German, which I revised and enlarged in terms of the ongoing German debate which at that time was at its peak. Especially important was a lengthy letter Bultmann had written on receipt of an off-print of my article "The Quest of the Historical Jesus Today," in which he anticipated in large part the guarded criticism he made public during that semester in his address of 25 July 1959 to the Heidelberg Academy of Sciences on "The Primitive Christian Kerygma and the Historical Jesus," published in English in *The Historical Jesus and the Kerygmatic Christ,* pp. 15–42. The resulting class lectures in turn became the basis for a much larger 192-page German edition of the book, under a title reverting back to that of the original address, *Kerygma und historischer Jesus* (Zürich and Stuttgart: Zwingli-Verlag, 1960). A quite inadequate French translation of the German edition by Étienne de Peyer was published without my having been consulted: *Le kérygme de l'église et le Jésus de l'histoire* (Nouvelle série théologique 11; Geneva: Labor et Fides, 1961).

The updating expansions of the German edition were not incorporated in the English edition, although some of this material has appeared in other forms. An essay mentioned as forthcoming on p. 121 of the English edition was published under the title "The Formal Structure of Jesus' Message" in *Current Issues in New Testament Interpretation: Essays in Honor of Otto A. Piper,* edited by William Klassen and Graydon F. Snyder (New York: Harper & Row, 1962), pp. 91–110, 273–84. The debate with Bultmann was summarized in a paper on "The Recent Debate on the 'New Quest'" that comprised part of a symposium on the "New Quest of the Historical Jesus" at the annual meeting of the National Association of Biblical

Instructors on 29–30 December 1961; it was published in *The Journal of Bible and Religion* 30 (1962), 198–208. These two essays are reprinted in the present volume as Chapters VI and VII.

The new quest reached its most valid formulation in 1962 in Gerhard Ebeling's response to Bultmann in his book *Theology and Proclamation: Dialogue with Bultmann.* This decisive phase of the discussion was incorporated in a second, again appreciably enlarged 264-page edition of *Kerygma und historischer Jesus* completed in the summer of 1965, again with the able assistance of Heinz-Dieter Knigge, and published in 1967. It also included, though largely relegated to long footnotes, detailed responses to the criticisms of Harvey and Ogden, since their essay had appeared in German already in 1962. It was my intention to translate this edition back into English. But a sabbatic year as Annual Professor at the American School of Oriental Research in Jerusalem in 1965–66 led instead to my gaining access to unpublished parts of the Nag Hammadi codices. On my return it seemed more important to make that otherwise inaccessible primary source material available to the scholarly community as rapidly as possible than it was to make accessible in English my own work which was already available in German. Hence my further involvement in the discussion was limited to such items as an Introduction to Albert Schweitzer's *Quest of the Historical Jesus* for the German edition of 1966 and the paperback American edition (New York: Macmillan, 1968), pp. xi–xxxiii, as well as an essay on "Jesus' Parables as God Happening" in *Jesus and the Historian: Written in Honor of Ernest Cadman Colwell,* edited by F. Thomas Trotter (Philadelphia: Westminster Press, 1968), pp. 134–50. These two essays are reprinted in the present volume as Chapters VIII and IX.

In the intervening period there has not only been the perennially ongoing, though somewhat disappointing, usual research on the historical Jesus, reported in great detail by Werner Georg Kümmel in the *Theologische Rundschau* 40 (1975), 289–336; 41 (1976), 197–258, 295–363; 43 (1978), 105–61, 233–65; 45 (1980), 40–84, 293–337; and 47 (1982), 136–65. Indeed the revolutionary epoch of the '60s brought with it still further contexts in which to translate Jesus. Suddenly the politicizing approach of S. G. F. Brandon in such works as his *Jesus and the Zealots: A Study of the Political*

Factor in Primitive Christianity (1967) and *The Trial of Jesus of Nazareth* (1968) took on contemporaneity. Oscar Cullmann's *Jesus and the Revolutionaries* (1970) and Martin Hengel's *Was Jesus a Revolutionist?* (1971) sought to calm all this down, a debate that found American expression in G. R. Edwards' *Jesus and the Politics of Violence* (1972). Gradually an approach more oriented to the social sciences began to emerge in Germany, in Gerd Theissen's *Sociology of Early Palestinian Christianity* (1978) and, not yet in English, the successor to Günther Bornkamm's *Jesus of Nazareth* with which the new quest had begun back in 1956 in the German paperback series of W. Kohlhammer: Luise Schottroff and Wolfgang Stegemann's *Jesus von Nazareth: Hoffnung der Armen* (*Jesus of Nazareth: Hope of the Poor*). They seek to establish precisely what the socio-economic status was of those who heard Jesus, so as to assess in these terms the reality of what happened in the public ministry of Jesus and continued in the congregations from which Q and Luke emanated. From the Parables Seminar of the Society of Biblical Literature has emerged a new focus on Jesus' message not as a coded theology, but as irreplacable loaded language, itself triggering the reality of what it is talking about; Jesus' metaphor shatters the familiar world of us all (what Jewish and Christian apocalypticism called the present evil aeon), thus freeing the attentive listener (he who has ears to hear) for God's reign, the strange new world that is not a world out in the sky somewhere that is about to come, has been delayed in coming, will nonetheless come at some predicted moment, or the like, but that is our shattered familiar world returned to us anew. I hope to get involved in the next stage of this rethinking of Jesus in terms of the collection of Jesus' sayings familiarly known as Q. Thus the quest of the historical Jesus has taken another turn, upsetting to some, exciting to some, challenging to all who understand what is taking place—the appropriate responses for every generation that confronts the historical Jesus.

quite different kind of quest based upon new premises, procedures and objectives, a quest which may well succeed in a way the other did not. For a new and promising point of departure has been worked out by precisely those scholars who are most acutely aware of the difficulties of the previous quest.[1] As a matter of fact this new development is recognized in its full significance only when one observes that it forms a central thrust in a second, 'post-Bultmannian' phase of post-war German theology.

Clearly the first phase of post-war German theology was the rise of the Bultmannian position to the centre of debate. The cumulative weight of Bultmann's prodigious career, focused into the concrete programme of demythologizing, burst like a meteor into the void caused by the attrition of the Nazi ideology, the war and post-war collapse, and the passing of such leading New Testament scholars as Lietzmann, Büchsel, Behm, von Soden, Loh-

---

of Christ' (*ExpT* LII, 1941–2, 60–65, 175–7, 248–51), with contributions by Vincent Taylor, C. J. Cadoux and T. W. Manson, is noteworthy for the unanimous rejection of the possibility of a real 'biography', and the almost equally unanimous assumption of a mediating position which is merely a sobered version of the original quest. Each contributor has subsequently published his life of Christ: Vincent Taylor, *The Life and Ministry of Jesus*, 1955; C. J. Cadoux, *Life of Jesus*, 1948; T. W. Manson, *The Servant-Messiah: A Study of the Public Ministry of Jesus*, 1953. A cross-section of views is found in Thomas S. Kepler, *Contemporary Thinking about Jesus; An Anthology*, 1944, and H. D. A. Major, T. W. Manson, C. J. Wright, *The Mission and Message of Jesus; An Exposition of the Gospels in the Light of Modern Research*, 1937. The most important American biography is probably still S. J. Case, *Jesus—A New Biography*, 1927. The difficulty of the quest found its classic English expression in R. H. Lightfoot's *History and Interpretation in the Gospels* (The Bampton Lectures for 1934). Steps in the direction of a new approach are found in R. C. Johnson, 'The Jesus of History and the Christian Faith', *Theology Today*, X, 1953, 170–84; W. Norman Pittenger, 'The Problem of the Historical Jesus', *Anglican Theological Review*, XXXVI, 1954, 89–93; R. H. Fuller, *The Mission and Achievement of Jesus*, 1954, and 'Some Problems of New Testament Christology', *Anglican Theological Review*, XXXVIII, 1956, 146–52; and the books of John Knox: *The Man Christ Jesus*, 1942; *Christ the Lord*, 1945; *On the Meaning of Christ*, 1947 (these now in one vol., *Jesus: Lord and Christ*, 1958); *The Death of Christ*, 1958. Cf. also my article, 'The Historical Jesus and the Church's Kerygma', *Religion in Life*, XXVI, 1956–7, 40–49.

[1] It is significant that these scholars feel most free to move toward a new quest when the context makes it clear that they accept the basic discoveries leading to the rejection of the nineteenth-century quest. Consequently they make a point of remaining critical toward treatments of Jesus which continue the original quest by neglecting the factors which brought it largely to

meyer, Kittel, Dibelius, and Schniewind. Such pupils of Bultmann as Ernst Käsemann (Tübingen), Günther Bornkamm (Heidelberg), Ernst Fuchs (Marburg), Erich Dinkler (Bonn), and Hans Conzelmann (Göttingen) have proven sufficiently distinguished to rise into the leading professorial positions, and a theological affinity to Gogarten and Tillich has provided a broad theological context. Bultmann himself provided a pre-established *rapprochement* with the dominant cultural trend in Germany centring in the existentialism of Martin Heidegger. His own monumental *Theology of the New Testament* provided the theological synthesis of the day, as did Barth's *Romans* a generation ago, and Harnack's *What is Christianity?* at the turn of the century. Consequently Germany is just as nearly 'Bultmannian' today as it was 'Barthian' a generation ago, 'Ritschlian' half a century or more ago, and 'Hegelian' still earlier; and Bultmann's works and ideas have

an end. This critical attitude is apparent, e.g. in Ernst Käsemann's reviews of the German editions of Lagrange's *L'Evangile de Jésus-Christ* (*VuF; Theol. Jahresbericht* for 1947-8 [1950], 218) and William Manson's *Jesus the Messiah* (*VuF; Theol. Jahresbericht* for 1953-5 [1956], 165-7). Cf. similarly Günther Bornkamm's review of Lagrange (*TLZ* LXXXII, 1957, 270 f.), and Hermann Diem's comments on Manson's work in his *Theologie II*, 1955, 77 f., 119 f. On the other hand Käsemann's review of the new edition of Bultmann's *Jesus* (*VuF; Theol. Jahresbericht* for 1949-50 [1952], 197) makes an initial effort to transcend the Bultmannian position in the direction of a new quest. Similarly a lecture to non-theologians ('Zum Thema der Nichtobjektivierbarkeit', *EvTh* XII, 1952-3, 455-66, esp. 463-6) reiterates the dominant contemporary German position opposing the conventional type of quest, while a lecture before 'old Marburgers' (i.e. Bultmannians) seeks to move beyond that consensus (cf. p. 12, n. 1 below). The turning-point of this lecture (133 f.), in re-evaluating the nineteenth-century quest and introducing the idea of a two-front war against docetism as well as historicism, echoes a lecture of 1933 by a leading form critic, Karl Ludwig Schmidt ('Das Christuszeugnis der synoptischen Evangelien', in *Jesus Christus im Zeugnis der Heiligen Schrift und der Kirche*, Beiheft 2 of *EvTh*, 2nd ed. 1936, 7-33). Similarly Käsemann's most recent attempt to move toward the historical Jesus ('Neutestamentliche Fragen von heute', *ZTK* LIV, 1957, 1-21, esp. 11 f.) is made in spite of the danger of a return to the nineteenth century seen in Stauffer's *Jesus: Gestalt und Geschichte* (and in the work of Joachim Jeremias), and is instigated by Günther Bornkamm's *Jesus of Nazareth* (and by the work of another Bultmannian Ernst Fuchs), and falls within the context of the first thoroughgoing criticism of Bultmann's *Theology of the New Testament* to come from within the Bultmannian group. Thus we observe a consistent effort to distinguish clearly any new quest from the original quest which still continues outside Germany.

become Germany's dominant theological export throughout the world.

One might well expect that the result of this first post-war phase would be a period of Bultmannian scholasticism. Instead we seem to be entering a new phase characterized by a critical re-study of the Bultmannian position by his leading pupils—itself a rare tribute to the spirit of free and critical scholarship represented by Bultmann. This second phase of post-war German theology may be designated as 'post-Bultmannian' in the stricter sense: led by outstanding pupils of Bultmann, it is based upon a thor-ough appreciation of the achievements of Bultmann's brilliant career, and could not have taken place without those achieve-ments. Yet it sees its task as that of carrying through a critical revision of Bultmann's position, out of which revision the theo-logical synthesis of the future will grow. The first part of this new programme to get seriously under way is with regard to the problem of the historical Jesus.

B. THE 'POST-BULTMANNIAN' QUEST OF THE HISTORICAL JESUS

The German repudiation of the quest of the historical Jesus at the opening of the century found its definitive crystallization in the scholarship of Rudolf Bultmann. His form-critical research tended to confirm the view that such a quest is impossible, and his existential theology carried through the thesis that such a quest is illegitimate. Therefore it is not surprising that the critical restudy of his position by his pupils should begin here.

The discussion was formally opened in 1953 by Ernst Käse-mann, who presented an address to a meeting of 'old Marburgers' (i.e. Bultmannians) on 'The Problem of the Historical Jesus'.[1] He moved beyond a recognition of the validity of much of Bult-mann's position, to argue that something *can* be known about the historical Jesus, and that we must concern ourselves with working

[1]'Das Problem des historischen Jesus', ZTK LI, 1954, 125–53. This view was already suggested in his address 'Probleme neutestamentlicher Arbeit in Deutschland', in *Die Freiheit des Evangeliums und die Ordnung der Gesellschaft* (*Beiträge zur EvTh* XV, 1952), 149–52. Cf. also note on p. 11 above.

working it out, if we do not wish ultimately to find ourselves committed to a mythological Lord. The crucial issue is identified in 'the question as to the continuity of the gospel in the discontinuity of the times and the variation of the *kerygma*',[1] i.e. whether the proclamation of the exalted Lord through the Church is in some kind of recognizable continuity with the preaching of the historical Jesus, and consequently whether the exalted Lord is in continuity with Jesus of Nazareth.

Käsemann's move toward reopening the quest of the historical Jesus has met with a rapid and largely favourable response from the various segments of German-language theology. Traditionally conservative theology has inherited liberalism's original position with regard to the historical Jesus.[2] It is therefore not surprising to find Käsemann's view advocated by spokesmen for Roman Catholicism,[3] Scandinavian theology,[4] and non-Bultmannian Germans.[5] And the new quest has found the support of Joachim Jeremias,[6] who perhaps more than any other is the custodian of the heritage of detailed and exacting philological, environmental research about Jesus, which is perhaps the most permanent contribution of the original quest. Furthermore, in typical German style, the current discussion has produced a doctoral dissertation,[7]

[1] *ZTK* LI, 1954, 152.

[2] This nonchalant reversal of position has not passed without comment, cf. Käsemann, *Beiträge zur EvTh* XV, 149; Hermann Diem, *Theologie: Dogmatik*, 1955, 76–79; Peter Biehl, *TR*, n.F. XXIV, 1957–8, 54–55; Vincent Taylor, *The Life and Ministry of Jesus*, 1945, 19–20.

[3] Franz Mussner, 'Der historische Jesus und der Christus des Glaubens', *BZ*, n.F. I, 1957, 224–52. René Marlé, *Bultmann et l'interprétation du Nouveau Testament* (*Théologie*, No. 33, 1956), Ch. V, 'Le problème de Jésus', 142–72.

[4] Nils Alstrup Dahl, 'Der historische Jesus als geschichtswissenschaftliches und theologisches Problem', *KuD* I, 1955, 104–32. Harald Riesenfeld, 'Evangelierna och den historiske Jesus', *Svensk Exegetisk Årsbok* XX, 1955, 25–57 (cf. also his opening address at the Oxford Congress on 'The Four Gospels in 1957', *The Gospel Tradition and its Beginnings; A Study in the Limits of 'Formgeschichte'*). Erik Sjöberg, *Der verborgene Menschensohn in den Evangelien*, 1955, 214–18.

[5] Otto Michel, 'Der "historische Jesus" und das theologische Gewissensproblem', *EvTh* XV, 1955, 349–63.

[6] 'Der gegenwärtige Stand der Debatte um das Problem des historischen Jesus', *Wissenschaftliche Zeitschrift der Ernst Moritz Arndt-Universität Greifswald. Gesellschafts- und sprachwissenschaftliche Reihe*, Nr. 3, VI, 1956–7, 165–70.

[7] Hans-Hinrich Jenssen, *Die Bedeutung des historischen Jesus Christus für die*

a contribution by a non-theologian,[1] a discussion of the discussion,[2] and an extremist who clearly went too far.[3] Certainly the most significant aspect of the continuing discussion is the response of leading representatives from the predominant Bultmannian and Barthian segments of German theology.

Käsemann's initial proposal of a new quest arose from the problem of the relation of Jesus' *message* to the Church's *kerygma*. This was soon followed from the Bultmannian side by a parallel proposal on the part of Ernst Fuchs,[4] who concentrated upon Jesus' *conduct* as 'the real context of his preaching'. 'What did

---

Entmythologisierung in der Predigt, a Berlin dissertation, unpublished but briefly summarized by the author, *TLZ* LXXXI, 1956, 491 f. Ch. III argues: 'The fact of the mere *existence* (*Dasein*) of a man to whom the *kerygma* appeals as "legitimation" does not free modern man, who is all too aware of the possibility of apotheosis in the history of religion, from the doubt that Christian faith too perhaps owes its existence only to human presumption. If on the other hand it could be shown that the application to Jesus of originally mythical categories of interpretation has its thoroughly justifiable point of departure in his concrete *kind* of existence (*Sosein*), then this would be a decisive pastoral aid. It is our thesis that there is this possibility of indicating such points of departure in the concrete kind of life Jesus lived, and that for pastoral reasons we must make full use of this possibility in preaching and catechetical instruction. Consequently we do not—as is so frequent today—regard demythologizing as a liberation from an appeal to the concrete kind of life Jesus Christ lived, but rather as a renewed and deepened return to it.'

[1] E. Heitsch, 'Die Aporie des historischen Jesus als Problem theologischer Hermeneutik', *ZTK* LIII, 1956, 193–210.

[2] Peter Biehl, 'Zur Frage nach dem historischen Jesus', *op. cit.,* 54–76.

[3] Ethelbert Stauffer, *Jesus: Gestalt und Geschichte,* 1957. Cf. the review by Wm. C. Robinson, Jr, in *Interpretation* XII, 1958, 82–83, and below. Not only the Bultmannians, but even such divergent viewpoints as the Barthian Hermann Diem (*Theologie* II, 77) and the Roman Catholic Rudolf Schnackenburg concur in the latter's judgement (*BZ*, n.F. I, 1957, 314): 'Scholarship will judge that Stauffer has fallen back into the error of the earlier "Lives of Jesus", and that his attempt has failed, even when he stimulates new approaches.'

[4] 'Die Frage nach dem historischen Jesus', *ZTK* LIII, 1956, 210–29, esp. 219 f. 'Glaube und Geschichte im Blick auf die Frage nach dem historischen Jesus. Eine Auseinandersetzung mit G. Bornkamms Buch über "Jesus von Nazareth",' *ZTK* LIV, 1957, 117–56. 'Bemerkungen zur Gleichnisauslegung', *TLZ* LXXIX, 1954, 345–8. *Hermeneutik,* 1954, esp. 219–30 ('Gleichnis und Parabel'). *Das Programm der Entmythologisierung,* 9, and *Das urchristliche Sakramentsverständnis,* 37–41 (Hefte 3, 1954, and 8, 1958, of the *Schriftenreihe der Kirchlich-Theologischen Sozietät in Württemberg*). 'Die der Theologie durch die historisch-kritische Methode auferlegte Besinnung', *EvTh* XVIII, 1958, 256–68. 'Jesus und der Glaube', *ZTK* LV, 1958, Heft 2.

Jesus do? We said he celebrated the eschatological meal with tax-gatherers and sinners (Matt. 11.19 par.), and we designated precisely this meal as the act of goodness supplied in advance to them all by Jesus. This means: Jesus forwent the publication of his own private eschatological experiences; rather he determined only to draw the consequences from them and to begin here on earth with the work of God visible only in heaven! This is why he celebrates his meal. *It is just this that is Jesus' real deed.*' What is here said of the eschatological meals open to all is then generalized to an interpretation of Jesus' conduct as a whole: 'This conduct is neither that of a prophet nor that of a sage, but rather the conduct of a man who dares to act in God's stead, by (as must always be added) calling near to him sinners who apart from him would have to flee from God.' This conduct, maintaining that God's will is a gracious will, by implication also claims to be divine action, and it was this claim latent in Jesus' conduct which led to opposition and to his death (Mark 3.6).

When Fuchs comes to Jesus' message, he presents it as dependent upon Jesus' action. For this view Fuchs appeals to the parables, which were often spoken in the setting of the eschatological meals: 'Jesus supplied his disciples with the interpretation of his parabolic language by an act of goodness.' 'It is consequently not the case, that first the parable clarifies Jesus' conduct —although Jesus makes use of it in defence of himself; rather it is the other way around: Jesus' conduct explains the will of God with a parable which can be read out of his conduct.' Thus in Jesus' mouth the parables are 'a witness to himself', and 'apply primarily to our relation to Jesus himself'. This approach to the parables is then generalized into an approach to all Jesus' teaching: 'For if we see this aright, then it is to be expected that certainly Jesus' words . . . generally reflect his conduct historically.' 'Jesus wishes only to be understood on the basis of his decision, his deed.' This concentration in Jesus' teaching upon his action made it possible for the disciples to conceive of his death also as divine action, which in turn led to the primitive Christian sacraments as custodians of 'Jesus' understanding of himself'. Thus

Fuchs has carried through with regard to Jesus' action the same thesis which Käsemann presented with regard to his message: in the message and action of Jesus is implicit an eschatological understanding of his person, which becomes explicit in the *kerygma* of the primitive Church.

The initiative of Käsemann and Fuchs in proposing a new quest of the historical Jesus has produced its first tangible results in the appearance in 1956 of Günther Bornkamm's monograph *Jesus von Nazareth.*[1] This is the first book on the historical Jesus to issue from the Bultmannian school since Bultmann's own *Jesus and the Word* appeared thirty years earlier. However the impetus provided by the proposal of a new quest is not only evident in the very fact that Bornkamm's book appeared, but is also evident in its distinctive divergences from Bultmann's own traditional presentation. For these divergences express the newly awakened concern for the message and conduct of Jesus in their relation to the *kerygma.*

Bornkamm does not confine his presentation to Jesus' 'word', as did Bultmann, but concerns himself as well with the events of Jesus' life, as did Fuchs. In addition to chapters on Jesus' disciples (Ch. VI) and his final journey to Jerusalem (Ch. VII), Bornkamm risks an introductory chapter which collects whatever general biographical information is available about Jesus into what amounts to a personality sketch. The significance of this chapter (III) lies in its attempt to describe the human impression Jesus made upon people in a way clearly suggestive of the meaning Jesus has for faith, as if a human contact with Jesus were—at least potentially—an encounter with the *kerygma.*

Buttressed by the context of Jesus' conduct,[2] Bornkamm's presentation of Jesus' message diverges from Bultmann's typical emphasis upon the future, of which Jesus' action in the present were but a sign calling for decision. Instead, a primary emphasis

[1]Cf. my review, *JBL* LXXVI, 1957, 310–13. The English translation of this book will be published by Hodder and Stoughton, in conjunction with Harpers, within the year. Page numbers here refer to the German edition.
[2]It is significant that Fuchs' key correlation between the eschatological meals and the parables is carried through, 74.

falls upon the present: 'Unmediated presence is always the characteristic of Jesus' words, appearance and action, within a world which . . . had lost the present, since it lived . . . between past and future, between traditions and promises or threats' (58). This is not to say that Bornkamm has moved to the position of 'realized eschatology' (91); rather he sees (with Bultmann) the tension between future and present as inherent in the involvement of the imperative in the indicative, i.e. inherent in the historical understanding of the self. But it does mean that he emphasizes more clearly than has been customary for Bultmann the continuity between Jesus' message and the Church's *kerygma*.

Bultmann's classical distinction between Jesus and Paul had been: What for Jesus is future is for Paul past and present, since the shift of aeons separates them, so that Jesus preached the law and the promise, while Paul preached the gospel.[1] This has become in Bornkamm the distinction between John the Baptist and Jesus. John is the 'sentinel at the frontier between the aeons' (51); the difference between John and Jesus is that 'between eleventh and twelfth hour' (67); and 'the contemporizing of this reality of God is the real mystery of Jesus' (62). Therefore Bornkamm's discussion of the messianic problem (Ch. VIII) does not confine itself to the view (shared with Bultmann) that Jesus made no claims to messianic titles, but goes on to explain the absence of any such special topic in Jesus' teaching by the view that 'the "messianic" aspect of his being is enclosed *in* his word and act, and in the unmediatedness of his historical appearance' (178). This leads to a final chapter (IX: 'Jesus Christ') in which a continuity between the historical Jesus and the Church's *kerygma* is sketched. In the Easter experience the disciples were assured 'that God himself had intervened with almighty hand in the wicked and rebellious activity of the world, and had snatched this Jesus of Nazareth from the power of sin and death which had risen up against him, and installed him as Lord of the world.' Easter 'is thus at the same time the inbreaking of the new world of God into this old world branded by sin and death, the setting up and beginning of his

[1] *GuV* I, 200 f., 316.

reign. . . . We note how here Jesus' own message of the coming reign of God rings out again in new form, only that he himself with his death and resurrection has now entered into this message and become its centre' (168 f.). Here it is clear that Jesus' eschatological message, including his eschatological interpretation of his own conduct, has been continued in christological terms by the Easter faith and the Christian *kerygma*.

Hans Conzelmann[1] has united these various lines of development into a unified view of Jesus' eschatology and his person, in which christology replaces chronology as the basic meaning of Jesus' message: the kingdom which Jesus proclaims is future, but the 'interim' is of no positive significance to him. Rather Jesus confronts man with an unmediated and consequently determinative encounter with the kingdom. This is the common significance of various themes which when taken literally could be contradictory: the nearness of the kingdom, the suddenness of its coming, and Jesus himself as the last sign. None of this is meant by Jesus temporally, but only existentially. Although the nearness is presented temporally, its 'meaning lies in qualifying the human situation in view of the coming of the kingdom'. Predictions of coming reward and punishment, like the present beatitudes and woes, represent the alternatives of salvation or lostness involved in one's present situation. Hence Jesus' message of salvation and his call for repentance 'form together the absolute determination of human existence'.

Put the other way round, 'existing means nothing more than comprehending the signs', i.e. Jesus' action. If Jesus' eschatology seems intentionally to ignore time, this is only because it intentionally centres in his person. He 'connects the hope of salvation with his person to the extent that he sees the kingdom effective in his deeds and understands his preaching as the last word of God before the end.' Thus his eschatology involves an 'indirect' christology: 'If the kingdom is *so* near that it casts *this* shadow, then the "observer" no longer has it before him, in the sense

[1]'Eschatologie: IV, im Urchristentum', *RGG*, 3rd ed., II, 1958, 665-72, esp. 666-8; 'Gegenwart und Zukunft in der synoptischen Tradition', *ZTK* LIV, 1957 (appeared Summer 1958), 277-96, esp. 286-8.

that he could still observe it from a certain distance; rather is he at that instant fully claimed. Jesus does not give a new answer to the question "When?"—in that case he would still be an apocalypticist—, but rather he supersedes this question as such.'

c. bultmann's shift in position

Certainly anyone who has followed this 'post-Bultmannian' development within Germany cannot fail to wonder how Bultmann himself reacts to this trend, a trend which certainly diverges from the 'classical' Bultmannian position, but which nonetheless works largely upon Bultmannian presuppositions and can in fact appeal to an undercurrent in Bultmann's writings which already moves in this direction.[1] It is therefore quite significant that a

[1]A summary of the classical Bultmannian position is found in the following quotation (*GuV* I, 208): 'So one may not go back behind the *kerygma*, using it as a "source", in order to reconstruct a "historical Jesus" with his "messianic consciousness", his "inwardness" or his "heroism". That would be precisely the Christ according to the flesh, who is gone. Not the historical Jesus, but Jesus Christ, the proclaimed, is the Lord.' However the various factors in this statement leading up to a repudiation of a quest of the historical Jesus do not, when analysed, necessitate this conclusion, except in terms of the original quest. The possibility of uniting these factors with the acceptance of a new kind of quest becomes visible from time to time in Bultmann's own writing. His *Jesus and the Word* of 1926 maintains in this regard a somewhat ambiguous role in the context of his total position. Käsemann (*ZTK* LI, 1954, 125) holds that *Jesus and the Word* intentionally avoids distinguishing between Jesus and the oldest *kerygma*, as if the relevance of *Jesus and the Word* lay for Bultmann in its inclusion of the *kerygma*; while Bultmann himself says (*Kerygma and Myth*, 1953, 117) that his book on Jesus is not *kerygma*. He can seem to express a complete lack of interest in Jesus: 'The Christ according to the flesh does not concern us; how things looked in Jesus' heart I do not know and do not wish to know' (*GuV* I, 101). However this remark of 1927 must be understood in terms of his rejection of psychologism and his disapproval of a personality cult, as in the preface to *Jesus and the Word* of 1926, where the positive alternative is given. In the case of great men, '*their* interest was not their personality, but their work', which he seeks to present in *Jesus and the Word*. In this preface he expresses a lack of interest in the question as to whether Jesus claimed for himself messianic titles. However this is because the answer to such a question would not provide a real solution to the problem of Jesus' significance, which Bultmann himself answers positively (*GuV* I, 1933, 266): 'Whether or not he knew himself as Messiah makes no difference. It would only indicate that he brought to consciousness the character of his action as decisive by making use of a Jewish concept of the day. But to be sure his call to decision implies a christology. . . . When the primitive Church names him the Messiah, she in her way brings to expression that she understood him.' Hence positive statements of the relation of Jesus'

recent article by Bultmann[1] seems to be by implication a defence of Käsemann's position against an initial criticism by the Barthian Hermann Diem:[2] Diem had maintained that when all is said and done Käsemann has presented Jesus as only proclaiming 'general religious and moral truths' about 'the freedom of the children of God', rather than a message in continuity with the Church's *kerygma*. For Käsemann doubts that Jesus claimed to be Son of Man and says instead: 'Jesus came . . . to say how things stand with the kingdom that has dawned, namely that God has drawn near man in grace and requirement. He brought and lived the freedom of the children of God, who remain children and free only so long as they find in the Father their Lord.'[3]

Bultmann points out that eternal truths, when used in concrete proclamation, can become historical encounter. Already in this sense he recognizes that Jesus' teachings were used by the primitive Church as kerygmatic proclamation of the exalted Lord: 'One can hardly object that Jesus' preaching was after all not Christian preaching, on the grounds that Christian preaching proclaims him, but was not proclaimed by him. Even if here we completely ignore the question, in what sense Jesus' preaching could perhaps after all be designated a hidden or secret Christian preaching, in any case his preaching was taken up into Christian preaching and became a part of the proclamation in which the Proclaimed is at the same time present as the Proclaimer' (246). However this is a purely formal use of Jesus' teachings, just as many 'general truths' can be used in concrete proclamation. Bultmann recognizes that the problem of the relation of Jesus' teaching to the Church's

message to the Church's *kerygma* do occur: *GuV* I, 205; *Theology of the New Testament* I, 1951 (Ger. ed. 1948), 42 ff. And this concern of Bultmann's for the historical Jesus has been on occasion detected, e.g. by Walther Eltester, *ZNTW* XXXIII, 1950-1, 276, and Peter Biehl, *TR*, n.F. XXIV, 1957-8, 76.

[1]'Allgemeine Wahrheit und christliche Verkündigung', *ZTK* LIV, 1957, 244-54. (This fascicle of *ZTK* actually appeared in Jan. 1958.) Bultmann had already shared in the move toward a new liberalism signalled by the reappearance of the *Zeitschrift für Theologie und Kirche* in 1950. Cf. his introduction to the semi-centennial edition of Harnack's *What is Christianity?* (1950; Eng. ed. 1957).

[2]*Theologie* II, 124.

[3]*ZTK* LI, 1954, 151.

kerygma—i.e. the by-passed question of the sense in which Jesus' preaching is Christian—goes deeper. 'This does not yet make it clear why the Proclaimer necessarily became the Proclaimed, unless it could be shown that Jesus' preaching of the law was differentiated from every other preaching of the law by being at the same time the proclamation of God's grace, which not only assumes freedom, but also grants it' (253).

At this point those accustomed to Bultmann's earlier distinction of Jesus from Paul in terms of law and gospel,[1] and his subsequent classification of Jesus within Judaism[2] as only a presupposition of New Testament theology,[3] would expect him simply to repeat that position. But instead, he lays hold of Fuchs' concept of Jesus' conduct as God's goodness in action, and comes to the conclusion that Jesus' message is after all grace, i.e. 'after all a hidden or secret Christian preaching': 'Such calls for decision as Matt. 11.6; Luke 12.8 f., are, by calling for decision with regard to his person, at the same time words of promise, of grace: it is at this very moment that the gift of freedom is offered to the hearer. If the one who calls for decision is the "glutton and drunkard, the friend of tax collectors and sinners" (Luke 7.34 f.; Matt. 11.19), does this not mean that he who proclaims the radical requirement of God at the same time speaks the word of grace? If the tax collectors and harlots enter the kingdom of God before the officially "righteous" (Matt. 21.31), then it is because those who understand God's requirement are those who have received grace. And when the condition runs: "Whoever does not receive the kingdom of God like a child shall not enter it" (Mark 10.15), then certainly the condition contains at the same time the assurance of grace' (254). Bultmann himself seems to have moved with the 'post-Bultmannian' move of his pupils[4] with regard to the historical Jesus and the *kerygma*.

[1] *GuV* I, 1933, 200 f.
[2] *Primitive Christianity in its Contemporary Setting,* 1956 (Ger. ed. 1949).
[3] *Theology of the New Testament* I, 3.
[4] This does not alter the fact that Bultmann's pupils conceive of the new quest as 'post-Bultmannian' rather than simply 'Bultmannian'; cf. the critical context in which it is presented by Käsemann, esp. 'Neutestamentliche Fragen von heute', *ZTK* LIV, 1957, 1–21.

When we apply this position to Diem's original criticism of Käsemann, that the latter presented Jesus as only teaching general truths rather than the *kerygma*, it becomes clear that Diem has overlooked the crucial point: Käsemann went beyond the view that Jesus *taught* God's fatherhood and man's freedom, to the assertion that 'God has *drawn near* man in grace and requirement,' and Jesus '*brought* and *lived* the freedom of the children of God'. Between the false alternatives of 'just general truths' or 'explicit claims to messianic titles' there lies in Jesus' public ministry a whole area of eschatological action accompanied by theological commentary which Diem overlooked, and wherein resides both the historical and the theological point of departure for the Church's *kerygma*, and thus the crucial area of research for a new quest of the historical Jesus.

D. THE BARTHIAN RAPPROCHEMENT

The movement we have sketched within the historical research of New Testament scholars largely under Bultmannian influence is to a certain extent parallel to the increasingly positive evaluation of history on the part of Karl Barth,[1] and a reawakening concern for the historical Jesus on the part of systematic theologians closely associated with him.[2] Perhaps the most significant instance of this trend is the shift of Hermann Diem from his initial attitude of considerable reserve to an acceptance of the basic position of Käsemann. Diem's basic position[3] is that the New Testament

---

[1] Cf. specifically the basic christological sections of his volumes on reconciliation (*Church Dogmatics* IV. 1, 2).

[2] E.g. Fritz Lieb, 'Die Geschichte Jesu Christi in Kerygma und Historie. Ein Beitrag zum Gespräch mit Rudolf Bultmann', in *Antwort* (Barth Festschrift, 1956), 582–95. Further '"Geschichte und Heilsgeschichte in der Theologie Rudolf Bultmanns"' (on Heinrich Ott's book of that title), *EvTh* XV, 1955, 507–22.

[3] *Theologie als kirchliche Wissenschaft. Handreichung zur Einübung ihrer Probleme*, 1951 (cited as *Theologie* I), esp. Para. 5: 'Die Aufgaben und Probleme für den Historiker', and Para. 6: 'Der Historiker als kirchlicher Theologe', 57–69; and Band II: *Dogmatik. Ihr Weg zwischen Historismus und Existentialismus*, 1955 (cited as *Theologie* II), esp. Para. 3: 'Die Bedeutung des historischen Jesus für Verkündigung, Lehre und Glauben der Kirche', and Para. 4: 'Die Geschichte von Jesus Christus, der sich selbst verkündigt', 76–131. Para. 4 has also been published separately (1955). With Diem's basic position cf. also Peter Biehl, *TR*, n.F. XXIV, 1957–8, 58–61.

proclaims a Jesus Christ who proclaims himself. 'This history of
the proclamation is the object of historical research in the New
Testament which we seek, and which is the only legitimate object
of such historical research according to the New Testament's
understanding of itself.'[1] But rather than implying by this, according to his original Barthian position,[2] that one cannot enquire behind the evangelist's message to that of Jesus,[3] Diem
now recognizes that 'we must search back to that first phase of
the history of the proclamation, the proclamation of the earthly
Jesus himself'.[4] For this historical question of the continuity of
the proclamation from Jesus to the Church is recognized as the
theological question as to whether the Church's Lord is a myth.
For Diem concedes that a negative answer to the historical question would 'negatively prejudice' the theological question as to
the truth of the gospel. Consequently he concerns himself with
the historical question sufficiently seriously to trace,[5] in one
instance, the term 'Son of Man' in the Gospels, the continuity

[1] *Der irdische Jesus und der Christus des Glaubens* (SgV 215, 1957), 9.
[2] Diem (*Theologie* II, 129) quotes Barth (*Church Dogmatics*, I. 2, 494): '... the
exegesis of canonical Scripture as such, the coherent exposition of Genesis,
Isaiah, the Gospel of Matthew, etc. according to their present status and com-
pass, is again recognized and undertaken as in the last resort the *only* possible
goal of biblical scholarship. . . . The *historical truth* which in its own way
biblical scholarship does have to mediate is the true *meaning and context of the
biblical texts as such*.' (Barth's italics.) Consequently Diem permits recourse
behind the text only to the extent needed to establish the 'meaning and context of the biblical texts as such', i.e. one can concern oneself with the
history of the origin of the present text only in order to establish how the
individual witnesses arrived at their present canonical form and are to be
understood (*Theologie* II, 130 f.).
[3] *Theologie* II, 117, 127, 129: 'From the very beginning we have declared
ourselves not interested in this historical reconstruction of Jesus' proclamation.' 'The history of Jesus Christ encounters us only in the history of the
proclamation of this history, and can be laid hold of historically only in the
latter. Consequently (the historian's) subject-matter can only be the history
of the proclamation present in the texts.' 'Consequently the task of this research would now no longer be to enquire of the text concerning a history
which lies behind it and on which it would report, but rather to enquire of
the history of the statements of the text itself. In the formation of the text
the history of the proclamation becomes visible, for the history of the text is
itself the only historically attainable segment of this history of the proclamation.'
[4] *Der irdische Jesus und der Christus des Glaubens*, 12.
[5] *Ibid.*, 15 f.

between Jesus' message and the Church's witness: although Jesus may never have called himself Son of Man, he did say that acquittal by the Son of Man in the eschatological judgement was dependent upon one's present relation to himself (Mark 8.38 par.). Thus the content of salvation is dependent on Jesus, and it was this which the Church explicated by attributing to him the title of bringer of salvation (i.e. the title Son of Man). Here Diem has clearly moved to the position of the advocates of the new quest, both by accepting—in terms almost identical with those of Käsemann—the theological validity of the new quest, and by adopting the basic method of the new quest, which consists in moving below the surface of terms and even concepts to the level of theological meaning and existential significance.[1]

From this survey of current German discussion we may conclude that the proposal of a new quest of the historical Jesus, originally made within the context of the 'post-Bultmannian' direction of leading pupils of Bultmann, has broadened itself, not only in traditionally conservative circles, but also by support from the Barthian side as well as from Bultmann himself.[2] A concen-

---

[1]A somewhat analogous direction is also indicated by Jeremias, 'Der gegenwärtige Stand der Debatte um das Problem des historischen Jesus', 169 f.: 'Everywhere in Jesus' proclamation we strike upon this ultimate claim, i.e. we strike upon the same claim for faith which the *kerygma* directs to us. Here something which is quite simple and obvious must be stated, since it is no longer obvious. Every sentence in the sources attests it to us, every verse in our Gospels hammers it in. Something has happened, something unique, something which never before existed. . . . There is no parallel for the authority which dares to address God with Abba. If we merely acknowledge the fact that the word "Abba" is Jesus' *ipsissima vox*—and I would not know how it could be contested—then, if this word is understood aright and not rendered harmless, we stand before Jesus' transcendent claim. . . . Thus example could be added to example, and the result is the same every time: when we use the critical means at our disposal with discipline and conscientiousness, we strike again and again, in our efforts concerning the historical Jesus, upon the ultimate: we are placed before God himself. . . . It is not as if [the act of] faith were taken from us or even facilitated, when exegesis shows us how his transcendent claim stands behind his every word and each of his deeds. . . . But it is true that the question of faith is inescapably posed at every turn by Jesus' words and deeds.'

[2]This *rapprochement* between German New Testament scholars largely operating upon Bultmannian presuppositions and German systematic theologians largely operating upon Barthian presuppositions is a result of the concern on both sides over the unhealthy separation of New Testament

tration of force seems to be in the making, which may well provide enough impetus to move beyond a mere proposal to a distinctive trait of theology during the coming generation.[1]

It is in this relatively propitious setting that the present work is presented, as a contribution to the new quest both by a clarification of its nature, and by an initial participation in the work of the new quest at a few significant points.

In order to enter into this discussion in such a way as to be able to make a fruitful contribution to it, it will be necessary (Ch. II) to recognize the degree of validity inherent in the arguments which brought the original quest to an end by pointing to its impossibility and illegitimacy. For only within the valid limits thus imposed can one seek in a relevant way (Ch. III) to define the sense in which a new quest may be possible, and to investigate (Ch. IV) the legitimacy of such a quest, i.e. the degree to which it is theologically permissible and necessary. Only then can one attempt (Ch. V) to get the actual work under way by laying hold of the central problem in terms of which the detailed research upon individual problems will gain its relevance.

---

research and systematic theology characteristic of Germany since the war. Cf. Käsemann, 'Probleme neutestamentlicher Arbeit in Deutschland', 138; Diem, *Theologie* II, 38 f. and *passim; Der irdische Jesus und der Christus des Glaubens,* 19. For a contribution to the discussion by a systematic theologian with Bultmannian presuppositions, cf. Gerhard Ebeling, *ZTK* LV, 1958, 64–109.

[1]Cf. e.g. Jeremias, 'Der gegenwärtige Stand der Debatte um das Problem des historischen Jesus', 168: 'As a matter of fact, then, the most recent theological development is moving beyond Bultmann at this very point. One sees that the question of the historical Jesus must be taken seriously, and thus the situation in contemporary New Testament research is after all not as disunited as it might seem at the first glance.'

II

THE IMPOSSIBILITY AND ILLEGITIMACY OF THE ORIGINAL QUEST

A. THE AMBIGUOUS TERM 'HISTORICAL JESUS'

'The quest of the historical Jesus' is an expression which has become familiar to us as the English title of Albert Schweitzer's book *Von Reimarus zu Wrede*. It is a poetic rendering of the German subtitle, which read literally: 'A History of Research upon the Life of Jesus'. Thus those who have read Schweitzer's book have come to sense that the expression 'historical Jesus' is closely related to modern historical research. Yet the extent to which the meaning of the term is inextricably related to historical research must be explained in some detail, if the concept is to be freed from the ambiguity which continues to haunt it.

The term 'historical Jesus' is not simply identical with 'Jesus' or 'Jesus of Nazareth', as if the adjective 'historical' were a meaningless addition. Rather the adjective is used in a technical sense, and makes a specific contribution to the total meaning of the expression. 'Historical' is used in the sense of 'things in the past which have been established by objective scholarship'.[1] Consequently the expression 'historical Jesus' comes to mean: 'What can be known of Jesus of Nazareth by means of the scientific methods of the historian.' Thus we have to do with a technical

---

[1] Cf. the definition of the noun 'history' from which this use of the adjective is derived, e.g. Diem, *Der irdische Jesus* . . ., 9: 'Under *Historie* we understand not the history itself which happened, but rather the ἱστορεῖν (investigation) of it, in the . . . sense of *learning about it, experiencing it, reporting about what is experienced*.' Similarly Barth defines *Historie*: 'the history which is available to man by being perceptible to him and comprehensible by him' (*KD* III.1, 84); 'ascertainable by the means and methods and especially, under the tacit presuppositions, of modern historical scholarship' (*KD* III.2, 535).

expression which must be recognized as such, and not automatically identified with the simple term 'Jesus'.

This technical meaning of the expression 'historical Jesus' may seem to us an unwarranted narrowing of the term 'history'. Yet such usage is nearest to the original, etymological meaning of the term 'history' (lit. 'research'). Such usage is somewhat similar to the scientist's use of the term 'nature' to refer to what in the world around us is subsumed under law by scientific research.[1] Now 'history' and 'nature' in this sense would envisage all of reality, if one assumed that objective historical scholarship and scientific research could, in theory at least, reach the whole of reality. In that case the technical usage of 'history' and 'nature' could be as comprehensive as the layman's normal meaning of 'history' as 'all that happened' and 'nature' as 'the whole world around us'.

This was in fact the assumption of the nineteenth-century quest of the historical Jesus. For this quest was initiated by the enlightenment in its effort to escape the limitations of dogma,[2] and thereby to gain access to the whole reality of the past. The quest

[1] The potentiality of this meaning inheres in the origin of the term as the Latin translation of the technical Greek term φύσις, whose etymological origin lay in the concept of growth. Thus 'nature' is the product of the growing process, which itself is grasped as conforming to law. This aspect is still echoed in the current definition (Funk and Wagnalls' New 'Standard' Dictionary of the English Language, 1952): 'A collective abstract term for the entire universe, and embracing all its existences, forces, and laws, regarded as constituting a system or unity which may be covered, however vaguely, by one conception and designated by a single term. In this meaning, however, we are obliged to recognize an attempt to blend two aspects or ways of regarding the universe which are more or less distinctly different, while both are necessary. These are: (1) The system of things and persons regarded as actually existent in space and time. . . . (2) The moulding or creative forces; the powers which account for the origins and changes of things, and for the production and evolution of the world, in accordance with some observable or purely conjectural plan or controlling ideas.' This last emphasis was brought to the centre of attention by Kant, who emphasized the epistemological aspect: 'We ourselves bring the order and conformity to law . . . into the phenomena which we call nature.' In this tradition K. Lasswitz (*Geschichte der Atomistik*, 1890, I, 80) defines nature as 'that which is objectified as temporal-spatial phenomenon by systematic thought, i.e. that which is conceptually established and thus guaranteed by law.' Cf. *Eislers Handwörterbuch der Philosophie* (2nd ed. 1922), s.v.

[2] This oft-forgotten origin of the quest has recently been emphasized by Jeremias, 'Der gegenwärtige Stand der Debatte um das Problem des historischen Jesus', 165 f.

of the historical Jesus was originally the quest after 'the Jesus of Nazareth who actually lived in first-century Palestine', unrestricted by the doctrinal presentations of him in Bible, creed and Church. One then proceeded to implement this alternative between orthodox christology and the Jesus of the enlightenment by appeal to the current alternatives in method. If the orthodox Christ was reached through faith and doctrine, it was readily assumed that 'the real Jesus of Nazareth' could be found by means of the newly-discovered historiography promising to narrate the past 'as it actually was'. Hence for the nineteenth century the two meanings of 'the historical Jesus' tended to coincide: 'Jesus of Nazareth as he actually was' coincided with 'the reconstruction of his biography by means of objective historical method'.

For the twentieth century this is no longer obvious. The reason for this change does not lie in any restriction of the historical-critical method in dealing with the objective data, as if there were one group of historical facts accessible to historiography, while other historical facts were in principle beyond the historian's reach.[1] Rather we have come to recognize that the objective factual level upon which the nineteenth century operated is only one dimension of history, and that a whole new dimension in the facts, a deeper and more central plane of meaning, had been largely bypassed. The nineteenth century saw the reality of the 'historical facts' as consisting largely in names, places, dates, occurrences, sequences, causes, effects—things which fall far short of being the actuality of history, if one understands by history the distinctively human, creative, unique, purposeful, which distinguishes man from nature. The dimension in which man actually exists, his 'world', the stance or outlook from which he acts, his understanding of his existence behind what he does, the way

---

[1]Such is, in fact, the view of Karl Barth (*KD* III.1, 84–88), but his view is here not characteristic of contemporary historiography. Cf. e.g. Bultmann's rejection of its use by Barth, in *Essays Philosophical and Theological*, 260 f.; Biehl's rejection of its use by Heinrich Ott (*Geschichte und Heilsgeschichte in der Theologie Rudolf Bultmanns*, 1955, 16), in his essay 'Welchen Sinn hat es, von "theologischer Ontologie" zu reden?', *ZTK*, LIII, 1956, 370; and Biehl's rejection of its use by Diem (*Theologie* II, 88), in his essay 'Zur Frage nach dem historischen Jesus', *TR*, n.F. XXIV, 1957–8, 59.

he meets his basic problems and the answer his life implies to the human dilemma, the significance he had as the environment of those who knew him, the continuing history his life produces, the possibility of existence which his life presents to me as an alternative—such matters as these have become central in an attempt to understand history. It is this deeper level of the reality of 'Jesus of Nazareth as he actually was' which was not reached by 'the reconstruction of his biography by means of objective historical method'. Consequently the two meanings of the term 'historical Jesus' no longer coincide.

Once it had become clear that nineteenth-century historical method had failed to penetrate the depths at which the reality of history lies, and consequently that its 'historical Jesus' failed to exhaust the reality of Jesus of Nazareth, it was inevitable that a re-study of historical method should follow, in an attempt to gain access to that deeper level of historical reality. But until such a method could be worked out and applied, and its results brought in, the only scientific historical reconstruction which was actually available remained that of the nineteenth century. For the time being at least, the only 'historical Jesus' available was the nineteenth-century reconstruction, now seen to fall far short of Jesus of Nazareth as he actually was. Consequently the twentieth century worked out its initial attitude toward the 'historical Jesus' in terms of the only available reconstruction, that of the nineteenth century with all its deficiencies.

This produced in the first place a recognition of the relativity of historical research even in the modern, post-enlightenment period. To say that medieval historians were subjective would not imply that historiography is inevitably subjective. But to say that the classical age of objective historical-critical research was itself historically conditioned and to this extent subjective, was to imply that historiography is inevitably limited as to the degree of objectivity and finality it can attain. Thus Lessing's old problem as to how 'accidental historical truths can serve as proofs for eternal rational truths' was deepened by the awareness that even our reconstruction of the 'historical truths' is 'accidental', i.e.

historically relative. All this was only augmented by the growing awareness in psychology, cultural anthropology, and existential-ism of the basic historicity of the self, so that one no longer assumed that the historical and relative could be readily removed as merely a surface defect on an essentially natural or changelessly rational selfhood. The problem of the historian's own historicity has become a fundamental problem. Quite apart from the assump-tions of Christian faith, it is easy to see that all that Jesus actually was is not likely to be fully grasped, objectively demonstrated, and definitively stated by historical research in any given period.[1] Now when we add to this the assumption that the historian's

[1]This conclusion about Jesus is in accord with the whole trend of his-torical research in our century. The view of F. M. Powicke, a central figure in British historiography during the first half of this century, is typical. In his address 'After Fifty Years' to the Historical Association in 1944 (*History*, XXIX, 1944, 2–16, reprinted in *Modern Historians and the Study of History*, 1955, 225–39), he said (229 f.): 'At the same time, as we look back over the last fifty years, all of us must be conscious of the *malaise* or discomfort which oppresses the thoughtful study of history. The his-torical student, especially if he is also a teacher of history, has never been so conscious of the significance of his subject. He is convinced, and rightly, of its importance and is beset by a public eager to know what it is all about; yet he can give no clear answers. This, at any rate, is the impression, probably the strongest impression, left upon my own mind, as I reflect upon the movement of the last half-century, and a most uncomfortable im-pression it is. The main reason for it is the susceptibility of all of us, whether we are historical students or not, to the sense of inadequacy to which I have already referred. The old smooth generalizations do not seem to fit, and the effort to make new ones is so faltering. . . . We are expected, willingly or unwillingly, to speak with assurance about the most mysterious and most intimate problem than can engage the mind of man, the experience of man as a social being throughout the centuries.' Similarly in his *History, Free-dom and Religion*, 1938, 15 f.: 'Just as nine-tenths of our personal experi-ence consists of instinctive or habitual acts, which we do not record even in our own memories, so it is in the past experience of peoples, nations, states. Even of what is left, the tenth part, some is consciously remembered, only to be forgotten as it is displaced by new experience, and some is too intimate to be shared with others; and so it is with peoples, nations, and states. . . . Just because history is so full of intelligence and of human purpose which eludes us, and is in its nature an incessant denial of fatalism, it can give us that sense of remoteness which we associate with fatalism. Sometimes, in the watches of the night, I have seen the whole of human experience, since man-kind, as a thinking animal, loosened the hold of matter upon him—human experience with its incessant, ant-like activity, its hopes and fears, its aspira-tions and its despair—as a great glacier moving imperceptibly, remorselessly, and myself as a tiny flake of frozen snow upon its lowest edge, explaining the nature and the laws of the vast mass, whence it came and whither it goes.'

subject matter is God, the impossibility of the situation is more than obvious. Thus the whole Ritschlian attempt to prove Christianity historically suddenly became absurd.[1] Consequently it seems incredibly naïve when today an advocate of positivistic historicism wishes to revive the attempt to prove historically the 'absoluteness of Jesus'.[2]

Since the twentieth century worked out its initial attitude toward the 'historical Jesus' in terms of the only available reconstruction, that of the nineteenth century with all its glaring limitations, it is not surprising to find as a second consequence a tendency to disassociate the expression 'the historical Jesus' from 'Jesus of Nazareth as he actually was', and to reserve the expression for: 'What can be known of Jesus of Nazareth by means of the scientific methods of the historian'.[3] 'The historical Jesus' comes really to mean no more than 'the historian's Jesus'. The clear implication is that 'Jesus of Nazareth as he actually was' may be considerably more than or quite different from 'the historical Jesus'.

It is in this sense that one must correctly understand statements which might seem shocking if used in the other sense of the term: 'We can know very little about the historical Jesus'. If by this one means that we can know very little about Jesus of Nazareth by means of the scientific methods of the historian, so that a modern biography of him is hardly possible, such a viewpoint need not trouble the believer, although it could be a topic of

---

Cf. also Benedetto Croce, *History as the Story of Liberty*, 1941, and R. G. Collingwood, *The Idea of History*, 1946.

[1] The classical document of this sudden reversal is Martin Kähler's *Der sogenannte historische Jesus und der geschichtliche, biblische Christus* (1892). This lecture has received more serious attention during the last generation than it did when it first appeared; the second edition of 1896 was reissued in 1928, and the original edition reappeared in 1953.

[2] E. Stauffer, 'Entmythologisierung oder Realtheologie?', *KuM* II, 27.

[3] Biehl, *TR*, n.F. XXIV, 1957–8, 55, gives a typical definition of 'der historische Jesus': 'Jesus, in so far as he can be made an object of historical-critical research'. It is clear that Bultmann is making use of this definition when e.g. he says (*Kerygma and Myth*, 117): 'The Jesus of history (Ger.: der historische Jesus) is not kerygma, any more than my book was. For in the kerygma Jesus encounters us as the Christ—that is, as the eschatological phenomenon *par excellence*.'

legitimate discussion among historians. For the believer's knowledge of Jesus has been hardly more dependent upon the historian's research than has his knowledge of God. Such research was as a matter of fact largely non-existent during the centuries of most fervent Christian faith. The same situation prevails with regard to another current statement: 'Christian faith is not interested in the historical Jesus.' This statement is to a considerable extent true, if one understands it correctly to mean that Christians throughout the ages have been largely ignorant of and not interested in 'what can be known of Jesus of Nazareth by means of the scientific methods of the historian'. The statement would become largely untrue only if one assumed it to be maintaining that Christian faith is not interested in Jesus of Nazareth.

B. THE END OF THE ORIGINAL QUEST

This discussion of the shifting meaning of the term 'historical Jesus' has already drawn attention to the basic shift in modern man's relation to history, as one of the broad and pervasive reasons why the quest came to an end. But there were also factors at work within the specific area of the study of Jesus which crystallized into the consensus that the quest is both impossible and illegitimate. It is to these factors within the discipline itself that we now wish to turn.

It is often said that Albert Schweitzer's *Quest of the Historical Jesus* marks the end of the quest. This is to a considerable extent true, if one does not take it to mean that his book *caused* the end of the quest. Undoubtedly his book was sufficiently shocking to give pause for thought. But neither of the main points he makes was such as to lead to more than a temporary suspension of the quest: 'The so-called historical Jesus of the nineteenth century biographies is really a modernization, in which Jesus is painted in the colours of modern bourgeois respectability and neo-Kantian moralism.'[1] However Schweitzer did not radicalize this insight

[1] An interesting confirmation of this philosophical origin of the prejudice Schweitzer detected in the original quest may be found in the comparison of the method of exegesis Kant proposed in 1798, and a methodological statement by one of the last representatives of nineteenth-century liberalism in

into a questioning of the objectivity of historical research as such, but himself presented a reconstruction of Jesus which he regarded as objective, simply because it lacked the Victorianism of

---

Germany, Hans Windisch. In *Der Streit der Fakultäten,* Kant proposed a higher form of exegesis, to supersede that current in his day. He summarized his argument as follows (108–11): 'What may be required of the *art* of biblical *interpretation* (hermeneutica sacra), since it may not be left to the laity (for it concerns a scientific system), is, in view of that which in religion is statutory: that the interpreter make clear to himself whether his statement should be understood as *authentic* or *doctrinal.*—In the first case the interpretation must be literally (philologically) appropriate to the meaning of the author; in the second case however the writer has the freedom to write into the text (philosophically) that meaning which it has in exegesis, from a moral, practical point of view (for the edification of the pupil); for faith in a mere historical sentence is dead in the sentence itself.—Although the first method may be important enough for the biblical scholar and indirectly also for the people from some practical point of view, yet the real objective of religious doctrine, to produce morally better men, can not only be missed thereby, but even hindered. . . . Therefore only the *doctrinal* interpretation, which does not need to know (empirically) what kind of meaning the holy author may have connected with his words, but rather what kind of doctrine the reason (*a priori*), in the interest of morals, can at the instigation of a saying read into the text of the Bible, only such a doctrinal interpretation is the sole evangelical, biblical method of teaching the people in true, inner and universal religion. . . . With regard to the religion of a people which has learned to reverence a holy Scripture, the doctrinal interpretation of it, which is related to the people's moral interest—edification, moral improvement, and thus blessedness—is at the same time the authentic interpretation: i.e. it is in this way that God wishes to have his will, revealed in the Bible, to be understood.' With this one can compare Hans Windisch's description of his own exegetical method (in his discussion with H. Jordan: 'Ein Briefwechsel über die Jesusfrage der Gegenwart', *ChrW* XXV, 1911, 988, quoted by Erik Beijer, 'Hans Windisch und seine Bedeutung für die neutestamentliche Wissenschaft', *ZNTW* XLVIII, 1957, 46 f.): 'The typical Jesus of modern criticism, according to the training I went through, is a man who shared many errors of his time, even with regard to religious questions; who was deeply saturated in eschatological ideas (his preaching of repentance and salvation is very intimately bound up with his expectation of the near end of the world); who however is able to lay hold also of modern hearts because of the strength of his divine seizure and because of the clarity and sharpness of his teaching. . . . I claim for myself the privilege, as do Bousset and Weinel, of modernizing the assumedly historical Jesus for practical use, i.e. to work out a figure which is similar to the Jesus of Herrmann's theology. I am fully aware that I am reading subjective interpretations into what is historically provable, and filling out gaps of scholarly research according to practical needs. Only in this procedure I have no inclination to draw near to the ecclesiastical dogma of Christ; rather I accentuate my difference.' These two quotations from Kant and Windisch are related to each other as prophecy and fulfilment, and tend to document this aspect of Schweitzer's thesis.

the classical lives of Christ. Nor did his insight lead him to doubt
the appropriateness of the sources for the kind of chronological
biography he and his predecessors tried to write. Instead he rejected the doubts of Wrede at this point, and to this extent is himself one of the last spokesmen for the nineteenth-century view of
the sources. From his point of view the rejection of the nineteenth-century biographies as modernizations need in no sense
involve a rejection of the quest itself, for the simple reason that an
initial prejudice once detected does not justify the permanent end
of a scholarly project.

The other main point of Schweitzer's presentation is that the
real Jesus of Nazareth was actually less modern than the Nicene
Christ one had originally intended to replace. Schweitzer put it
bluntly: Jesus was the high water mark of Jewish apocalypticism.
Thus the theological value of the original quest in proving the
Ritschlian system was reversed. Schweitzer had little personal
sympathy for eschatology, and saw in it no potentiality for theology today. Consequently his construction was characterized by
a crudity and misunderstanding inevitable in any appraisal of
history from an inner distance. He remained a Ritschlian in his
heart, and never dreamed that he would live to see Jesus' eschatology become the core of modern theology. For theology has out-
lived the initial shock, and, in the movement stemming from Karl
Barth, has learned to understand eschatology existentially from
within. Thus Jesus, rather than becoming a liability to modern
theology, has become the inescapable factor forcing almost every
modern theology into some positive relationship to eschatology.
Jesus' theology is anything but irrelevant or meaningless for
theological thought today. It is clear that neither of the most
striking conclusions of Schweitzer's work was such as to explain
why the quest of the historical Jesus came largely to an end a
generation or more ago.

The real cause behind the end of the quest is to be found in a
series of basic shifts which were taking place in New Testament
scholarship at the opening of the century. These shifts when taken
together formed a decisive cleft between nineteenth- and twenti-

eth-century scholarship, and indicated the *impossibility* and *illegitimacy* of the quest of the historical Jesus. It is to these factors that we consequently turn.

C. THE SOURCES AND THE 'IMPOSSIBILITY' OF THE ORIGINAL QUEST

The *possibility* of the original quest resided primarily in its view of the oldest sources as the same kind of objective, positivistic historiography which the nineteenth century itself aspired to write. The basic reorientation consisted in the discovery that the Gospels are the devotional literature of the primitive Church, rather than the products of scholarship. Thus the function which the tradition about Jesus performed in the life and worship of the Church came to be recognized as the organizing principle in the formation of the individual stories and sayings, and in the formation of the Gospels themselves. This insight, already at home in Old Testament research, was carried over to the New Testament by Wellhausen. The Gospels are primary sources for the history of the early Church, and only secondarily sources for the history of Jesus.[1] Consequently the *Sitz im Leben* of each tradition must be first identified, as the key to the direction in which the tradition would be inclined to develop. Only by discounting this tendency can one then hope to disengage the oldest level in the tradition, and thus come to speak about Jesus of Nazareth in distinction from the Church's kerygmatic presentation of him. This basic methodological insight was implemented by the results of detailed analysis: William Wrede[2] demonstrated that Mark is not writing with the objectivity or even the interests of a modern historian, but rather as a theologian of the 'Messianic secret'. Karl Ludwig Schmidt[3] demonstrated that the order of events in the Gospels is not based upon a memory of the order of Jesus'

[1]This particular formulation was used by Wellhausen of Mark 8–10 and Q, but is sufficiently characteristic of his whole position in his *Einleitung in die drei ersten Evangelien* (1906, 2nd ed. 1911) to serve Bultmann ('The New Approach to the Synoptic Problem', *The Journal of Religion* VI, 1926, 341) as a summary of Wellhausen's whole position.

[2]*Das Messiasgeheimnis in den Evangelien,* 1901.

[3]*Der Rahmen der Geschichte Jesu,* 1919.

public ministry inherent in the material, but rather is largely the contribution of the redactional process, which assembled unrelated stories, sayings, and small individual collections for devotional purposes, and then arranged them topically or theologically without any serious interest in chronology or geography. The basic theses of these works have not been disproved, and therefore must continue to be presupposed in current scholarship conversant with them.

It is often assumed that the original quest came to an end in Germany because of the rise of form criticism. Since form criticism has been widely rejected in the English-speaking world, the inference is readily drawn that the original quest can properly continue untroubled.[1] However the basic assumption is in error. It was not form criticism, but rather the revolution in the generation preceding form criticism, which brought the original quest to an end. Form criticism was an outstanding attempt to implement some of those insights, but they themselves are more basic and have proved to be more lasting that has form criticism itself.

The form critic conjectured that one way to identify the *Sitz im Leben* of the gospel tradition would be to classify the material on purely formal grounds, and then to identify the function in the Church's life responsible for the rise of each identified form. This procedure is methodologically sound, but did not in practice arrive at ultimately conclusive results. This was due to the indistinctness of the formal structure of much of the material, and the difficulty of making a clear correlation between formal tendencies and their setting in the Church's life. Consequently when the form critics came to discuss the historicity of the gospel tradition, a question for which their method was at best only indirectly relevant, they tended to arrive at the conclusion which their general orientation suggested, rather than a conclusion which

[1]Vincent Taylor (*ExpT* LIII, 1941–2, 61 f.) cites rejections of form criticism by F. C. Burkitt, F. W. Howard, A. H. McNeile, and C. H. Dodd, and then remarks: 'Important, however, as these judgements are, they are opinions and no more. No one has built upon them. The universities of Great Britain are silent.'

form criticism as such required. Thus their views as to the material's historicity ranged from the more conservative position of Albertz to the mediating position of Dibelius and the radical position of Bultmann.[1] A second consequence of the inconclusiveness of the results of form criticism is that the mention of their 'forms' has largely passed out of the scholarly discussion of gospel passages, even in Germany. Thus one may say that form criticism, as applied to the gospel tradition, has to a large extent passed out of vogue. Yet it is all the more striking that the basic orientation with regard to the Gospels, of which form criticism was but one manifestation, continues as the basis of twentieth-century scholarship.

This basic reorientation is to the effect that *all* the tradition about Jesus survived only in so far as it served some function in the life and worship of the primitive Church. History survived only as *kerygma*. It is this insight which reversed our understanding of the scholar's situation with regard to the relation of factual detail and theological interpretation in the gospels. If the nineteenth century presupposed the detailed historicity of the Synoptic Gospels except where 'doctrinal tampering' was so obvious as to be inescapable (they had in mind such things as 'Paulinisms' and the miraculous), the twentieth century presupposes the kerygmatic nature of the Gospels, and feels really confident in asserting the historicity of its details only where their origin cannot be ex-

[1]Vincent Taylor (*The Formation of the Gospel Tradition*, 1933, vi) pointed out that the negative results often held to inhere in form criticism are 'not the necessary trend of the method; on the contrary, when its limitations are recognized, Form-Criticism seems . . . to furnish constructive suggestions which in many ways confirm the historical trustworthiness of the Gospel tradition.' Similarly F. C. Grant observes in his review of Dibelius' *Die Botschaft von Jesus Christus* (*Anglican Theol. Review* XVIII, 1936, 103): 'Form-Criticism has not done away with our knowledge of the historical Jesus; on the contrary, it has brought him and the earliest body of his followers far closer to us than ever before.' Cf. also M. M. Parvis, 'NT Criticism in the World-Wars Period', in *The Study of the Bible Today and Tomorrow* (ed. by Harold R. Willoughby, 1947), esp. pp. 61–68. Jeremias ('Der gegenwartige Stand der Debatte um das Problem des historischen Jesus', 168) lists form criticism among the better equipment we now have for a quest, and states: 'It is much too little known and observed that the essential significance of form criticism is that it aids us in removing a Hellenistic layer which had placed itself over the older Palestinian tradition.'

plained in terms of the life of the Church.[1] In the nineteenth century the burden of proof lay upon the scholar who saw theological interpolations in historical sources; in the twentieth century the burden of proof lies upon the scholar who sees objective factual source material in the primitive Church's book of common worship. The result is obvious: the burden of proof has shifted over to the person who maintains the possibility of the quest. This situation does not necessitate the further inference that such a quest is impossible; but it does explain how such a position seemed from a scholarly point of view 'safest', easiest to defend.

D. THE KERYGMA AND THE 'ILLEGITIMACY' OF THE ORIGINAL QUEST

If we wished to summarize in one word these considerations which led to the view that the quest was impossible, we could speak of the discovery of the *kerygma* at the centre of the Gospels. It is only here that we reach the unifying factor in all the elements bringing the quest to an end. For as a matter of fact the discovery of the *kerygma* had an even more pervasive effect upon our problem than has been stated thus far. The *kerygma* came gradually to be recognized as the centre not only of the Gospels, but also of primitive Christianity itself. Furthermore it has increasingly come to replace the theological centrality of the 'historical Jesus' in leading theological systems of our day. It was this rise of the

[1]Cf. my discussion of the resultant methodological difficulties, 'The Historical Jesus and the Church's Kerygma', *Religion in Life* XXVI, 1956–7, 40–49. The broad effect of this methodological aspect can be seen from the quotation by Vincent Taylor (*ExpT* LIII, 1941–2, 60 f.) of the method proposed by S. J. Case in his *Jesus—A New Biography*, 1927, 115: 'Every statement in the records is to be judged by the degree of its suitableness to the distinctive environment of Jesus, on the one hand, and to that of the framers of Gospel tradition at one or another stage in the history of Christianity on the other.' Taylor draws the obvious inference: 'It is not surprising that, with such a test as "our safest guide", the results were extremely meagre.' T. W. Manson observes (*ExpT* LIII, 1941–2, 249: 'Of any story or teaching we may ask concerning its "Sitz im Leben"—is it a "Sitz im Leben Jesu" or a "Sitz im Leben der alten Kitche"? It is sometimes overlooked that an affirmative answer to the latter alternative does not automatically carry with it a negative answer to the former.' This is of course correct; but Manson himself has failed to observe that it does automatically shift the burden of proof: since the historian now works backward from the date of composition rather

kerygma to the centre of our understanding of primitive Christianity, and to the normative position in contemporary theology, which was the underlying cause for questioning even the *legitimacy* of the original quest. It is this second aspect of the role of the *kerygma* in the problem of the historical Jesus which still remains to be examined in some detail.

If the nineteenth-century view of history found its meaningful expression in 'the historical Jesus', the twentieth century has found its approach to history already anticipated in the *kerygma*. We have already noted how the positivistic understanding of history as consisting of brute facts gave way to an understanding of history centring in the profound intentions, stances, and concepts of existence held by persons in the past, as the well-springs of their outward actions. Historical methodology shifted accordingly from a primary concern for recording the past 'wie es eigentlich gewesen', i.e. cataloguing with objective detachment facts in sequence and with proper casual relationships. Instead, the historian's task was seen to consist in understanding those deeplying intentions of the past, by involving one's selfhood in an encounter in which one's own intentions and views of existence are put in question, and perhaps altered or even radically reversed. Now the *kerygma* is formally analogous to this new approach to the historian's task, for it consists in an initial understanding of the deeper meaning of Jesus. Therefore the *kerygma*,

---

than forward from Jesus' lifetime in his search for a historical 'cause' of the material before him, the detection of such a sufficient 'cause' in the life of the Church would place the burden of proof upon the person who wished to affirm the existence of another 'cause' of the item under consideration lying still farther back, i.e. back in the life of Jesus. For an acute formulation of these difficulties within the context of the new quest cf. Käsemann, *ZTK* LI, 1954, 144: 'We wish to characterize the embarrassment of critical research only in a few rough lines: the historical reliability of the synoptic tradition has become doubtful all along the line; yet for working out the authentic material going back to Jesus we are largely lacking in an essential presupposition, namely a survey of the earliest stage of the primitive Church, and are almost completely lacking in sufficient and valid criteria. Only in one single case do we have relatively firm ground under our feet, namely when for some reason a tradition can neither be derived from Judaism nor attributed to primitive Christianity, and especially when Jewish Christianity has toned down or bent the material it received as too daring.'

rather than brute facts of Jesus' external biography, was identified as our primary historical source for understanding his meaning. Of course this does not mean that the historian automatically accepts the *kerygma* as the correct interpretation of Jesus' meaning, for it, like any other interpretation, is subject to critical re-examination. But it does mean that we have moved beyond the initial conclusion that the kerygmatized Gospels are incompatible with the historian's objectives, to the recognition that they in their way are doing something similar to what the modern historian in his way would like to do.

Just as the *kerygma* provided a *rapprochement* to the current view of history and historiography, it also provided the unifying factor between the twentieth-century reconstruction of primitive Christianity and its own systematic theological reflection. This becomes apparent when one scans the interrelated course of New Testament research and systematic thought in this century. The century opened with the older generation still following the Ritschlian approach to God in terms of ethical idealism,[1] and to Jesus as the historical fact exemplifying that ideal. However Ritschlianism was already giving way to the *religionsgeschichtliche Schule*, whose philosophy of religion centred in a decided preference for cultic experience over ethical action, and whose historical reconstruction saw primitive Christianity orientated like other Hellenistic religions to the cult's dying and rising Lord, rather than to the Jesus of the Sermon on the Mount. This school combined its theological and historical positions into the normative statement that Christianity centres in a numinous experience of the dying and rising Lord, not in the ethical experience of the historical Jesus. Christ the

---

[1]This neo-Kantian background of Ritschlianism became explicit as early as Wilhelm Herrmann's *Die Religion im Verhaltnis zum Welterkennen und zur Sittlichkeit*, 1879, which marked the shift away from the basis of the mediating theology in idealistic metaphysics to the neo-Kantian connexion of religion with ethics (cf. my work *Das Problem des Heiligen Geistes bei Wilhelm Herrmann*, 1952). This union is still a commonplace at the end of the Ritschlian period, e.g. in Harnack's position in his debate with Barth of 1923 (cf. Vol. 3 of Barth's collected essays, *Theologische Fragen und Antworten*, 1957, 8): 'If God and world (life in God and worldly life) are absolute contradictions, how is education to God, i.e. to the good, possible? But how is education possible without historical knowledge and high esteem of morality?'

Lord is the cult symbol of Christianity, but it would be an instance of the genetic fallacy to concern oneself with problems related to the historical origin of that symbol, i.e. its relation to the historical Jesus.

Between the wars the *religionsgeschichtliche Schule* faded away, and its historical reconstruction underwent a transformation in terms of more current theological orientations. The emphasis of comparative religion on the point that primitive Christianity centred in a dying and rising divinity was subsequently transformed, for instance by C. H. Dodd, into the emphasis on the point that the original *kerygma* had at its centre Christ's death and resurrection. And under Barthian influence, Rudolf Otto's 'numinous' experience of the *tremendum* and *fascinans* was clarified as an existential encounter with the proclamation of Jesus' death and resurrection, i.e. as judgement and grace.[1] Thus the *kerygma* became recognized as central in both senses of the term: as the content of the message and as the act of preaching.[2]

[1] This is e.g. the avenue by which Bultmann shifted from the comparative religious school into the contemporary discussion. Cf. *GuV* I, 22, and his review of Barth's *Romans*, *ChrW* XXXVI, 1922, 320.

[2] C. F. Evans, 'The Kerygma', *JTS*, n.s. VII, 1956, 26, in his polemic against Dodd's view, attempts to eliminate from the NT the usage of κήρυγμα to designate the content of the message. The same thesis is presented over against Bultmann by Kurt Goldammer, 'Der *Kerygma*-Begriff in der ältesten christlichen Literatur', *ZNTW* XLVIII, 1957, 80 f. However the complete elimination of the meaning 'content of the message' cannot be carried through in I Cor. 1.21, in view of the context, vv. 18, 23 (cf. G. Friedrich in *TWNT* III, 715). It is true that the same term is used in 2.4 to designate the act of preaching, rather than the content. But it becomes unnecessary to harmonize the meaning in 1.21 with that of 2.4, once one has recognized that Paul is in 2.4 (as frequently elsewhere) applying the *content* of the *kerygma* (repeated in 2.2) to his own existence, in this case his existence as *preacher* (cf. an existential application already in 1.26–31). Thus the use of the two meanings of the term in one context (1.21; 2.4) is due to Paul's recognizing that the past action of God in Christ (the content of the *kerygma*) recurs in his presence existence (the act of preaching). Of course it is of considerably more importance than debating the NT usage of the term, to recognize that the *kerygma* of primitive Christianity, whatever they may or may not have called it, did have in it these two aspects of 'recital of past event' and 'recurrence of present event'. This point is well made by William Baird, 'What is the Kerygma? A Study of I Cor. 15.3–8 and Gal. 1.11–17', *JBL* LXXVI, 1957, 181–91. Much the same point with regard to the tradition had already been made by Oscar Cullmann, 'The Tradition', in *The Early Church*, 55–99, a reprint of his article '*Kyrios* as Designation for the Oral Tradition concerning

These two aspects of the term correspond respectively to the contemporary historical reconstruction of primitive Christianity and to the normative centre of contemporary theology, so that the term *kerygma* comes to represent the unifying element in the contemporary situation: historically speaking, the central content of primitive Christian preaching was God's eschatological action centring in the saving event of cross and resurrection. Theologically speaking, this saving event proclaimed by the *kerygma* shows itself to be eschatological precisely by recurring in the proclamation of the *kerygma* itself: the act of proclaiming Jesus' death and resurrection becomes God's act calling upon me to accept my death and receive resurrected life.[1] Believing the witness about God's past action in Christ coincides with the occur-

---

Jesus (*Paradosis* and *Kyrios*)', *Scottish Journal of Theology* III, 1950, 180–97 (cf. my review, *JBL* LXXV, 1956, 238–9).

[1] The coinciding of the witness to past event with the present recurrence of the event in Paul's theology has been worked out by Bultmann (*Theology of the New Testament* I, 292 ff.), who presents this as basic to the whole biblical concept of the Word of God (*GuV* I, 287 f.): '*Thus the relation to history is a constitutive character of the Word of God in the* OT. And whatever historical events may be named, irrespective of whether one's fantasy moves *via* the delivery from Egypt back even to patriarchal times, or whether God's acts in the most recent past are named, history is conceived of as a unity, as unified action of God, out of which each Now arises, and which gives to each Now and thus to each Word of God spoken to Now its character. In this sense *the Word as call* (for decision) *is at the same time communication* (of information), and both form a unity, since what is communicated, *the history, itself calls in the Now*. Consequently obedient submission under the Word encountered now is at the same time faithfulness to what God did to the people and thus to the individual. *Faith is obedience, which is at the same time faithfulness and trust.* Thus the communicating of the past does not have the meaning of a historical report, but rather is a call, in which the past is contemporized. The contemporizing of history takes place neither in poetic recollection, nor in scholarly reconstruction, but rather in a calling tradition, in which the history itself "becomes vocal", becomes the Word.' A remarkably similar position as to the nature of history is taken by R. G. Collingwood (*The Idea of History*, 1946, 158): 'The historian, if he thinks his past is a dead past, is certainly making a mistake; but Oakeshott (*Experience and its Modes*, 1933, 111) supposes that there is no third alternative to the disjunction that the past is either a dead past or not past at all but simply present. The third alternative is that it should be a living past, a past which, because it was thought and not mere natural event, can be re-enacted in the present and in that re-enactment known as past.' Cf. also paragraph 76 of Martin Heidegger's *Sein und Zeit*, 1927: 'Der existenziale Ursprung der Historie aus der Geschichtlichkeit des Daseins.'

rence of this divine action in my present life. Herein resides the unity of God's action in history, and ultimately the meaningfulness of the Trinity. Thus both as witness to past event and as experience of present event, the *kerygma* is central in primitive Christianity and contemporary theology. It is for this reason that the *kerygma* has become a whole unified theological position which has just as nearly swept the field in twentieth-century theology as did the theology of the historical Jesus in the nineteenth century.

The historian's detection of the *kerygma* at the centre of the Gospels found a formal analogy in the contemporary view of historiography as concerned with underlying meaning, and this correlation led to the view that the kind of quest of the historical Jesus envisaged by the nineteenth century not only *cannot* succeed, but is hardly appropriate to the intention of the Gospels and the goal of modern historiography. The theologian's recognition that the *kerygma* provides the normative pattern of contemporary religious experience also found a formal analogy in the contemporary view of existence, and it is *this* correlation which gave impetus to the view that the kind of quest which the nineteenth century envisaged *ought not* to succeed.

Christianity began with the call of the eschatological *kerygma* to break with the 'present evil aeon' and to commit oneself existentially to the 'aeon to come', which has drawn so near as to be already the horizon of present existence (e.g. Matt. 4.17; Rom. 12.2). God's judgement upon this world must be accepted as God's judgement upon myself, while the kingdom breaking in and destroying the present evil aeon is accepted as the grace of God in my life. Thus the *kerygma* proclaims the death in which resides life (Mark 8.35), a *kerygma* incarnated in Jesus and therefore shifting terminologically from Jesus' own eschatological message into the Church's christological *kerygma*: this death in which life resides is Jesus' death, and becomes available only in dying and rising with him. This meant for the earliest disciples a basic renunciation of the struggle for existence, implemented by a complete break with the power structure of society: the automatic prerogatives of the chosen people, the security of the holy tradition, the comfort of established religious organization and clergy—all such props, controlled by man and as a result constantly available to him for securing his existence, were in principle eliminated. Judaism's 'confidence in the flesh' was revealed as the basic rebellion of the *homo religiosus* against God (e.g. Phil. 3; Rom. 10.3). Man must build his existence upon that which is beyond his control and available only as God's gift (*ubi et quando visum est deo*), upon a world which is transcendent by being basically future, and present only as the eschatological miracle, the gift of transcendence. Thus 'faith', the pattern of contemporary religious experience which is to relate us to God through Christ, cannot by its very nature be built upon 'the present evil aeon', with all that it provides of worldly security under man's control and invariably at his disposal; by definition 'faith' is the life given in death, and consequently has its basis beyond our control, is lived out of the future, is 'an act of faith'.

Now it became increasingly clear that 'the historical Jesus', the scholarly reconstruction of Jesus' biography by means of objective historical method, was just such an attempt to build one's existence upon that which is under man's control and invariably at his disposal. The historical Jesus as a proven divine fact is a worldly security with which the *homo religiosus* arms himself in his effort to become self-sufficient before God, just as did the Jew in Paul's day by appeal to the law. Whereas the *kerygma* calls for existential commitment to the meaning of Jesus, the original quest was an attempt to avoid the risk of faith by supplying objectively verified proof for its 'faith'. To require an objective legitimization of the saving event prior to faith is to take offence at the offence of Christianity and to perpetuate the unbelieving flight to security, i.e. the reverse of faith. For faith involves the rejection of worldly security as righteousness by works. Thus one has come to recognize the worldliness of the 'historicism' and 'psychologism' upon which the original quest was built. To this extent the original quest came to be regarded as theologically illegitimate.

The classical document for this radical shift in the theological appraisal of the quest is the debate in 1923 between Harnack and Barth.[1] For Harnack, the 'content of the gospel' consisted in concepts which must be disengaged from the historical ambiguities of the Bible and then grasped intellectually, a task which can only be performed by 'historical knowledge and critical reflection'. This same rationalistic approach to the gospel was applied to the believer's knowledge of Jesus: 'If the person of Jesus Christ stands at the centre of the gospel, how can the basis for a reliable and communal knowledge of this person be gained other than through critical historical study, if one is not to trade a dreamed-up Christ for the real one? But how is this study to be made except by scholarly theology?' To this Barth replied: 'The reliability and communal nature of the knowledge of the person of Jesus Christ as the centre of the *gospel* can be no other than the reliability and communal nature of the *faith* awakened by God. Critical historical study signifies the deserved and necessary end of those 'bases' of such knowledge which are no bases since they are not laid by God himself. The man who does not yet know (and that *still* means all of us) that we know Christ *no* longer according to the flesh, can learn it from critical biblical scholarship: the more radically he is shocked, the better it is both for him and for the cause. And this may then perhaps be the service which "historical knowledge" can perform for the real task of theology.' Barth's basic position was that the 'theme of theology' is 'God's revelation', rather than any given concepts in the history of ideas. Consequently the fundamental role of historical critical scholarship would be quite different from that which Harnack conceived it to be: 'Historical knowledge could then of course say that the communicating of the "content of the gospel", at least according to its own statement, can be carried out only by an action of this "content" *himself*. "Critical reflection" could lead to the result that this statement made by the gospel is based in the

[1] In *Die Christliche Welt*, reprinted in the third volume of Barth's *Gesammelte Vorträge* which is entitled *Theologische Fragen und Antworten*, 1957, 'Ein Briefwechsel mit Adolf von Harnack', 7–31.

nature of the case (the relation between God and man), and consequently is to be seriously respected.' Bultmann[1] promptly shifted away from liberalism to the position of Barth, and the rejection of the quest on theological grounds gradually became a commonplace of contemporary theology.

Now the theological considerations leading to the rejection of the original quest as illegitimate correspond formally to the general pattern of existentialistic thought in our day. For existentialism usually conceives of inauthentic existence as man's attempt to avoid the 'awful freedom' of his historicity, and to find security in his human nature, which is understood quite rationalistically: the individual is a particular, comfortably subsumed under a universal. Inauthentic existence is a life built upon conformity, the herd instinct, the tradition, that which is objectively available and controllable. The original quest was thus one way of implementing such a proclivity toward inauthentic existence.[2]

This is not to say that authentic existence as understood by existentialism is materially the same as eschatological existence, but only that there is a formal analogy. For both viewpoints authentic existence is selfhood constituted by commitment, and consists in constant *engagement*. The nature of the commitment can vary as sharply as do Faust and Jesus; the 'world' in which one is *engagé* can vary as radically as do 'the present evil aeon' and the kingdom of God. The formal analogy affects the substance at

---

[1]'Die liberale Theologie und die jungste theologische Bewegung', *TB* III, 1924, 73–86, reprinted in *GuV* I, 1–25. For this specific point cf. p. 3 f.

[2]Martin Heidegger, *Sein und Zeit*, 1927, 395: 'The question as to whether history has as its object the listing of unique, "individual" affairs or also "laws" has already gone astray at the root. The theme of history is neither the purely unique occurrence nor some generality floating above it, but rather the possibility which was factually existent. This is not reproduced as such, i.e. really understood historically, when it is perverted into the pallor of a supra-historical pattern. Only factual authentic historicity, as determined fate, is able so to open up the history which has been, that in the repetition the "power" of the possible strikes into one's factual existence, i.e. comes to it as its futurity. . . . In no science are the "universal validity" of the standards and the claims of "universality" which the impersonal "one" and its common sense requires, *less* possible criteria of "truth" than in authentic history.

only one point: a Christian content without the form of commitment and *engagement* becomes a this-worldly Christendom at ease in Zion, a dead orthodoxy, a white-washed tomb, a tinkling cymbal, and ceases really to be the Christian content. A Jesus whose role is established in terms of this world is not the eschatological Messiah transcending this world.

This formal analogy between Christian existence and existentialism draws attention to another aspect of 'historicism' which is theologically illegitimate. Sometimes historical critical scholars absolutized their method of objectivity into a permanent avoidance of existential encounter with the history they were supposedly studying. But existentialism insists that one should be *engagé*, with one's whole selfhood at stake, in the 'world' in which one moves. And the *kerygma* calls for a total encounter with the person of Jesus, in which the self is put in radical decision. Therefore it can only regard as illegitimate a scholarly career which becomes in the long run no more than a distracting fascination with historical details about Jesus, details which may occupy the memory, move the emotions, prod the conscience, or stimulate the intellect, but fail to put the self in radical decision. This insight in no sense invalidated the role of detailed and exacting research. But it did mean that the historian's personal authenticity could not be found in increasingly narrowed specialization; rather this came to be recognized as an escape mechanism in a situation where one's research had actually become existentially meaningless. Thus both forms which the historical study of Jesus took at the opening of the century—the attempt to prove historically his absoluteness, and the ultimate lack of interest in him as a possible understanding of one's own existence, came to be recognized as illegitimate. In each of these various ways the temper of our day united with the course of theological and historical reflection to bring the quest of the historical Jesus to an end.

III

THE POSSIBILITY OF A NEW QUEST

If the rise of the *kerygma* meant that we cannot and ought not continue the quest of the historical Jesus, any reappraisal of the problem must concentrate upon these two aspects. Therefore we first inquire as to whether we *can* renew the quest of the historical Jesus.

A. THE 'HISTORICAL SECTION' OF THE KERYGMA?

The more one catches sight of the decisive role the *kerygma* played in bringing the quest to an end, the more one recognizes the relevance of C. H. Dodd's attempt to show that the *kerygma* contained something corresponding to a life of Jesus, namely a sketch of the public ministry.[1] However his competent presentation only served to show the difficulties inherent in such an avenue toward reconciling the *kerygma* and the quest of the historical Jesus.

First of all, he neglected the fact that the *kerygma* receives its tremendous authority in theology today not simply from its position in the history of ideas, i.e. not simply as precedent, but rather from its existential function as a call to faith, in which God calls upon me to accept his judgement upon me in Jesus' death, and to live from his grace in Jesus' resurrection. Even if the *kerygma* as historical precedent contained details of Jesus' bio-

[1]The relevance of his attempt is evident, e.g. from the following statement by Hermann Diem, *Theologie* II, 78: 'The life and preaching of the historical Jesus are available for us only in the post-Easter *kerygma*, and are so covered over by it that it is impossible to reconstruct out of it again a history of Jesus. The Synoptics are of course of the opinion that they are giving historical factual reports, although measured by our modern meaning of history they operate in a naïvely uncritical way. But their reporting exclusively served the *kerygma*, which concentrated on cross and resurrection.'

graphy, just as it contained at times mythological motifs from Hellenistic syncretism, the *kerygma* as eschatological event does not impose upon me the thought patterns with which it originally operated. For Dodd's approach to succeed, it would be necessary to show that the inclusion of details from Jesus' life is not part of the *adiaphora*, i.e. not just one means among others of emphasizing the incarnation, but rather that it is indispensable for conveying the existential meaning of the *kerygma*, i.e. is constitutive of the *kerygma* as eschatological event. This is difficult in view of the fact that apart from Acts the *kerygma* is almost totally lacking in biographical facts, and that in Acts the facts listed vary from sermon to sermon.[1]

The way in which Dodd attempts to reconcile the *kerygma* and the quest is in the second place misleading, since it interprets the 'historical section of the *kerygma*' (47)[2] in terms of a positivistic view of history, rather than in terms of the theological approach to history which actually characterized primitive Christianity. For Dodd characterizes this 'historical section' as presenting the 'historical facts of the life of Jesus' (31), a 'comprehensive summary of the facts of the ministry of Jesus' (28), so that the average reader would be misled into the assumption that the *kerygma* was concerned with the objectively verifiable 'data' (29) of the historian. To begin with, this language suggests considerably more 'data' than are actually to be found in the rather meagre factual detail of the sermons in Acts, not to speak of the almost complete absence of such detail in kerygmatic texts outside Acts. But even more important, the direction in which this 'historical section' is interpreted is in terms of the *Sitz im Leben* of the historian, rather than

[1]Somewhat analogous is the widespread modern viewpoint that certain facts are essential to the *kerygma*, and an almost equally widespread dissensus as to which these essential facts are. This point has been made by William Baird (*JBL* LXXVI, 1957, 182), who points to this discrepancy within the agreement of A. Hunter, C. T. Craig, F. V. Filson, T. F. Glasson, and B. Gärtner. E. L. Allen, 'The Lost Kerygma', *New Testament Studies* III, 1957, 349–53, has shown that the most impressive list of facts in the *kerygma*, the list of appearances in I Cor. 15.3 ff., seems to have been largely 'lost' prior to the writing of the resurrection narratives of the Gospels.

[2]Numbers refer to pages of *The Apostolic Preaching and its Development*, 1936, 2nd ed. 1944.

in terms of the *Sitz im Leben* of the primitive Christian. It may be that kerygmatic allusions to Jesus' humility, meekness, gentleness, love, forgiveness and obedience derive from historical memory of Jesus;[1] but the 'historical value' which such material may have is far from its kerygmatic meaning, which is more accurately stated by Bultmann, in language actually intended to state the significance of the pre-existence in the *kerygma*: 'That Jesus, the historical person, did this service for us, and that he did it not out of personal sympathy and loveableness, but rather by God acting in him, in that God established his love for us through Jesus dying for us sinners (Rom. 5.6–8).'[2]

One need only read the kerygmatic hymn in Phil. 2.6–11 to see the role this 'historical section of the *kerygma*' originally played:

I

6 Who being in the form of God
  Did not count equality with God a thing to be grasped
7 But emptied himself,
  Taking the form of a servant.

II

Being born in the likeness of man
And being found in human form
8 He humbled himself
Becoming obedient unto death (i.e. the death of the cross).

III

9 Therefore God has highly exalted him
  And bestowed on him the name which is above every name,
10 That at the name of Jesus every knee should bow,
    (in heaven and on earth and under the earth)
11 And every tongue confess: JESUS CHRIST IS LORD
    (to the glory of God the Father).[3]

[1] So Dodd, *History and the Gospel*, 1938, Ch. II. One should observe that this possibility is far from proven by Dodd, who contents himself with the demonstration that these motifs do not derive from OT prophecy.

[2] *GuV* I, 213.

[3] This strophic arrangement was proposed by Joachim Jeremias, 'Zur Gedankenführung in den paulinischen Briefen', *Studia Paulina*, 1953, 152–4, and was accepted by Otto Michel, 'Zur Exegese von Phil. 2.5–11', *Theologie als Glaubenswagnis*, 1954, 79–95. It was arrived at independently by L. Cerfaux, 'L'hymne au Christ-Serviteur de Dieu', *Miscellanea historica in honorem Alberti de Meyer*, 1946, 117–30, although without any of Jeremias' deletions from the Pauline text.

Although no facts from Jesus' life are reported, his humiliation is emphasized as the indispensable presupposition of his exaltation. It is this meaning of humiliation which keeps the 'historical section of the *kerygma*' from attempting to legitimize the *kerygma* with objectively demonstrable 'signs'. For not only did Jesus reject such an insistence upon legitimizing signs, but Paul explicitly recognized the rejection of such signs as inherent in the existential meaning of the *kerygma* (I Cor. 1.17–25).[1] Consequently when details do on occasion come to be introduced into the 'historical section of the *kerygma*', the normative significance of their introduction should not be seen in terms of positivistic historiography. Rather is it necessary to seek to trace the original kerygmatic meaning at work in this procedure, in order to reach a valid kerygmatic approach to the Gospels and a normative basis for a modern quest of the historical Jesus.

The central strophe in the hymn of Phil. 2.6–11 presents Jesus' earthly life in the lowest possible terms,[2] precisely because the first strophe about the Pre-existent[3] and the third strophe about

[1] An interesting parallel is to be found in the case of Paul's discussion of the 'signs' legitimizing himself, in II Cor. 10–13. Here he begins by listing facts which positively demonstrate his superiority—but all under the admission 'I am speaking as a fool', i.e. such a method is contrary to the *kerygma*. Then he shifts to speaking paradoxically of his humiliation, as the only Christian way of speaking of one's own history.

[2] Käsemann, 'Kritische Analyse von Phil. 2.5–11', ZTK XLVII, 1950, 334 ff., rightly accentuates this aspect of the hymn.

[3] Cf. Bultmann, *GuV* I, 213: 'That Jesus, the historical person, did this service for us (sc. of renewing us to a new understanding of ourselves in obedience and love), and that he did it not out of personal sympathy and loveableness, but rather by God acting in him, in that God established his love for us through Jesus dying for us sinners (Rom. 5.6–8)—that is the meaning of language about the Preexistent.' *Kerygma and Myth*, 35: 'Our interest in the events of his life, and above all in the cross, is more than an academic concern with the history of the past. We can see meaning in them only when we ask what God is trying to say to each one of us through them. Again, the figure of Jesus cannot be understood simply from his context in human evolution or history. In mythological language, this means that he stems from eternity, his origin transcends both history and nature.' One may question whether, with Jeremias, the whole of strophe I in Phil. 2.6–11 treats of the Pre-existent, or whether, with Käsemann (ZTK XLVII, 1950, 334 ff.), incarnation is not rather already involved in the last half of strophe I.

the Exalted[1] point to the meaningfulness of his (and therefore our) very ambiguous historical existence. Although pre-existence and exaltation are, so to speak, chronologically separate from the life, they reveal the life's whence and whither, and are thus a way of expressing its meaning. This method is quite common in kerygmatic texts of the briefer 'humiliation—exaltation' type (Rom. 1.3–4; I Tim. 3.16; I Peter 3.18b), as well as in kerygmatic texts with much the same 'pre-existence—humiliation—exaltation' pattern as Phil. 2.6–11 (e.g. Col. 1.15–20; Heb. 1.2 ff.; II Cor. 8.9; Rom. 10.6–9; I Cor. 8.6). Even though the 'historical section' or humiliation seems even to disappear from some of these kerygmatic texts, their original intention was to emphasize the meaningfulness of Jesus' historicity or humiliation, and only with gnosticism was this original meaning lost.

Consequently the introduction of details into the 'historical section of the *kerygma*' is valid only[2] as an impressive way of witnessing to this kerygmatic message, that in suffering lies glory, in death resides life, in judgement is to be found grace. Whereas the *kerygma* customarily describes this 'exaltation to be found in humiliation' by stating the exaltation *outside* the 'historical section', sometimes the *kerygma* superimposes the exaltation *upon* the

---

[1]Lohmeyer, *Kyrios Jesus. Eine Untersuchung zu Phil. 2.5–11*, 1928, 56: 'The name Jesus seems to have been chosen in order to remain in the realm of the historical.' Käsemann (*ZTK* XLVII, 1950, 354) locates the same emphasis in the meaning of the whole hymn: 'The scope of the whole, according to the analysis here carried through, is: the obedient one is the Cosmocrator. As such he is criterion and κριτής of all history. In the last judgement there stands only this theme for discussion, whether we were obedient or not. . . . This distinguishes the Christian *kerygma* from myth, that the obedient one, and he alone, determines the cosmos and its history in this way. And what is meant here by obedience has become clear from the interpretation of vv. 7–8, namely this, that lowliness is laid hold of as the possibility of freedom. The myth, which was and is always interested in apotheosis, never proclaimed this. Here is its limit, and here it is demonstrated that the primitive Christian message is only making use for its own purposes of the myth's categories.'

[2]Cf. the *Sachkritik* advocated here by Bultmann (*GuV* I, 54; *Kerygma and Myth*, 112; *Theology of the New Testament* I, 295) with regard to I Cor. 15.5, and by Ernst Haenchen (*Die Apostelgeschichte*, 1956, 154) with regard to Acts 2.22. For a divergent exegesis of I Cor. 15.5 cf., in addition to Karl Barth, *The Resurrection of the Dead*, 1933, 131 ff.: Ernst Fuchs, *Hermeneutik*, 1954, 185, and *ZTK* LIII, 1956, 212. Cf. also Diem's attempt to mediate, *Theologie* II, 112 f.

humiliation, so that life becomes visible *in* death, glory *in* suffering, grace *in* judgement, the exaltation *in* the humiliation, the resurrection glory *in* the 'historical section'. The statements about Jesus 'in the flesh', originally intended to designate only the humiliation half of the paradox, come to express both sides of it. 'Put to death in the flesh' (I Peter 3.18) becomes '*Revealed* in the flesh' (I Tim. 3.16).[1] And the statement of Jesus' this-worldly origin 'according to the flesh' is not only *followed* by a statement about his other-worldly origin 'according to the Spirit', but also includes *within* the this-worldly side an allusion to the messianic lineage (Rom. 1.3; 9.5; Ignatius, *Smyrn.* 1.1), so that both sides of the paradox are present within the 'historical section'.[2] Another expression for Jesus' this-worldly origin is 'born of a woman' (Gal. 4.4), and this too comes to express both sides of the paradox, in the expression 'born of a virgin' (Ignatius, *Smyrn.* 1.1; Justin, *Dial.* 85.2; *Apol.* 31.7; 32.14).[3]

Now this trend within the kerygmatic tradition is the move-

[1]Yet the lowly half of the paradox is still retained, in that the line presents a contrasting pair to the exaltation line: 'Justified in the Spirit'. For the antithetic structure of the whole cf. Eduard Schweizer, *Erniedrigung und Erhöhung bei Jesus und seinen Nachfolgern*, 1955, 63–66; *TWNT* VI, 414. The shift from 'put to death' to 'revealed' may be due to the influence of the kerygmatic type designated by N. A. Dahl ('Formgeschichtliche Beobachtungen zur Christusverkündigung in der Gemeindepredigt', *Neutestamentliche Studien für Rudolf Bultmann*, *ZNTW*, Beiheft 21, 1954, 4 f.) as 'revelation-pattern': 'present from eternity on—now revealed'. For a sub-form 'speaks of the mystery which was earlier hidden, but now has been revealed, I Cor. 2.6 ff.; Col. 1.26 f.; Eph. 3.4–7, 8–11; Rom. 16.25 f.' When one recalls (cf. Eduard Norden, *Agnostos Theos*, 1923, 255 f., nn. 5 and 6) the great similarity of I Tim. 3.16 to Rom. 16.25 f. and Col. 1.26 f., where 'revealed' also introduces the transition, the historical origin of this kerygmatic development beyond I Peter 3.18 is explained. Cf. also II *Clem.* 14.2. (An English translation of *Erniedrigung und Erhöhung* will shortly appear in the same series as the present work. Page references here are to the German edition.)

[2]Eduard Schweizer, 'Röm. 1.3 f. und der Gegensatz vom Fleisch und Geist vor und bei Paulus', *EvTh* XIV, 1955, 563–71, and *Erniedrigung und Erhöhung*, 56, sees only the humiliation in the expression; cf. also *TWNT* VI, 414 f. Hans Conzelmann called my attention to the dialectic within the humiliation line itself, as a criticism of Schweizer's presentation.

[3]The lowly half of the paradox is also retained in this expression. In Ignatius, *Smyrn.* 1.1 this is evident from the addition of 'truly', which is used in the brief chapter three times to stress the reality of Jesus' humanity over against docetism. Since the immediately preceding context is a contrasting pair, one may recognize in the immediately following allusion to Jesus'

ment which logically leads to the writing of Gospels.[1] This is most apparent in the case of the Gospel of John. For this Gospel, more self-consciously and explicitly than the others, speaks of Jesus in terms of the *kerygma*. Therefore we should not be surprised to see the Gospel of John consciously superimposing the glory of pre-existence and exaltation upon the 'historical section'. The pre-existent glory 'still' shines in the earthly life: 'The word became flesh, and dwelt among us, and we beheld his glory' (1.14). And the glory of exaltation is 'already' in the earthly life: The cross is 'already' Jesus' 'glorification' (7.39; 12.16; 13.31;

---

pair, one may recognize in the immediately following allusion to Jesus' baptism the 'exaltation' (Spirit) line corresponding to the 'humiliation' of birth, so that the 'flesh-Spirit' pattern evident in the preceding context of David and God's son is repeated of birth by Mary and baptism by the Spirit; in view of I Peter 3.18; I Tim. 3.16, one may even sense the same 'flesh-Spirit' pattern in the following context treating of death and resurrection.—In the first passage from Justin (*Dial.* 85.2), the expression 'born of a virgin' falls within the humiliation half of an a b b a pattern:

> This son of God and firstborn of all creation,
> Both born through a virgin and become passible man,
> Both crucified under Pontius Pilate by your people and killed,
> Both raised from the dead and ascended into heaven.

In the second passage (*Apol.* 31.7), 'begotten through a virgin and made man' (at the incarnation) stands in contrast to 'being and being called son of God' (at the ascension). In the third passage (*Apol.* 32.14), 'through a virgin of the seed of Jacob' stands over against 'through the power of God'.—A similar use of 'Mary' to suggest both humiliation and exaltation may be observed in Ignatius (*Eph.* 18.2):

> By Mary, according to the dispensation of God,
> Of the seed of David, and also of the Holy Spirit.

Here the virginity is clearly recognized, but is listed (19.1) with the birth and death as the mystery which remained hidden until the ascension. In *Eph.* 7.2 'both of Mary and of God' is an antithetic pair corresponding to 'both flesh and spirit, both born and not born'. 'Mary' occurs in anti-docetic polemic to emphasize Jesus' humanity in *Trall.* 9.1.

[1] Thus this discussion should serve as a contribution to the solution of a problem to which T. W. Manson called attention in his lecture on 'The Life of Jesus: A Study of the Available Materials' (*Bulletin of the John Rylands Library* XXVII, 1942–3, 337). He observes correctly that the *kerygma* makes only 'bare mention' of Jesus' ministry 'in the most general terms, without details'. Then he observes: 'Nevertheless, before the end of the first century we have gospels which offer a narrative of the Ministry. We have what Luke calls in his Preface a *diegesis* of the things that had happened, a detailed narrative that links the Ministry with the Passion. How was the transition from *kerygma* to *diegesis* made? There lies one of the most fascinating as it is one of the most vital of Gospel problems.'

17.1, 5) and 'exaltation' (3.14; 8.28; 12.32–34). Similarly the synoptic tradition embedded the exaltation within the humiliation, most clearly in the transfiguration scene, but also in Jesus' miracles, brilliant teachings, and victorious debates. And here too, just as in the case of the sermons in Acts (2.22; 10.38), the use of various Jewish and Hellenistic styles of narrating the divine in history[1] should not mislead us as to the normative kerygmatic significance which is to be maintained throughout this transition from '*kerygma*' to 'narrative'. In the narrative, just as in the *kerygma*, we are confronted with paradox: exaltation in humiliation, life in death, the kingdom of God in the present evil aeon, the eschatological in history. This kerygmatic meaning of the 'historical section' is constitutive of the Gospel as a literary form. This is apparent in Mark's 'messianic secret'[2] and finds expression in the modern definition of the Gospels as 'passion narratives with long introductions'.[3]

[1] Cf. e.g. the discussion of motifs in the miracle stories borrowed from the common stock of the Hellenistic world for portraying the divine man, in Dibelius' *From Tradition to Gospel*, 1934, Ch. IV.

[2] This point has been most clearly made by Hans Conzelmann (*ZTK* LIV, 1957, 293–5), in his reversal of Wrede's explanation of the Marcan 'messianic secret': Mark's 'construction consisted not in forcing unmessianic units into the christological framework of faith, but rather in taking a mass of material already understood in a christological sense and composing it according to the *kerygma* (understood in terms of the secrecy christology). The idea of the secret does not derive from historical, pragmatic considerations. Rather it expresses a positive understanding of revelation, as is apparent e.g. in the passage Mark 4.10–12, composed by Mark himself. It is not the *un*messianic character of the elements of the tradition, but rather their messianic character, which gives difficulty to the evangelist, in view of which he has trouble enough in carrying through his theological doctrine. This is apparent in the literary and even logical violence of such passages as 4.10 ff.; 8.31–33 (in view of the confession to Christ in his source!). . . . The concept of secrecy is apparently supplied by the tradition as a *theological* conception, and in turn provides the possibility of conceiving the material, in form so divergent, under one unified point of view. *The theory of secrecy is the hermeneutic presupposition of the form 'Gospel'*.

[3] Ernst Fuchs (*ZTK* LIII, 1956, 225) has amplified in a twofold sense Martin Kähler's famous definition of the Gospels as passion narratives projected back upon the public ministry. On the one hand the passion does not need to be 'projected back', for it was already in the public ministry. And on the other hand: 'The Gospels are in reality not only passion narratives, but first of all the proclamation of the resurrection, and they are this from the very beginning.'

The paradox inherent in the *kerygma* and the Gospels is beyond objective verification by the historian. Neither the *kerygma*, nor the kerygmatic Gospels, can legitimately be used to lead us into a positivistic approach to the quest of the historical Jesus.

When the emphasis laid by the *kerygma* upon the historicity or humiliation of Jesus has been misunderstood in terms of nine-teenth-century historiography, it is almost inevitable that one would search in the *kerygma* for the implementation of that kind of historiography. Dodd is only carrying out this logical conse-quence when he seeks to find a chronology of the public ministry in the *kerygma*; and the failure of this attempt should confirm the thesis that the basic meaning of Jesus' historicity for the *kerygma* has been misunderstood. Outside Acts, the kerygmatic texts con-tain no factual details from the public ministry. In the sermons of Acts, the few details from the public ministry provide no chrono-logical information. We can infer from Acts 10.37; 13.24 f. that the public ministry's beginning at John the Baptist preceded its end on the cross; but since one knows *a priori* that the beginning precedes the end, this element reflects no more chronological information or interests than does the hymn of Phil. 2.6–11, where we can infer that the incarnation preceded the death. In two sermons of Acts various elements of the public ministry are mentioned, but without chronological order: the 'mighty works and wonders and signs' of 2.22 are not different facts occurring in that order in the public ministry; the only 'order' one might sense is a certain parallel to the order in the immediately preceding prophecy from Joel 2.28–32. Acts 10.38 says that Jesus 'went about doing good and healing all that were oppressed by the devil, for God was with him'. This Lucan formulation includes no chrono-logical sequence; or should we assume that 'doing good' refers to one phase of the public ministry, which was then followed by another, in which 'doing good' was superseded by exorcisms? If so, one would then arrive at the reverse of the Marcan order!

The complete absence from the *kerygma* of a chronology for the public ministry should have been sufficient evidence to indicate that the kind of historicity in which the *kerygma* was interested

differed basically from that with which Dodd was occupied. But
it is indicative of Dodd's intellectual stature that he nonetheless carried through the logic of his position, and does actually
present us with a kerygmatic chronology of the public ministry.
This is worked out in an essay on 'The Framework of the Gospel
Narrative',[1] which is one of the rare serious attempts to refute
Karl Ludwig Schmidt's argument that the Marcan order is not
chronological. Schmidt and others had called attention to the
generalizing summaries ('*Sammelberichte*') introduced into the
Gospel by Mark to hold the narrative together. Dodd now unites
all these '*Sammelberichte*' into a continuous text, and defines this as
a kerygmatic chronology of the public ministry. Now ingenious
though this solution is, it fails, by being a pure conjecture composed of a series of less likely alternatives.

One must first assume that the various '*Sammelberichte*' be-
longed together as a continuous outline, in the order in which they
occur in Mark. But no evidence for this 'original' form in which
they circulated is given, and one of the '*Sammelberichte*' is omitted
by Dodd himself as unfit for this construction. One must then
assume that the order of the reconstructed unit is chronological.
But for this assumption one has neither the support of any other
kerygmatic text, nor the support of the Gospels. For Dodd is
attempting to refute the dominant view since Schmidt of the non-
chronological order of the Gospels, and it would clearly be an
argument in a circle to assume the chronological order of the
Gospels in the argument. Dodd must next maintain that the
'*Sammelberichte*' are not, as has been generally supposed,[2] Marcan
creations, but rather comprise a pre-Marcan kerygmatic tradition.

[1]This essay of 1932 is reprinted in the volume *New Testament Studies,* 1–11.
[2]The view of Henry J. Cadbury, 'The Summaries in Acts', *The Beginnings
of Christianity*, V, 1933, 393, is typical: 'The summaries in the gospels,
whether of teaching or healing or both, are not so primitive as the individual
stories, and have been largely distilled out of them. They are an indication
of an individual author. Their purpose is that of generalizing and of thus
filling the lacuna which is felt when a continuous narrative is to be made out
of detached scenes. They represent the latest part of Mark, and specially
reveal his editorial motives. The later evangelists use these sections of Mark
with great freedom. Desiring a still more connected story they show a tendency to repeat and multiply them.'

Dodd's argument here is to the effect that Mark does not actually follow this reconstructed outline; it is assumed that he attempted to do so, and consequently that his failure indicates that the outline was not his own, but came to him from the tradition. However the case for the existence of the conjectured 'outline' really requires for its proof some such objective indication of its existence as would be provided by Mark following it in his narrative. The fact that Mark does not follow the order of the hypothetical outline certainly points to a more obvious inference than the pre-Marcan origin of the hypothetical document: namely, its non-existence. Mark did not follow the outline of the collected '*Sammelberichte*' simply because he was unaware of them as assembled into a chronological outline by Dodd, but knew of them only as he himself presents them: a series of independent generalizing summaries, probably, like the *kerygma* and the Gospels, primarily topical in nature. Dodd's whole thesis with regard to a kerygmatic chronology fails for lack of the confirming evidence required to establish a position which would reverse the course of scholarship, and thus must move against the stream of current views as to the probabilities in the case.[1]

[1] This problem of using an evangelist's presentation of the *kerygma* to prove that his Gospel conforms to an earlier kerygmatic pattern is also being felt increasingly in the case of Luke and the sermons of Acts. When Dodd wrote on the sermons in Acts, de Zwaan had published (in *The Beginnings of Christianity* II, 1922, 30–65) a critical study of Torrey's theory of an Aramaic origin of Acts (*The Composition and Date of Acts*, 1915) and had conceded the existence of Aramaic source material at least behind the speeches. It was upon this that Dodd built (*The Apostolic Preaching*, 20). But scholarly opinion with regard to the speeches of Acts has shifted sharply since the publication in 1949 of Dibelius' 'Die Reden der Apostelgeschichte und die antike Geschichtsschreibung' (*Studies in the Acts of the Apostles*, 1956, 138–85), which is really only a confirmation of Henry J. Cadbury's thesis, 'The Speeches of Acts', *The Beginnings of Christianity* V, 1933, 402–27. Their argument that the composition of the speeches is the work of Luke has gained wide support, and provides the basis for the most recent important commentary, by Ernst Haenchen (*Die Apostelgeschichte*, 1956, e.g. 152 f.; cf. also his essay 'Tradition und Komposition in der Apostelgeschichte,' ZTK LII, 1955, 205–25), as well as for the forthcoming commentary in the *Handbuch zum Neuen Testament* series by Hans Conzelmann. A somewhat extreme example of the new trend is found in C. F. Evans' article on 'The Kerygma' (*JTS*, n.s. VII, 1956, 25–41). Yet it is characteristic of the new period that J. A. T. Robinson, in his soberer answer to Evans ('The Most Primitive Christology of All?' *JTS*, n.s.

B. 'NEW SOURCES'?

The original quest had been brought to an end by the rise of the *kerygma* to the centre of twentieth-century theology. Credit for the centrality of the *kerygma* is largely due, at least in the English-speaking world, to C. H. Dodd. Yet the new spirit, once conjured up, was no longer at the service of the master, and failed to provide him with a new basis for the old quest. Perhaps sensing this situation, the most forthright German attempt to revive the positivistic kind of quest,[1] although carried through by a strong supporter of the *kerygma*,[2] has sought its basis elsewhere. This is the significance of the life of Jesus by Ethelbert Stauffer, which is due to appear in English within the year.[3]

VII, 1956, 177–89), assumes the burden of proof for his case that in some instances the sermons contain pre-Lucan tradition. The striking unity in the outlines in the sermons of Acts has led Eduard Schweizer (in conjunction with Hans Conzelmann) to the conclusion that the outline is Luke's contribution ('Zu den Reden der Apostelgeschichte', *TZ* XIII, 1957, 1–11), although he holds that Luke made use of older traditions, especially in the christological section of the sermons (cf. *Erniedrigung und Erhöhung bei Jesus und seinen Nachfolgern,* 1955, sections 6a and 12k). Even when more conservative conclusions along the lines of Dodd are reached, e.g. by Bo Reicke ('A Synopsis of Early Christian Preaching', *The Root of the Vine,* ed. A. Fridrichsen, 1953, 138–41; *Glaube und Leben der Urgemeinde,* 1957, *passim*) and Etienne Trocmé (*Le 'Livre des Actes' et l'histoire,* 1957, 207–14), it is upon the assumption of Lucan composition with use of a traditional form, rather than upon the assumption of early sources incorporated into Acts. Cf. Trocmé, 16: 'Since about 1930 there has been an increasing tendency to abandon the idea of extended sources, and to prefer the hypothesis of the use by the author *ad Theophilum* of isolated accounts, often very brief, which he received either in writing or in oral form. The only source going beyond the range of popular narration in length and content remains the 'diary' of the second part (of Acts). H. W. Beyer, O. Bauernfeind, M. Dibelius, W. L. Knox, W. G. Kümmel, W. Michaelis have defended these ideas, with various nuances.' An even sharper view of the shift in scholarly opinion is given by Haenchen, *Die Apostelgeschichte,* 30–41.

[1]Stauffer explicitly states (*Jesus: Gestalt und Geschichte,* 12) that he proposes to write a 'positivistic' history of Jesus, with facts, chronological sequence, and causal relationships, 'so wie es eigentlich gewesen ist' (*ibid.,* 7; cf. also *KuM,* II, 17).

[2]Cf. his *New Testament Theology,* esp. part three on 'The Creeds of the Primitive Church', and the appendices.

[3]This translation of *Jesus: Gestalt und Geschichte* (1957) is being published by SCM Press, London, and Alfred Knopf, New York. Page numbers in the present discussion refer to the German edition.

Initially impressed by the current consensus as to the kerygmatic nature of the Gospels (7), Stauffer bases the possibility of a positivistic quest upon the existence of new sources (8). These are of three kinds.

First are 'indirect' sources: increased knowledge of Palestinian conditions. However this is not basically a new kind of source, but is actually what Ernst Renan a century ago entitled 'the fifth gospel'. And the bulk of this information was collected by Gustav Dalman and Joachim Jeremias toward the opening of the present century, before the modernization of Palestine obscured the tradition of the past. Thus we are not dealing with a new source which has arisen during the last generation, outdating the current position that the quest is impossible, but rather with an old source used by the original quest; and, although one may speak of a quantitative increase of accumulated research, the source itself is less intact now than when the quest came to an end.

Nor is the way in which Stauffer uses this source basically new. He speaks (8) of 'synchronizing' this material with the Gospels to achieve a chronology. But the indirect sources have no chronology of Jesus' life to be synchronized with the Gospels; information about Palestine is merely used (16-18) to identify the season or year fitting Gospel allusions (e.g. harvest in the spring; 15th year of Tiberius as A.D. 28). *Given* the order of the Gospels as chronological, one's knowledge of Palestine could help to set up dates or seasons.[1] But what is here presupposed is precisely what today cannot be presupposed, that the Gospels are in chronological order. What is really synchronized is the Fourth Gospel with the synoptics, much as in the lives of Christ of the nineteenth cen-

[1]The view of Philip Carrington (*The Primitive Christian Calendar; A Study in the Making of the Marcan Gospel* I, 1952), to the effect that the dates one would be setting up are those of the primitive Church's liturgical year, is completely ignored. It is generally agreed that Carrington has gone much too far in carrying through the liturgical implications of the kerygmatic nature of the Gospels. Cf. e.g. T. W. Manson's review, *JTS*, n.s. IV, 1953, 78; Vincent Taylor, *The Life and Ministry of Jesus*, 40-43; and my *Problem of History in Mark*, 1957, 12. Yet it is suprising that Stauffer, who begins by conceding their kerygmatic nature, never even considers this possibility, which could account for any correspondences between Palestinian seasons and Marcan sequence.

tury.[1] One must conclude that the first 'new source' has not helped Stauffer to disprove the present consensus; instead the consensus has been ignored, and the traditional sources, i.e. the Gospels, used in a pre-Schmidt fashion.

The second kind of 'new source' is found in the Jewish (i.e. Rabbinic) polemics against Jesus, which again can hardly be called a 'new source'. Since the Jewish sources have the reverse prejudice to that of the Christian sources, Stauffer assumes (9–10) that one has historical fact when the two agree. The Achilles' heel of this argument is the dependence of Rabbinic allusions to Jesus upon the Christian witness. Stauffer seeks to avoid this difficulty by arguing that if the Jews took over a Christian view, the view must be historically accurate. However this argument would be valid only if one assumed that the Jews were historical critics, rather than polemicists. Where the facts were damaging, they had to deny their historicity or hide them; but where they could easily be given an anti-Christian meaning (as in the case of the virgin birth), they could be left standing. Thus the omission or adoption of Christian views about Jesus in the Rabbinic tradition has no direct bearing upon their historicity.[2]

[1]Compare the review by John J. Vincent (*TZ* XIII, 1957, 366): 'Indeed, the reader is continually confronted with matters of a conjectural or debatable character, not always with justification. This applies particularly to the chronological scheme proposed, which is really the fitting of Synoptic elements into a basically Johannine framework.'

[2]Perhaps recognizing this problem, Stauffer also tries to prove that the Jews had independent sources. Cf. the 'Exkurs', 147 f., and his article 'Messias oder Menschensohn', *Novum Testamentum* I, 1956, 81–103. He asserts that the Jewish polemic cited in the Gospels is obviously independent of Christian influence, since the Gospels had not yet been written. But Stauffer here ignores the pre-Gospel oral tradition, upon which such Jewish polemics could be based. We know that this Jewish polemic was in contact with the oral Christian tradition, for it survived as part of the oral Christian tradition incorporated in the Gospels. And it is antecedently improbable that a polemical tradition would arise apart from contact with those against whom the polemic was directed. Upon this crumbling base Stauffer then builds the thesis that the Jewish tradition up to A.D. 500 was independent of Christian influence, simply because it continues the same 'independent' arguments cited in the Gospels. This he bolsters by observing that some points in the Gospels are ignored in Jewish polemic of the second century (Jesus' claim to the specific title Messiah; the near end of the world; Judas; the trial before Pilate). Now various explanations for these omissions could probably be

Stauffer's third 'new source' is the literature of Jewish apocalypticism (10 f.). However this too is no 'new source', but rather a source which played a major role in the last phase of the original quest, culminating in the work of Johannes Weiss and Albert Schweitzer. One might assume that Stauffer had in mind the newly discovered Qumran texts. However these have for him only a negative significance (11). The legalism of Qumran identifies Jesus' legalistic sayings as inauthentic, introduced into the tradition in the re-Judaizing process carried on by Baptist and Palestinian Christian forces.

None of Stauffer's 'new sources' actually adds new information specifically about Jesus. They are merely used to argue for the historicity of the Christian sources. In this sense they are not so much new sources for the life of Jesus as new arguments; except that the arguments are not new. For the 'new sources' are not used to disprove the kerygmatic nature of the New Testament sources and their resultant partiality, which Stauffer began (7 f.) by fully conceding, and then as fully ignores. What *is* new in Stauffer is the programmatic revival of the positivistic understanding of history. He says the *Verbum Dei incarnatum* is a *nudum factum,* and the *quaestio prima* of all theological research is the reconstruction of the history of Jesus, which can solve among other things the problem of the absoluteness of Jesus. In his view of history, as well as in his view of the sources, Stauffer

given (e.g. a Jewish conspiracy of silence—cf. *TWNT* III, 287; V, 696; the decline of eschatological tension in Judaism and Christianity during the second century; the dubious apologetic value of the Jewish traitor; unwillingness to allude to Roman jurisdiction over Palestine). But it is probably more re.evant to recall how scanty the *Christian* citations from the Gospels are in the second century, so that the omission of a few elements by the *Rabbinic* sources should not be unusual. His argument from silence becomes absurd when one recalls the amount of source material upon which it is built. To quote T. W. Manson (*Bulletin of the John Rylands Library* XXVII, 1942–3, 327): 'One point is worth noting: it is that the farther we go back in the Jewish tradition the more scanty the references to Jesus become. The later Jewish romances are of some size; the Talmudic references are considerably less in extent; and, when we come to the Mishnah, there are no direct references at all. (There are a few possible veiled allusions but nothing that can be regarded as an absolutely certain reference to Jesus. The passages usually quoted in this connexion are *Yebamoth,* iv.13; *Aboth,* v.19; *Sanhedrin,* x.1 f.)'

shares the outlook of nineteenth-century liberalism, except that
he replaces the critical approach with the conservative principle:
in dubio pro tradito.[1] His basic weakness is that he has ignored the
intervening fifty years, whereas real progress in scholarship, precisely when progress means a shift in direction, comes by means
of profound understanding of the valid reasons behind the current position, including the valid reasons it had for rejecting
an older view to which we must now in some legitimate sense
return. For a return must always be a transformation, accepting
the valid arguments levelled against the original position, and
accepting the valid achievements of the intervening period.

Whereas Stauffer made much of 'new sources' which are hardly
new, there is a source which he does not mention which *is* quite
new. Among the Coptic gnostic manuscripts discovered in
Egypt at Nag Hammadi in 1945 was a copy of the Gospel of
Thomas. This apocryphal gospel is mentioned in patristic allusions,[2] and has been more[3] or less[4] identified with a late and purely
fanciful infancy narrative known for some time. However,
according to preliminary reports, the Gospel of Thomas from
Nag Hammadi[5] actually contains a considerable body of *sayings*
of Jesus, some of which are not purely of gnostic invention, but
are of a type similar to those in the Synoptics. Thus an increase
in the quantity of authentic sayings of Jesus may be reasonably
anticipated. Yet the nature of the collection does not seem to be
such as to alter basically the kind of history or biography of
Jesus which is possible. For we apparently have to do with a
collection of individual, unrelated sayings apart from their historical setting or chronological order, and reflecting the gnostic
tendencies and outlook of the Jewish Christian Church venerating
James. Thus the Gospel of Thomas only adds to the type of
material already available from Oxyrhynchus Papyri 1 and 654.

[1]*KuM* II, 22, 27, 28.
[2]Cf. M. R. James, *The Apocryphal New Testament*, 1924, 14–16.
[3]*Ibid.*, 49 ff.
[4]Cf. Edgar Hennecke, *Neutestamentliche Apokryphen*, 2nd ed., 1924, 93 ff.
[5]Published in part in *Neutestamentliche Apokryphen*,[3] ed. W. Schneemelcher, and in full by G. Quispel *et al*. Cf. the latter's preliminary report, 'Unknown Sayings of Jesus', *Universitas* (Quarterly Eng. lang. ed.) II, 1958, 123–30.

C. A NEW VIEW OF THE GOSPELS?

Neither the *kerygma* nor new source material has provided the possibility of a return to the type of quest attempted by the nineteenth century. Nor does such a possibility reside in any general shift in scholarly evaluation of the Gospels.[1] If form criticism served to draw attention to the theology of the Church in the formative period of the oral tradition, scholarship today is concentrating upon the influence of the evangelists' theologies upon the Gospels.[2] And one of the outstanding conclusions of this recent research is that 'Luke the historian' is not a positivistic historian supplying us with the kind of objectively verified chronological, geographical, psychological, developmental information previously assumed, but rather is a theologian of history, presenting us with the construction of history which is meaningful to him. There has been a gradual trend toward recognizing historical aspects of the Fourth Gospel; yet this trend has not led to the conclusion that the Fourth Gospel provides a degree of historical objectivity not found in the synoptics, but at most that it falls within the same general category of 'theology

[1]This needs to be particularly emphasized in view of the ambiguous position of Harald Riesenfeld's pamphlet, *The Gospel and its Beginnings; A Study in the Limits of 'Formgeschichte'*, 1957. The thesis of this work by Sweden's leading New Testament professor is quite clear: the *Sitz im Leben* of the synoptic material was a Christian rabbinate, going back to Jesus himself. Jesus limited his teaching in form and extent to what could be memorized, and had his disciples learn it by heart. Even the narratives of Jesus' deeds were largely formulated by Jesus, with the understandable exception of the passion narrative. Paul memorized this tradition during his fortnight in Jerusalem. Jesus also originated the Johannine meditations. Now this thesis not only matches in undocumented construction the excesses of the form criticism it is intended to disprove, but also does not reflect the actual status of New Testament research at the present time. Hence as the address inaugurating a Congress on 'The Four Gospels in 1957' (held at Oxford in September, 1957) it could lead to an inaccurate view of the current situation on the part of those not familiar with the literature in the field.

[2]Significant recent contributions are: Ernst Fuchs, 'Jesu Selbstzeugnis nach Matthäus 5', *ZTK* LI, 1954, 14-34; Günther Bornkamm, 'Kirche und Enderwartung im Matthäus-Evangelium', *The Background of the New Testament and its Eschatology*, Studies in honour of C. H. Dodd, 1956, 222-60; Willi Marxsen, *Der Evangelist Markus; Studien zur Redaktionsgeschichte des Evangeliums*, 1956; Hans Conzelmann, *Die Mitte der Zeit; Studien zur Theologie des Lukas*, 1954, 2nd ed. 1957.

of history' as do the Synoptics.[1] It must also be recognized that we have to do with an inverse ratio: the increase in the degree of historicity attributed to specific points in John has been accompanied by a diminution in the degree of historicity which could be attributed to the divergent view of the Synoptics.

We do find in current discussion various positive statements as to the historical reliability of factual material in the Gospels, not only on the part of writers from whom such might be anticipated,[2] but also from among the Bultmannian group itself.[3] Although this is a new emphasis, coinciding with the proposal that the quest be reopened, it is actually not a basic reassessment of the situation with regard to the sources. For even a generation ago, when the emphasis was upon the impossibility of the older kind of quest, the existence of some historical information about Jesus was conceded by Bultmann.[4] And on the other hand the

[1]Cf. e.g. the appendix in C. H. Dodd's *The Interpretation of the Fourth Gospel,* 1953: 'Some Considerations upon the Historical Aspect of the Fourth Gospel', 444–53.

[2]Cf. e.g. Vincent Taylor's list of six reasons why radical scepticism seems to him excessive, *The Life and Ministry of Jesus,* 36–37, and Joachim Jeremias' list of five ways in which the danger of modernization can be avoided, 'Der gegenwärtige Stand der Debatte um das Problem des historischen Jesus', 168 f.

[3]E.g. Käsemann, *ZTK* LI, 1954, 152: 'There are after all pieces in the synoptic tradition which the historian must simply acknowledge as authentic, if he wishes to remain a historian.' Similarly Bornkamm, *Jesus of Nazareth,* 10, says he 'cannot share the degree of scepticism' of those who say that 'only a white spot can be indicated . . . on the map of the real history of Jesus, which was formerly drawn so confidently'.

[4]Cf. e.g. his essay 'The New Approach to the Synoptic Problem', *The Journal of Religion* VI, 1926, 337–62, esp. 343: 'This conclusion (of form criticism), however, is not simply a negative one. It has also its positive significance, since critical analysis has brought out portions which can be regarded as original traditions.' Further (350): 'There is no reason to doubt that many genuine utterances attributed to Jesus in these (controversial) discourses rest back upon accurate historical recollection' (although not the scenes in which the sayings are placed). Further (357 f.): 'In these (prophetic and apocalyptic) utterances also it is possible to detect with some probability genuine words of Jesus, for there can be no doubt that Jesus appeared as prophet and announcer of the coming Kingdom of God.' Therefore Bultmann could write his *Jesus and the Word* in the same year without putting 'Jesus' in quotation marks, since, as he explains in his introduction, he holds that in the oldest layer of the tradition we encounter Jesus himself. One often reads a quotation from this same introduction (e.g. in Vincent Taylor, *ExpT* LIII, 1941-2, 60; Erik Sjöberg, *Der verborgene Menschensohn in den Evangelien*

modern Bultmannians reopening the quest have not rejected the Bultmannian view of the sources as primarily kerygmatic and only secondarily custodians of factual detail for historians of posterity.[1] The mid-century has brought no basic revolution in our view of the sources, such as characterized the turn of the century. The cause for the reawakened interest in the quest of the historical Jesus lies elsewhere.

D. A NEW CONCEPT OF HISTORY AND THE SELF

If the possibility of resuming the quest lies neither in the *kerygma,* nor in new sources, nor in a new view of the Gospels, such a possibility *has* been latent in the radically different understanding of history and of human existence which distinguishes the present from the quest which ended in failure. 'Historicism' is gone as the ideological core of historiography, and with it is gone the centrality of the chronicle. 'Psychologism' is gone as the ideological core of biography, and with it is gone the centrality of the *curriculum vitae.* Consequently the kind of history and biography at-

---

1955, 214: 'I am of the opinion, that of the life and personality of Jesus we know next to nothing, since the Christian sources have no interest in these things and are overgrown by legend, and since other sources about Jesus do not exist.' But one rarely finds quoted the accompanying statement: 'Little as we know of his life and personality, we know enough of his proclamation to be able to make for ourselves a connected picture of it.' Nor do most readers of that quotation understand the technical sense in which Bultmann there uses the terms 'life' and 'personality'. By a 'life' he means a chronological, developmental biography. It is this in which the sources have no interest, and which we consequently cannot reconstruct. And by 'personality' Bultmann has in mind (cf. *GuV* I, 212 f.) a personality cult, a psychological study, a fascination with Jesus' charm, whereas, as he points out, no great personage in history wishes to be evaluated in such terms, 'for *their* interest was not their personality, but their work'. Thus the well-known quotation is far from a sweeping denial of our ability to know historically about Jesus, and is in harmony with the other positive statements made in the same year.

[1]Cf. e.g. Käsemann, 'Zum Thema der Nichtobjektivierbarkeit', *EvTh* XII, 1952–3, 465: 'Although in fact individual details may reach back to an earlier stage, in principle our Christian history begins with the Easter faith of the disciples. What lies behind, even and especially the historical Jesus, is available today only through reconstruction.' Similarly Bornkamm, *Jesus von Nazareth*, 5: 'To be sure the difficulties in arriving at tolerably assured historical knowledge in the area of the tradition about Jesus have become greater and greater. This has to do with the nature of the sources.'

tempted unsuccessfully for Jesus by the nineteenth century is now seen to be based upon a false understanding of the nature of history and the self. As a result it has become *a completely open question,* as to whether a kind of history or biography of Jesus, consistent with the contemporary view of history and human existence, is possible.

This open question has been obscured during the past generation by the necessary polemics against the impossible and misguided kind of quest. But these polemics have been successful enough for the urgent task of our day no longer to be their mechanical perpetuation, but rather the investigation of the possibility of writing the kind of history or biography of Jesus consistent with our modern understanding of history and human existence.

Nineteenth-century historiography and biography were modelled after the natural sciences, e.g. in their effort to establish causal relationships and to classify the particular in terms of the general. Today it is widely recognized that this method placed a premium upon the admixture of nature in history and man, while largely bypassing the distinctively historical and human, where transcendence, if at all, is to be found. It was primarily Wilhelm Dilthey who introduced the modern period by posing for historiography the 'question about the scientific knowledge of individual persons, the great forms of singular human existence'.[1] Today history is increasingly understood as essentially the unique and creative, whose reality would not *be* apart from the event in which it becomes, and whose truth could not be *known* by Platonic recollection or inference from a rational principle, but only through historical encounter. History is the act of intention, the commitment, the meaning for the participants, behind the external occurrence. In such intention and commitment the self of the participant actualizes itself, and in this act of self-actualization the

[1]'Die Entstehung der Hermeneutik' (1900), *Ges. Schr.* V, 317. Dilthey is becoming increasingly known in the English-speaking world through such works as H. A. Hodges, *Wilhelm Dilthey; An Introduction,* 1944; R. G. Collingwood, *The Idea of History,* 1946, 171–6; Rudolf Bultmann, *History and Eschatology* (Gifford Lectures, 1957), 123 ff.

self is revealed. Hence it is the task of modern historiography to grasp such acts of intention, such commitments, such meaning, such self-actualization; and it is the task of modern biography to lay hold of the selfhood which is therein revealed.

This implication of the modern view of history for biography is only strengthened when one turns to the modern concept of selfhood, and its more direct implications for biography. The self is not simply one's personality, resultant upon (and to be explained by) the various influences and ingredients present in one's heritage and development. Rather selfhood is constituted by commitment to a context, from which commitment one's existence arises. One's empirical *habitus* is the inescapable medium through which the self expresses itself, but is not identical with the self, even when one seems to make it so. For even if one avoids commitment and merely drifts with life's tide, or even if the commitment is merely to hold to one's own past or absolutize one's personality, the resultant selfhood is decisively qualified by the mood of inauthenticity in the one case, or by one or the other form of doctrinaire self-assertion in the other. Consequently it would be a basic misunderstanding of selfhood, to describe the causal relationships and cultural ingredients composing the personality, and assume one had understood the self. Selfhood results from implicit or explicit commitment to a kind of existence, and is to be understood only in terms of that commitment, i.e. by laying hold of the understanding of existence in terms of which the self is constituted.

To be sure, neither the modern view of history nor the modern view of existence involves necessarily a dimension of transcendence. To this extent the classical philologian Ernst Heitsch[1] is correct in sensing that the historian's awareness *'tua res agitur'* is 'nuanced in a particular way' by the New Testament scholar: 'It is a matter of *thy blessedness,* however one may understand this.' The secular historian does not have this particular and narrow concentration of interest, but thinks of *'tua res agitur'* in the comprehensive sense that 'nothing human is foreign to thee'. Yet it is

[1]*ZTK* LIII, 1956, 193.

precisely because of this complete openness to all that is human, that the historian must open himself to encounter with humans who understand their existence as lived out of transcendence.

The first effect of the modern view of history and human existence upon New Testament study was, as we have seen, to focus attention upon the *kerygma* as the New Testament statement of Jesus' history and selfhood. This involved also a positive appraisal of the kerygmatic nature of the Gospels, so that one came to recognize the legitimacy in their procedure of transforming the *ipsissima verba* and brute facts into kerygmatic meaning. Thus the modern approach to history and the self made it easy to emphasize the rarity of unaltered sayings and scenes.

There is however another aspect which is equally true, and yet has not been equally emphasized. If the Church's *kerygma* reduced the quantity of unaltered material, it deserves credit for the quality of the unaltered material. The kind of material which the 'kerygmatizing' process would leave *unaltered* is the kind of material which fits best the needs of research based upon the modern view of history and the self. For the kerygmatic interest of the primitive Church would leave unaltered precisely those sayings and scenes in which Jesus made his intention and understanding of existence most apparent to them. Of course the very fact that the earliest Church could on occasion go on saying it in Jesus' way makes it difficult to be certain that any given saying originated with Jesus rather than in this earliest phase of the Church. And areas where Jesus differed from his first disciples would tend to have disappeared from the tradition. Yet in spite of such difficulties, the 'kerygmatic' quality of the material the primitive Church preserved unaltered means that this material is especially suitable for modern research concerned with encountering the meaning of history and the existential selfhood of persons.

Now that the modern view of history and the self has become formally more analogous to the approach of the *kerygma,* we need no longer consider it disastrous that the chronology and causalities of the public ministry are gone. For we have, for example, in the parables, in the beatitudes and woes, and in the sayings on the kingdom, exorcism, John the Baptist and the law, sufficient insight into Jesus' intention to encounter his historical action, and enough insight into the understanding of existence presupposed in his intention to encounter his selfhood. 'If it is by the finger of God that I cast out demons, then the kingdom of God has come upon you' (Luke 11.20). 'From the days of John the Baptist until now the kingdom of heaven has suffered violence, and men of violence take it by force' (Matt. 11.12). Such authentic sayings, whose exact wording cannot well be reconstructed, whose translation is uncertain, whose out-of-date thought patterns are obvious, are none the less more important historical sources for encountering Jesus' history and person than would be the chronological and psychological material the original quest sought in vain. Consequently Jesus' history and selfhood *are* accessible to modern historiography and biography. And *that* is the crucial significance of Käsemann's remark: 'There are after all pieces in the synoptic tradition which the historian must simply acknowledge as authentic, if he wishes to remain a historian.' *This* kind of quest of the historical Jesus *is* possible.

The positive relevance of the modern view of history and the self to the problem of Jesus has not gone completely undetected. As a matter of fact, Bultmann's *Jesus and the Word* of 1926 was prefaced with a classic statement of the modern view of history, and on this basis he states that his book reflects his own encounter with the historical Jesus, and may mediate an encounter with the historical Jesus on the part of the reader. And Käsemann's brief analysis of the authentic sayings of Jesus[1] concludes that, in spite of the absence of messianic titles, Jesus' understanding of his existence can be deduced from his intentions revealed in his sayings. We have already noted how Fuchs derives his understanding of Jesus' work and person from his conduct and its interpretation in the parables.[2] Similarly Bornkamm[3] recognizes that the possi-

[1] *ZTK* LI, 1954, 144–51.
[2] He also derives Jesus' selfhood from his call for decision (*ZTK* LIII, 1956, 221 f., 227): 'This requirement is simply the echo of that decision which Jesus himself had made. We must understand Jesus' conduct as equally determined by a decision, and consequently we can infer from what he re-

bility of his *Jesus of Nazareth* resides in a new view of history. 'If the Gospels do not speak of the history of Jesus in the sense of a reproducible *curriculum vitae* with its experiences and stages, its outward and inward development, yet they none the less speak of history as occurrence and event. Of such history the Gospels provide information which is more than abundant.' And his presentation of 'The messianic question'[1] is permeated by the new view of existence, when he explains that Jesus presented no independent doctrine of his person precisely because 'the "messianic" aspect of his being is enclosed *in* his word and act, and in the immediateness of his historical appearance'. It is consequently not surprising that Peter Biehl[2] has introduced into the discussion of a new quest a thematic discussion of the interpretation of history in terms of the historicity of the self, as found in Martin Heidegger and R. G. Collingwood.

It is apparent that a new quest of the historical Jesus cannot be built upon the effort to deny the impossibilities inherent in the original quest; rather a new quest must be built upon the fact that the sources *do* make possible a new kind of quest working in terms of the modern view of history and the self. Whether one wishes to designate this possible task of historical research a history or life of Jesus, or whether one prefers to reserve these terms for the kind of history or life envisaged by the nineteenth century, is not of crucial importance. The German ability to distinguish between *Historie* and *Geschichte* has made it possible, from Bultmann's *Jesus and the Word* on, to look upon oneself as presenting the history (*Geschichte*) of Jesus. Such has not been the case with the terms 'life', 'biography', and '*bios*', which continue to be avoided,[3] for

---

quired what he himself did.' 'Believing on Jesus means now in content repeating Jesus' decision . . . Jesus' person now became the content of faith.' Cf. also his essay 'Jesus Christus in Person. Zum Problem der Geschichtlichkeit der Offenbarung', *Festschrift Rudolf Bultmann*, 1949, 48–73.
[3] *Jesus of Nazareth*, 24–26.

[1] *Ibid.*, Ch. VIII, esp. 163.   [2] TR, n.F. XXIV, 1957–8, 69 ff.
[3] Cf. Käsemann, *ZTK* LI, 1954, 132; Bornkamm, *Jesus of Nazareth*, 9; and even Stauffer, *Jesus: Gestalt und Geschichte*, 12. It is interesting that Maurice Goguel entitled the second edition of his *Life of Jesus* merely *Jésus* (1950).

the reason Käsemann gives:[1] 'In a life of Jesus one simply cannot give up outer and inner development.' Since usage determines meaning, it may be that such a nineteenth-century definition of biography is still accurate.[2] But this should not obscure the crucial fact that Jesus' understanding of his existence, his self-hood, and thus in the higher sense his life, is a possible subject of historical research.

[1] *ZTK* LI, 1954, 151.
[2] Cf. Martin Kähler's definition (*Der sogenannte historische Jesus und der geschichtliche, biblische Christus* (1892, reprinted 1953), 23: 'More recent biography seeks its strength in psychological analysis, in demonstrating the quantity of causes and the causal chain out of which the appearance and performance of the person being portrayed has arisen.' The continuation of this definition in the modern period is evident, e.g. in the statement of D. W. Riddle ('Jesus in Modern Research', *The Journal of Religion* XVII, 1937, 177) that we know 'general features' of Jesus, but not such as to write a 'biography', or in the ambiguous statement of C. J. Cadoux ('Is it Possible to Write a Life of Christ?', *ExpT* LIII, 1941–2, 177): 'We do not possess for the life of Jesus anything approaching that knowledge of chronology which is usually deemed necessary for a "biography". . . . I do not concur in the modern view that it is impossible to write a life of Christ.'

IV

THE LEGITIMACY OF A NEW QUEST

A. THE RELEVANCE OF THE THEOLOGICAL QUESTION

The historian may well feel that the *possibility* of a new quest is itself sufficient basis for its *legitimacy*, simply because any possible subject of research is a legitimate topic for the free, inquiring mind. This is certainly true, and one may consequently expect to see from time to time research in this field which is motivated merely by man's insatiable desire to know. However this stimulus would not be such as to provide a concentration of research comparable to that of the original quest, nor could this stimulus produce a new quest which would be a distinctive characteristic of our day, in comparison with other topics where the possibilities of success are much greater. If a new quest of the historical Jesus is to be undertaken on any large scale, it must have some specific impetus in terms of the meaningful concerns of our day, comparable with those which characterized the original quest and its abrupt discontinuation.

The original quest cannot be explained merely in terms of the availability of modern historiography since the eighteenth century. The historical-critical method supplied the means, but not the driving power. An initial impetus had come from the anticlericalism inherent in much of the enlightenment.[1] But the bulk of the lives of Jesus in the nineteenth century were motivated on the one hand by a desire to overcome the mythological interpretation of David Friedrich Strauss,[2] and on the other hand by

[1]This is the motive of H. S. Reimarus' *Von dem Zweck Jesu und seiner Jünger*, published by Lessing in 1778.

[2]The statement by Willibald Beyschlag (*Das Leben Jesu*, Part I, 3rd ed., 1893, v) is typical: 'Ever since I, as a 21-year-old theological student, let Strauss' *Life of Jesus* with its critique, so superior as to methods and yet so unsatisfying in its conclusions, have its effect upon me, it has been my inner motivation to rebuild for myself in a new, defensible way on scientific grounds the world of faith apparently sinking in these flames.'

the attempt to replace orthodoxy with the Ritschlian system.[1] Similarly the discontinuation of the quest was not due simply to the historical difficulties involved, but rather in great measure to certain theological considerations. It is sometimes assumed that Bultmann's theological position is primarily due to his negative historical conclusions, from which *impasse* he then retreated into Barthianism. However Bultmann has explicitly denied that his move towards Barthianism was due to the negative results of his form criticism.[2] As we have seen, it was Barth himself[3] who called attention to the positive theological significance of radical criticism in eliminating worldly proof as a false support to faith, a position which Bultmann only echoed.[4] Now this positive evaluation of radical criticism in terms of the nature of faith has deep roots in the Marburg tradition out of which both Barth and Bultmann came,[5] but had been radicalized by the discovery of Kierkegaard.[6]

[1]This is in substance the thesis of Albert Schweitzer's *Quest of the Historical Jesus*.

[2]*GuV* I, 101 (1927): 'Wiser persons such as P. Althaus and F. Traub have even detected that I have saved myself from my scepticism (by flight) to Barth and Gogarten. They must excuse me if their wisdom strikes me as comical. I have never felt uncomfortable in my critical radicalism, but instead quite comfortable. But I often have the impression that my conservative colleagues in New Testament feel quite uncomfortable; for I see them always involved in salvage operations. I quietly let it burn; for I see that what is there burning are all the phantasies of the life-of-Jesus-theology, the *Christos kata sarka* itself.'

[3]In the debate with Harnack in *Die Christliche Welt* of 1923, reprinted in Barth's *Theologische Fragen und Antworten*, 1957, 13.

[4]*GuV* I, 4 (1924). Cf. also Bultmann's interpretation of Barth's position, in his review of Barth's *Romans* (*ChrW* XXXVI, 1922, 369): 'Barth rejects this (Ritschlian) answer, not only because he knows that NT research has been largely led to the admission: "Of Jesus' inner life we are hardly able to know anything, as good as nothing." Rather it is because Jesus as a man belongs to psychic, historical reality, to the "world", and we are in no way helped by such psychic, historical perceptibility.'

[5]Cf. e.g. the remark of Martin Rade at the burial of their teacher Wilhelm Herrmann: 'Often it appeared as if research could not turn out radical enough for him.' (*ChrW* XXXVI, 1922, 75). Since Herrmann was primarily concerned with achieving an understanding of faith in terms of encounter rather than of scientific proof, one may detect here the origin of Barth's position. Cf. Barth's lecture, 'Die dogmatische Prinzipienlehre bei Wilhelm Herrmann', 1925, reprinted in Vol. 2 of his *Gesammelte Vorträge, Die Theologie und die Kirche*, 240–84.

[6]Cf. the *Concluding Unscientific Postscript*, Ch. I, 'The Historical Point of

In the case of Bultmann, this theological background was strengthened by his training in the comparative religious school. Here Christianity centres in the cult symbol 'Christ the Lord', whose relation to Jesus of Nazareth was both historically questionable and theologically irrelevant. This position had found its classic expression in Wilhelm Bousset's *Kyrios Christos* of 1913.[1] And Bultmann was sufficiently rooted in this tradition to be entrusted with the editing of the second, posthumous edition, which appeared in the same year as Bultmann's own *Geschichte der synoptischen Tradition,* 1921. Consequently it would be erroneous to see Bultmann's theological position with regard to Jesus as a belated appendix to his historical position; if one were unwilling to concede that the theological and historical factors are inextricably intertwined,[2] then one could equally well argue the priority of the theological. Bultmann himself likes to present his position in terms of Pauline and Johannine theology.

If a new quest of the historical Jesus is to become a significant aspect of theological scholarship during the coming generation, the role which this research will play in the theological thought of our day must be made equally clear. Man's quest for meaningful existence is his highest stimulus to scholarly enquiry; consequently a serious quest of the historical Jesus must have meaning in terms of man's quest for meaningful existence. This does not

---

View,' Para. 1, 'The Holy Scriptures,' esp. 30 ff.: 'While faith has hitherto had a profitable schoolmaster in the existing uncertainty, it would have in the new certainty its most dangerous enemy. For if passion is eliminated, faith no longer exists, and certainty and passion do not go together. . . . For whose sake is it that the proof is sought? Faith does not need it; aye, it must even regard the proof as its enemy.' Already Kierkegaard applied this to the problem of the historical Jesus: 'If the contemporary generation had left nothing behind except the words: "We have believed that in such and such a year God showed himself in the puny form of a servant, taught and lived among us, and then died"—that would be more than enough' (cited by Diem, *Theologie* II, 22).

[1]E.g. (75 of 2nd ed.): 'For the purely historical is really never able to make an impression, but rather only the living present symbol, in which one's own convictions are transfigured and presented.'

[2]Cf. Barth, *Church Dogmatics* I, 2, 493 f.; Ernst Fuchs, 'Probleme der neutestamentlichen Theologie', *VuF, Theol. Jahresbericht* for 1942–6 (1947), 168; Hermann Diem, *Theologie* I, 66.

mean that such a quest should presuppose a given christology,[1] or that it should be oblivious of the peril of modernizing Jesus, this time perhaps in terms of existentialism.[2] It merely means that we must be quite realistic about the day and age in which we live, and its likelihood of producing a new quest. Unless the trend toward regarding the quest of the historical Jesus as theologically irrelevant or even illegitimate is reversed, i.e. unless a new quest becomes for us theologically legitimate and even indispensable, it probably will not enlist the active participation of the strongest intellects and best-equipped specialists, upon whom its success is completely dependent.

B. THE PERMISSIVENESS OF A NEW QUEST

The discussion of the theological propriety of a new quest must naturally begin with the point at which the original quest was seen to be illegitimate. It is illegitimate to dodge the call of the *kerygma* for existential faith in the saving event, by an attempt to provide an objectively verified proof of its historicity. To require an objective legitimization of the saving event prior to faith is to take offence at the offence of Christianity and to perpetuate the unbelieving flight to security. This would signify the reverse of faith, since faith involves the rejection of worldly security as righteousness by works. This line of criticism is a valid identification of the worldliness latent in the 'historicism' and 'psychologism' of the original quest, and must therefore be recognized as a valid theological objection to it.

However it should be equally apparent that this veto upon the original quest does not apply to the modern view of history and historiography which would be presupposed in a new quest. For the objectivity of modern historiography consists precisely in one's openness for the encounter, one's willingness to place one's

[1]This point is well made e.g. by C. J. Cadoux, *ExpT* LIII, 1941–2, 175.

[2]Cf. e.g. Pierre Prigent, 'Les grandes étapes de la vie de Jésus', *Bulletin trimestriel de la Faculté de Théologie protestante de Paris*, 21ème Année, No. 59, March 1958, 28: 'We smile today at the humanistic portrait of Jesus which the nineteenth century painted. But do you think that the same smile will not rise on the lips of those who detect tomorrow, in certain recent works, Jesus the existentialist?'

intentions and views of existence in question, i.e. to learn something basically new about existence and thus to have one's own existence modified or radically altered. Nor can the end result of such historical research be a proven *kerygma* dispensing with the necessity for existential commitment. E.g. from the treatments of Bultmann, Käsemann, Fuchs and Bornkamm it has not become a proved fact that God acted in Jesus' intentions or that Jesus is saviour. At most it has been established that Jesus intended to confront the hearer inescapably with the God who is near when he proclaimed 'Repent, for God's reign is near', i.e. that he intended a historical encounter with himself to be an eschatological encounter with God, and that he consequently understood his existence as that of bringer of eschatological salvation. The historical Jesus does not legitimize the *kerygma* with a proven divine fact, but instead confronts us with action and a self which, like the exorcisms, may be understood either as God's Spirit (Mark 3.29; Matt. 12.28), or Beelzebub (Mark 3.22), or insanity (Mark 3.21). The historical Jesus confronts us with existential decision, just as the *kerygma* does. Consequently it is anachronistic to oppose the quest today on the assumption that such a quest is designed to avoid the commitment of faith. That may have been the existential significance of the original quest, but can hardly be the meaning of the quest today for a person aware of what is currently known about historiography and the historical Jesus.

Throughout the generation which emphasized the antithesis between faith in the *kerygma* and interest in the historical Jesus, it seems to have been the fact of the Gospels which kept alive some awareness of the parallelism between the two. For the initial discussion concerning the theological relevance of a new quest has taken place to a large extent in terms of an exegesis of the evangelists' intention:[1] the evangelists undoubtedly insisted upon the

---

[1]This approach was anticipated by Karl Ludwig Schmidt, 'Das Christuszeugnis der synoptischen Evangelien', a lecture of 1933-4 published in Beiheft 2 of *EvTh*, 7-33. Käsemann appropriates it in the decisive section of his essay 'Das Problem des historischen Jesus' (*ZTK* LI, 1954, 125-53), on 'The Meaning of the Historical in our Gospels', 138-44 (cf. also 133 f.), upon which the following summary is primarily based. This approach has been

relevance of history for faith. This relevance resided in the identification in the *kerygma* of the humiliated Jesus and the exalted Lord. Now it is characteristic of twentieth-century theology to emphasize one aspect of this identification: the historical Jesus cannot be isolated from the Christ of faith, as the original quest attempted to do. Yet, as the evangelists point out, the other aspect of the identification is equally important: the Christ of faith cannot be separated from the historical Jesus, if we do not wish to find 'a myth in the place of history, a heavenly being in the place of the Nazarene'.

This emphasis upon the humiliation, i.e. the historical in the *kerygma,* is in turn rooted in the eschatological orientation of primitive Christianity. Here again we are accustomed to a one-sided view, in this case with regard to the relation of eschatology and history: the eschatological interpretation placed upon Jesus is largely responsible for the introduction of non-historical material into the Gospels. Yet it is equally true that the eschatological interpretation placed upon Jesus gave to the historical its theological relevance for the evangelists, and thus prevented the disappearance of Jesus into mythology. It is this theological relevance of the historical Jesus for the eschatology of the evangelists which has been examined in some detail:

1. Primitive Christianity experienced Jesus as a unique action of God, creating a situation in which man has an unique opportunity to lay hold of eschatological existence. Revelation was not for them an idea always available to rational reflection, nor was salvation a permanent potentiality of the human spirit. Rather in the last hour God encounters man with a free and gracious opportunity of eschatological existence, a chance which man neglects at his own peril and which therefore places him in ultimate decision. This is what Jesus' earthly life had meant to his followers, and Easter only confirmed this significance. It was this dramatic contingency of the revelation, which found expression in the recording of the concrete history of Jesus in the Gospels.

taken over by Bornkamm, *Jesus von Nazareth,* 20–23, Ernst Fuchs, *Festschrift Rudolf Bultmann,* 54, and Fritz Lieb, *Antwort,* 583.

2. The Fourth Gospel especially is concerned to preserve this awareness of the historicity of revelation, in an environment sufficiently gnostic in its view of religious experience to dissolve Jesus into docetism. In order to dramatize earthly, corporeal existence as the realm of revelation, in order to emphasize the divine condescension of revelation, the Fourth Gospel portrays present religious experience in terms of Jesus' life. The evangelist implements this purpose by drawing attention to the ambiguity, the offence, the hiddenness, which characterized the revelation even in Jesus' life, as if to say: Today it is the same. The Church still remains exposed to the ambiguity of history, the possibility of offence, in spite of having risen with Christ; for the resurrection glory is really the transcendence of his historical existence.

3. By way of contrast the Synoptics betray more of the 'pastness' of Jesus. This may not be due merely to their weaker theological talents, but may indicate a positive insight: although history is determined by present possibilities and decisions, it cannot be dissolved into a series of present situations. Our present possibilities and decisions are determined to a large extent by events of the past, which opened or closed doors for the present. Thus our present situation is part of a larger *kairos,* dating from a past in which the present situation is, so to speak, predestined. In this sense the Christian *kairos* is rooted in the historical Jesus, who is *extra nos,* given prior to faith and determining our present, as the history upon which our existence is constituted.

This clarification of the theological meaning involved in emphasizing Jesus' historicity by writing Gospels does not automatically provide a compelling motivation for a new quest of the historical Jesus. For this meaning expressed in the writing of Gospels was already inherent in the *kerygma,* e.g. in its emphasis upon the humiliation, and can find expression in various forms of Christian experience, e.g. in the experience of Francis of Assisi. Nor does the writing of Gospels form an exact precedent to a quest of the historical Jesus. A quest of the historical Jesus involves an attempt to disengage information about the historical Jesus from its kerygmatic colouring, and thus to mediate an encounter with the historical Jesus distinct from the encounter with the *kerygma*. The Gospels however do not present the historical Jesus in distinction from the *kerygma,* but rather present a kerygmatized history of Jesus.[1]

At the most the discussion of the writing of Gospels presents a parallel in terms of New Testament 'historiography' to the view discussed above, that modern historiography is not in principle a contradiction of faith, but could be used to implement faith's openness to historical encounter. Although the methods of New Testament 'historiography' and modern historiography are quite different, the same or similar kerygmatic motives which produced the one could lead us to a legitimate use of the other. Thus the discussion of the theological meaning of writing Gospels explicates the theological *permissiveness* of a new quest. But the actual *impetus* leading scholarship to make use of this permission resides elsewhere.

C. THE IMPETUS PROVIDED BY DEMYTHOLOGIZING

The debate on demythologizing has been under way since 1941, and it is this movement which is to a large extent responsible for the impetus leading to a new quest of the historical Jesus. As we have seen, it was from among the advocates of demythologizing that the initial proposals of a new quest have come. For the demythologizing of the *kerygma* has drawn attention to a clear alternative inherent in Christian theology:[2] in the process of demythologizing, the objectified language of the *kerygma* loses its own concreteness, and becomes, so to speak, transparent, so that its existential meaning may be grasped. But when the *kerygma* is thus rendered transparent, what is it which then becomes visible

[1]Cf. Heitsch (*ZTK* LIII, 1956, 195): 'To be sure one may say that primitive Christianity did not let the phenomenon of the historical Jesus completely disappear. But does this history (*Historie*) really have relevance for faith? Certainly only as kerygmatized history (in secular language: as history presented in a biased way under the authority of the *kerygma*)! And to be sure, if I accept kerygmatized history as historical, then it simply *must* be relevant to faith, since it was in fact the content of faith which was built into the history.'

[2]Cf., e.g. the Hegelian distinction between the 'Christ-principle' and the 'Christ-person'.

through it? Does one encounter in the *kerygma* a symbolized principle, or interpreted history?

The first alternative conceives of the *kerygma* much as did the comparative-religious school, i.e. as a symbol objectifying a given type of piety, which in turn is the principle or essence of the religion.[1] To be sure this Christian principle would no longer consist in a variant upon Hellenistic mysticism, but would rather be in terms of the historicity of human existence. But in any case the *kerygma* is the objectivation of a truth, not of an event. Or, if one concedes that the witness to an event is essential to the *kerygma*, one must then classify the *kerygma* as essentially mythological, so that 'demythologizing' involves 'dekerygmatizing'.[2]

Now the concept of the *kerygma* as a religious symbol was familiar to Bultmann from his background in the comparative-religious school. Yet it was precisely within his comparative-religious research that he moved away from that basic position. Primitive Christianity is rooted in Jewish eschatology, rather than in Hellenistic mysticism. Consequently it conceives of salvation in terms of the meaning of history, rather than in terms of escape from history. As a result, the myths of the mystery religions were irrelevant for such a Jew as Paul, until he encountered the view that the myth had happened in history. Although Bultmann agrees fully with Bousset that the concepts Paul used in his christology were taken over from the mystery religions rather than handed down from Jesus, he is not misled by this fact into ignoring the decisive role Jesus' historicity plays in the theology of Paul: 'The historical person of Jesus makes Paul's preaching gospel.'[3]

Not only did the coming of the Messiah mean that the eschatological age had dawned, i.e. that eschatological existence was

[1]Classical instances of this position are found in Ernst Troeltsch, *Die Bedeutung der Geschichtlichkeit Jesu für den Glauben,* 1911, and Wilhelm Bousset, *Kyrios Christos,* 1913.

[2]This alternative is presented by Fritz Buri, 'Entmythologisierung oder Entkerygmatisierung der Theologie,' *KuM* II, 85–101, and 'Theologie der Existenz,' *KuM* III, 83–91, and by Schubert M. Ogden, 'Bultmann's Project of Demythologization and the Problem of Theology and Philosophy', *The Journal of Religion* XXXVII, 1957, 156–73.

[3]*GuV* I, 202 ff.

possible within history. It also meant that the Pharisaic 'plan of salvation' had simply been by-passed by God, i.e. it meant the replacement of man's presumptive potentiality of self-salvation by the gift of salvation. The Judaism of which Paul had been so proud gave way to his discovery of the present evil aeon, where the egocentric dilemma is such that even the holy law is used self-centredly and only increases man's sin. Thus the eschatological event was God's judgement upon human pride, as well as God's grace giving meaning to human life. Consequently the eschatological event revealed the absence of man's natural possibility of salvation, and thereby only accentuated the indispensability of God's saving intervention. The myth of a mystery religion (or the symbol of the comparative-religious school) could only point out what *ought* to be; as the 'law' of the Hellenistic world it would simply be a new legalism ending like the Jewish law in despair (Rom. 7). Only as witness to God's intervention in history could the myth or symbol be the good news that eschatological existence is possible within history. In this way Bultmann's study of the New Testament *kerygma* compelled him to move beyond the view of it as the objectification of a religious idea, and come to recognize in its 'happened-ness' its essence.[1]

This role in which the *kerygma* played in the thought of Paul finds a parallel in the dilemma confronting modern man, and this parallel has doubtlessly facilitated the appropriation of the Pauline position by the Bultmannian group. This is particularly apparent in the case of Ernst Fuchs: 'We could object that such encounters (*horribile dictu* even with ourselves!) are after all inherent in the meaning of history in general! Why is a Jesus necessary, then, if historical decisions are possible at any time? But how do things stand today (1944) for instance, with the European cultural synthesis demanded by Troeltsch? After all, even in the existence of a single individual, there are often enough decisions which make history. But how do we know that we have thereby achieved the existence that comes from God? And when man becomes conscious of his guilt towards his neighbour, what right has he to

[1] Cf. *Kerygma and Myth*, 14 f., 29 f.

take himself seriously in what he still has?' 'We are sinners, if we think we are in a position to cope with the guilt of our existence. That is the meaning of the talk about righteousness by works.'[1]

This same sentiment is characteristic enough of our day to have found eloquent expression in W. H. Auden's *Christmas Oratorio*.[2]

> Alone, alone, about a dreadful wood
> Of conscious evil runs a lost mankind,
> Dreading to find its Father lest it find
> The Goodness it has dreaded is not good:
> Alone, alone, about our dreadful wood.
>
> Where is that Law for which we broke our own,
> Where now that Justice for which Flesh resigned
> Her hereditary right to passion, Mind
> His will to absolute power? Gone. Gone.
> Where is that Law for which we broke our own?
>
> The Pilgrim Way has led to the Abyss.
> Was it to meet such grinning evidence
> We left our richly odoured ignorance?
> Was the triumphant answer to be this?
> The Pilgrim Way has led to the Abyss.
>
> We who must die demand a miracle.
> How could the Eternal do a temporal act,
> The Infinite become a finite fact?
> Nothing can save us that is possible:
> We who must die demand a miracle.

[1]'Jesus Christus in Person; Zum Problem der Geschichtlichkeit der Offenbarung', *Festschrift Rudolf Bultmann*, 53, 63. One should note how in this context the problem of Jesus arises. Cf. also Fuchs' comment on Buri's position (*TLZ* LXXXII, 1957, 275): 'It seems to me that one must ask here whether "existence" is given so simply in unhistorical fashion or independent of all history—or whether Buri is not here illuminating an existence which is what it is from the history of Christian reality, i.e. which presupposes that revelation in Jesus which conditions and bears this history.' This latter point is made more clearly in a different context by Peter Biehl (*TR*, n.F. XXIV, 1956-7, 71): 'The traditional question in the philosophy of history, as to the supratemporal meaning of history, which can only be answered when history has reached its end, is a secularized form of Christian cosmic eschatology: similarly the possibility of historical knowledge correctly understood is opened up where Christ is understood by each individual already as the end of history, i.e. where the *historicity of man* comes into view, in Paul and John. Once this possibility is opened up, then it is in principle open also to secular (existentialistic) reflection.'

[2]From *For the Time Being*, Random House, New York, 1944; Faber and Faber, London, 1945, 65 f.

Thus the first assumption as to the purpose of demythologizing, namely that the *kerygma* is a religious symbol objectifying a human potentiality for authentic existence, fails precisely because of what the *kerygma* symbolizes. An unhistorical symbol can hardly symbolize transcendence within history. And the objectification of a human capacity can hardly symbolize man's incapacity before God. Buri is quite correct in recognizing that his alternative is not a demythologization of the *kerygma,* but an elimination of the *kerygma.* But what he has not adequately recognized is that it is not merely an elimination of the 'happened-ness' of the *kerygma,* but thereby also of the existential meaning of the *kerygma.*

Now Bultmann has recognized that the *kerygma* is not a symbol in the same sense as other religious symbols, precisely because of what it symbolizes: as the symbol for transcendence within history it cannot be an unhistorical symbol. Consequently Bultmann emphasizes—in this context at least—that the *kerygma* is a witness to the meaning of Jesus. Thus the other answer to the question 'what the *kerygma* dissolves into' when it is demythologized, is: into the meaning of Jesus of Nazareth. What is encountered when the objectified language of the *kerygma* becomes transparent is Jesus of Nazareth, as the act of God in which transcendence is made a possibility of human existence. The *kerygma* is not the objectification of a new, 'Christian' religious principle, but rather the objectification of a historical encounter with God.[1]

From this position at which Bultmann has arrived it is only one step to the 'post-Bultmannian' recognition that the actual demythologizing which went on within the primitive Church was the 'historicizing' process taking place within the *kerygma* and leading to the writing of Gospels, as has been discussed above. It is simply because Germany's leading exegetes have correctly understood the demythologized meaning of the New Testament *kerygma,* that they have looked through the *kerygma* not directly to a principle

[1]Peter Biehl, 'Welchen Sinn hat es, von "theologischer Ontologie" zu reden?', *ZTK* LIII, 1956, 363, reports: 'On Jan. 30, 1954, in a discussion with Buri before the Basel student body, Bultmann succeeded quite well in showing that his concept of *kerygma* is not a "mythological vestige" in his thought.'

inherent in human nature, but rather to Jesus as the event in which transcendence becomes possible.[1]

D. THE NECESSITY OF A NEW QUEST

The theological necessity of a new quest resides in the resultant situation in which theology finds itself today. It is committed to a *kerygma* which locates its saving event in a historical person to whom we have a second avenue of access provided by the rise of scientific historiography since the enlightenment. Apart from this concrete situation, there is no theological necessity for a quest of the historical Jesus, since Jesus can be encountered in the *kerygma*. In this sense faith is not dependent on historiography, which as a matter of fact has been all but non-existent with regard to Jesus during most of the centuries of Christian faith. Yet theological responsibility is in terms of the situation in which we find ourselves placed, and it is an inescapable part of the situation in which we exist that the quest of the historical Jesus has taken place, and in fact has neither proved historically fruitless, nor been brought completely to a halt even among those most opposed to it as an ideological orientation.[2] Thus the problem of the two avenues of

---

[1]Fuchs, *Das Programm der Entmythologisierung*, 1954, 9: 'The encounter with Jesus himself, no more and no less, is the force at work in the so-called demythologizing. Today demythologizing, at least in the area of New Testament scholarship, is encounter with Jesus. I know that I am here going beyond the stage which the debate has reached in recent years. We have made progress.' (Cf. also his concern with the historical Jesus in the context of the quotation on p. 83 above, and his critical position toward Buri, *TLZ* LXXXII, 1957, 275.) Bornkamm, *Jesus von Nazareth*, 20: 'The Gospels signify the *repudiation of myth*, and in so far as its concepts are still or again admitted into the thought of primitive Christian faith, give it once for all the function of interpreting the history of Jesus as the history of God with the world.' Similarly, Käsemann, *ZTK* LIV, 1957, 11: 'Fuchs, G. Bornkamm and I see ourselves compelled to restrict the assertion that Easter founded the Christian *kerygma*; we must enquire as to the meaning of the historical Jesus for faith.'

[2]Both of these latter aspects were recognized by Käsemann in his proposal of a new quest (*ZTK* LI, 1954, 152, 133). Heitsch (*ZTK* LIII, 1956, 195) has most clearly recognized the problem of two avenues of approach to Jesus: 'For here lies a problem which seems to us a decisive problem, namely that rather than one, there are two entities which must be taken from the tradition, both of which have their own requirements and call upon our thinking to take some stand.'

encounter with Jesus must be faced, if we are to theologize realistically in the situation in which we find ourselves.

These two avenues of access to the same person create a situation which has not existed in the Church since the time of the original disciples, who had both their Easter faith and their factual memory of Jesus. They responded to this situation by intuitively explicating their memory until they found in it the *kerygma,* i.e. by 'kerygmatizing' their memory. Thus they largely precluded their situation for the following generations, until we today attempt to disengage their historical information about Jesus from the *kerygma* in terms of which they remembered him. At least to some extent we are thereby returning ourselves to their original situation, which they met by writing the Gospels. It is not their precedent which compels us to express our faith as did they, which in any case would be in many regards impossible. Rather there is an inner logic in the common situation, in which the necessity for a new quest resides. It is this inner logic to which we therefore turn.

The current limitation of New Testament research to the *kerygma* has a significant formal deficiency: it sees Jesus only in terms determined by the Christian encounter, and thus obscures formally the concreteness of his historical reality. If current research upon the New Testament *kerygma* serves to draw attention to the historicity of the proclaimed word of God, as treasure in such earthen vessels as Jewish or Hellenistic thought patterns, research upon Jesus' message would serve formally to draw attention to the flesh of the incarnation. The shock of seeing the all-too-familiar Christ of the traditional gospel within the context of Jewish eschatological sects is comparable to that experienced in portraits, e.g. by Picasso, where half the face is the normal full-face mask, while the other half is cut away, providing insight into what is going on within the head; when one returns to the traditional half of the portrait, one must recall that this conventional view and that 'subliminal' view are together the reality of the person. The formal error of the nineteenth-century quest was to assume that in the Jesus 'according to the flesh' one could see undialectically, unparadoxically, unoffensively Jesus as Lord, whereas one can only see Jesus 'born of a woman, born under the law'. But the formal error of the last generation in eliminating the quest has been to ignore the relevance for the Christian dialectic, paradox, and offence, of seeing Jesus causally bound within the historical reconstruction of first-century Judaism, and yet encountering in him transcendence: 'born of a woman, born under the law, to redeem those who were under the law.'

The *kerygma*, no matter how many mythological concepts it may have made use of in getting its message across, is not proclaiming mythological ideas, but rather the existential meaningfulness of a historical person. Although one may concede that the *kerygma* is not concerned with a Jesus 'according to the flesh', if by this one means a historically proven Lord,[1] it is equally apparent that the *kerygma* is centrally concerned with a Jesus 'in the flesh',[2] in the sense that the heavenly Lord was 'born of a

[1]This is in fact the direction in which the expression moves in contemporary discussion, so that the expression becomes the New Testament equivalent to the technical meaning of the term 'historical Jesus' discussed above. Cf. e.g. Karl Barth, *The Resurrection of the Dead*, 1933, 65 (translation corrected according to Ger. ed. of 1924, 34): 'For what we call the historical Jesus, a Jesus pure and simple, who is not the Lord Jesus, but an earthly phenomenon among others to be objectively discovered, detached from His *Lordship* in the Church of God, apart from the *revelation* given in Jesus to the Church and at first to the apostles—this abstraction was for Paul (and not for him alone) an impossibility. The thought that Jesus should and could be first regarded by himself, in order then to recognize Him as Lord, could at most be for him a painful recollection of his former error. *This* Jesus, who is not the Lord, who is known *after the flesh* (II Cor. 5.16), was in fact the foe whom he persecuted; he no longer knows Him.' Bultmann (*GuV* I, 207) means by 'Christ according to the flesh' 'a phenomenon of the world which one finds given at one's disposal'. From his *Theology of the New Testament* I, 238 f., it is apparent that he, like Barth, expounds II Cor. 5.16 with 'according to the flesh' modifying the verb 'know', so that the epistemological problem is presupposed in the concept 'Christ according to the flesh'. Hence the expression is not used to negate the significance of Jesus' historicity, but rather to negate the importance of the historian's (or disciple's) reconstruction of the historical Jesus. Cf. also Otto Michel, ' "Erkennen dem Fleisch nach" (II Kor. 5.16)', *EvTh* XIV, 1954, 22–29.

[2]The expression is itself kerygmatic: I Tim. 3.16; I John 4.2; II John 7; Ignatius, *Smyrn.* 1.2 and *Eph.* 7.2 (*v.l.*). In I Peter 3.18, a kerygmatic text quite parallel with I Tim. 3.16, the expression occurs without the preposition (cf. also 4.1). In Rom. 8.3 the concept of sin is added to that of the flesh, which necessitates the cautious circumlocution 'in the likeness of sinful flesh', which is clearly equivalent to the original expression 'in the flesh' occurring in the same verse. Other equivalent expressions are: 'in the days of his flesh' in

woman, born under the law', a historical person. This emphasis in the *kerygma* upon the historicity of Jesus is existentially indispensable, precisely because the *kerygma,* while freeing us from a life 'according to the flesh', proclaims the meaningfulness of life 'in the flesh'.[1]

It is this concern of the *kerygma* for the historicity of Jesus which necessitates a new quest. For how can the indispensable historicity of Jesus be affirmed, while at the same time maintaining the irrelevance of what a historical encounter with him would mean, once this has become a real possibility due to the rise of modern historiography? Such a position cannot fail to lead to the conclusion that the Jesus of the *kerygma* could equally well be only a myth, for one has in fact declared the meaning of his historical person irrelevant. Nor can the requirement of the *kerygma* be met by the observation that Jesus' historicity is beyond question, since one no longer needs to take seriously the unrealistic attacks on his historicity by Bruno Bauer, Albert Kalthoff, Peter Jensen, W. B. Smith, Arthur Drews, P.-L. Couchoud,[2] and, most recently, Communist propaganda.[3] For a myth does not become historical simply by appropriating the name of a historical personage.[4]

Heb. 5.7; the adjective 'fleshy' in Ignatius, *Eph.* 7.2; the genealogical use of 'according to the flesh' in Rom. 1.3; 9.5; Ignatius, *Smyrn.* 1.1 and *Eph.* 20.2; and the expression 'became flesh' in John 1.14 and II *Clem.* 9.5. Note also the emphasis upon Jesus' 'flesh' in Col. 1.22; 2.11; Heb. 10.20; John 6.51–56.

[1]The expression 'in the flesh' is simply an idiom referring to life in the world (II Cor. 10.3; Gal. 2.20; Phil. 1.22). But it comes to be used to point to the *meaningfulness* of life in the world, by drawing the parallel between man's life in the world and Jesus' life in the world: compare Rom. 8.4–13 with 8.3, Col. 1.24 with 1.22, I Peter 4.1, 6 with 3.18.

[2]Cf. the survey of this view since the enlightenment, presented by Goguel, *Jésus,* 39–45. The very absence of recent defences of Jesus' historicity is indicative of the fact that such radically critical positions are untenable and need no longer be taken seriously.

[3]A. P. Gagarin, *Die Entstehung und der Klassencharacter des Christentums,* tr. from the Russian, Dietz Verlag, Berlin, 1955.

[4]Cf. Erik Sjöberg, *Der verborgene Menschensohn in den Evangelien,* 1955, 216: 'Even if Jesus was a historical person, but we could know nothing about this historical person, then the Jesus preached in the Church and portrayed in the Gospels is nevertheless actually a mythological figure. For then he has nothing in common with the Jesus of history, who remains unknown to us, except for the name. Here the New Testament message is much more radically mythological than is presupposed in the contemporary discussion about "demythologizing" the gospel.'

This can be illustrated with regard to the cross, whose historicity in the normal sense of the word is not doubted. For in spite of this factuality of the cross, it would none the less be a purely mythological *kerygma*—i.e. a *kerygma* speaking of a selfhood which never existed—if Jesus' death were looked upon only as a physical, biological occurrence, as accidental or involuntary, i.e. as completely distinct from his existential selfhood. Only Jesus' death as his own existential act of accepting his death and living out of transcendence is really a historical event in distinction from a natural occurrence.[1] Hence the cross would be misunderstood if its chronological distinctness from the public ministry were looked upon as a basic theological separation from the public ministry, as is all too easy in reaction against Ritschlianism. For example the cross must be interpreted as Jesus' climatic actualization of his message, 'Repent, for God's reign is near'. For this message means a radical break with the present evil aeon, which in turn involves the acceptance of one's own death to and in this world. The revelation that transcendence resides in such a death as this, would be the eschatological saving event in history, just as the Easter *kerygma* claims to be.[2] Yet how can this relation of Jesus' death to his existential selfhood be investigated other than in terms of a new quest of the historical Jesus?

Hence the decisive point with regard to the *kerygma* and history is not whether the *kerygma* preserves detailed historical memories

[1]Note the theological concern to speak of Jesus being 'given over' to death or 'betrayed' (both παραδιδόναι), not only by God or Jesus' opponents, but also reflexively by himself: Gal. 2.20; Eph. 5.2., 25; cf. also Gal. 1.4. This view is expressed by the Gospels in their narrative of the journey to Jerusalem, where Jesus teaches the *kerygma* as his intention. In Gethsemane, the Last Supper, and the passion narrative this intention is given dramatic presentation. Käsemann in his 'Kritische Analyse von Phil. 2.5–11' (*ZTK* XLVII, 1950, 313–60) has pointed out that the hymn in Phil. 2.6–11 does not have in view the personality traits of the human, but rather the theological saving acts of the redeemer 'in suprahistorical, mythical framework' (342). Yet he emphasizes (336) that the reflexive pronoun ('emptied himself', 'humbled himself') 'points to Christ's own will and describes the occurrence as his act.' Cf. also Fritz Lieb, *Antwort*, 586.

[2]Cf. Paul Tillich, *Systematic Theology* I, 136: 'The acceptance of the cross, both during his life and at the end of it, is the decisive test of his unity with God, of his complete transparency to the ground of being.'

about Jesus, but rather that the *kerygma* is decidedly an evaluation of the historical person. The *kerygma* does not commit one to assume the historicity of this or that scene in Jesus' life, but it does commit one to a specific understanding of his life. Thus the *kerygma* is largely uninterested in historiography of the nineteenth-century kind, for the *kerygma* does not lie on the level of objectively verifiable fact. But it is decisively interested in historiography of the twentieth-century kind, for the *kerygma* consists in the meaning of a certain historical event, and thus coincides with the goal of modern historiography.

It is because modern historiography mediates an existential encounter with Jesus, an encounter also mediated by the *kerygma*, that modern historiography is of great importance to Christian faith. Käsemann's essay reopening the question of the historical Jesus was instigated[1] by Bultmann's procedure of placing Jesus' message outside primitive Christianity and putting it back into Judaism,[2] as only a presupposition of New Testament theology.[3] Although this classification may be justified and of no great import when limited to the level of the history of ideas, it becomes the crucial issue of the person of Jesus when one recognizes, as does Bultmann in the preface to his *Jesus and the Word,* that it is in the message that one encounters existentially the intention, the understanding of existence constituting the self, and thus the person.[4] If such encounter is not (like the encounter with the *kerygma*) the

[1]*ZTK* LI, 1954, 125 f.
[2]In *Primitive Christianity in its Contemporary Setting* (Ger. ed, 1949).
[3]In his *Theology of the New Testament* I (Ger. ed. 1948).
[4]It is in this sense that one is to understand the crucial importance of Jesus' message throughout Käsemann's basic essay (*ZTK* LI, 1954): 'Most of all, the New Testament itself gives us a right to this question (sc. about the historical Jesus), in so far as the Gospels attribute their *kerygma,* wherever it may come from, to none other than the earthly Jesus, and consequently attribute to him authority which is undeniably exceptional' (133). 'What is of concern to me is the proof that out of the darkness of the history of Jesus, characteristic traits of his proclamation become relatively recognizable, and primitive Christianity combined its own gospel with that proclamation. . . . The question of the historical Jesus is legitimately the question of the continuity of the gospel in the discontinuity of the times and in the variation of the *kerygma.* . . . The gospel is bound to the one who before and after Easter revealed himself to his own as Lord, by placing them before the God who is near and thus setting them in the freedom and responsibility of faith' (152).

eschatological event, i.e. 'Christian', then one must conclude that the message, intention, self, i.e. person, of the historical Jesus is different from what the *kerygma* says his reality is.

This would open the Jesus of the *kerygma* to the same destructive criticism which Bultmann[1] levelled against Barth's 'believer' who does not even know he believes: 'Isn't the *paradox overstretched?* If faith is separated from every psychic occurrence, if it is beyond the consciousness, is it still anything real at all? Is not all the talk about such faith just speculation, and absurd speculation at that? What is the point of talking about my 'self' which is never my self? What is the point of this faith of which I am not aware, of which I can at most believe that I have it? Is this identity which is claimed between my visible self and my invisible self not in fact a speculation as in gnosticism or anthroposophism, which also speak of relations of my self to higher worlds, relations which are real beyond my consciousness and which are in reality highly indifferent to me? . . . A faith beyond consciousness is after all not the 'impossible possibility', but in *every* sense an 'absurdity'. Is not an incarnation beyond Jesus' historical existence equally an absurdity? Bultmann's procedure of eliminating Jesus' message from primitive Christianity means ultimately that 'Christian faith is understood as faith in the exalted Lord for whom the historical Jesus as such no longer possesses constitutive significance'.[2]

This is not to say that faith hangs upon the question in the history of ideas as to whether Jesus appropriated any specific title available in his culture, or whether he ever spoke as does the *kerygma* in terms of his death and resurrection. But it does mean to say that when the evangelists attribute both to him, they are not merely harmonizing, or changing the *kerygma* into a system invented by Jesus, or betraying their lack of historical ability, but are also stating—admittedly on the externalized level of the history of ideas, and therefore in inadequate form, but nonetheless stating—that the *kerygma* is talking not about a myth, but about the historical existence presupposed in the message of Jesus of Nazareth.

[1]*ChrW* XXXVI, 1922, 358.
[2]Käsemann, *ZTK* LI, 1954, 126.

Although this historical existence could not be proved objectively by any quantity of authentic sayings of Jesus, were they ever so orthodox, yet that historical existence can be encountered historically and understood existentially. And if in the encounter with Jesus one is confronted with the *skandalon* of recognizing in this all-too-human Jewish eschatological message the eternal word of God, and consequently of breaking with the present evil aeon so as to live now out of the grace of God, i.e. if in encountering Jesus one is confronted with the same existential decision as that posed by the *kerygma,* one has proved all that can be proved by a new quest of the historical Jesus: not that the *kerygma* is true, but rather that the existential decision with regard to the *kerygma* is an existential decision with regard to Jesus.

V

THE PROCEDURE OF A NEW QUEST

A. THE PURPOSE AND PROBLEM OF A NEW QUEST

A new quest of the historical Jesus cannot be simply a continuation of the original quest. This fact is most apparent with regard to purpose. For the various factors which motivated the original quest have disappeared with it. The secularization of the West has so advanced that anti-clericalism rarely enlists the best talents of the day. Nor are the Church's opponents likely to be sufficiently embedded in the Christian tradition to be able to participate in biblical scholarship. For specialization has advanced to the degree where membership in the intelligentsia no longer qualifies for participation in the quest of the historical Jesus.[1] Nor can the wish to replace orthodoxy with a more modern theology be a compelling motivation, simply because the hold of orthodoxy upon Western civilization has been so clearly broken that only a Don Quixote would choose to tilt in such a tournament. On the other hand we no longer have an Arthur Drews or P.-L. Couchoud compelling the scholarly world to argue Jesus' historicity. The age of rationalism is past, with its apologetic interest in proving the historicity of the miracle stories by eliminating the miraculous element. For we see that this would merely eliminate the eschatological meaning of Jesus' life to which they in their way attest. Nor do we think that Jesus' personality can be reconstructed as a factor of real relevance to theology today. For apart from the difficulties inherent in the sources, modern man is too rudely awakened to his problems to be lulled by the winsomeness of the charming personality which may (or may not) have been Jesus'. Nor do we hold that an accurate reconstruction of Jesus' teaching can produce an ethical or theological system estab-

[1]This generalization is confirmed by the most recent attempt, that of Robert Graves in *King Jesus*, 1946, and *The Nazarene Gospel Restored*, 1954.

lishing the validity of Christianity. We recognize as basic, that historiography cannot and should not prove a *kerygma* which proclaims
Jesus as *eschatological* event calling for *existential* commitment.

The purpose of a new quest must derive from the factors which
have made such a quest possible and necessary, a generation after
the original purposes had lost their driving force and the original
quest had consequently come to an end. A new quest must be
undertaken because the *kerygma* claims to mediate an existential
encounter with a historical person, Jesus, who can also be encountered through the mediation of modern historiography. A
new quest cannot verify the truth of the *kerygma*, that this person
actually lived out of transcendence and actually makes transcendence available to me in my historical existence. But it can test
whether this kerygmatic understanding of Jesus' existence corresponds to the understanding of existence implicit in Jesus' history,
as encountered through modern historiography. If the *kerygma*'s
identification of *its* understanding of existence with *Jesus*' existence
is valid, then this kerygmatic understanding of existence should
become apparent as the result of modern historical research upon
Jesus. For such research has as a legitimate goal the clarification
of an understanding of existence occurring in history, as a possible
understanding of my existence. Hence the purpose of a new quest
of the historical Jesus would be to test the validity of the *kerygma*'s
identification of *its* understanding of existence with *Jesus*' existence.

As a purposeful undertaking, a new quest of the historical Jesus
would revolve around a central problem area determined by its
purpose. This is not to say that the innumerable detailed problems
involved in research would disappear, or no longer call for solution, but rather that the solution of individual difficulties would
be primarily relevant in terms of implementing the solution of a
focal problem. In the case of a new quest, this focal problem would
consist in using the available source material and current historical
method in such a way as to arrive at an understanding of Jesus'
historical action and existential selfhood, in terms which can be
compared with the *kerygma*.

It is out of this focal problem that the distinctive individual problems of a new quest arise. One seeks an encounter with the whole person, comparable to the totality of interpretation one has in the *kerygma*. Yet the totality of the person is not to be sought in terms of chronological and developmental continuity, which is not only unattainable, but also is a different order of 'wholeness' from that needed to draw a comparison with the *kerygma*. Rather the whole person is reached through encounter with individual sayings and actions in which Jesus' intention and selfhood are latent. Hence the relation of each saying or scene to the whole would be a problem of constant relevance.

The Gospels have in their way met this problem, not only by placing the *kerygma* on Jesus' lips, but also by presenting individual units from the tradition in such a way that the whole gospel becomes visible: At the call of Levi, we hear (Mark 2.17): 'I came not to call the righteous, but sinners'; at the healing of the deaf-mute, we hear (Mark 7.37): 'He has done all things well; he even makes the deaf hear and the dumb speak.' Thus such traditions become kerygmatic, not by appropriating the traditional language of the Church's *kerygma,* but in a distinctive way: They retain a concrete story about Jesus, but expand its horizon until the universal saving significance of the heavenly Lord becomes visible in the earthly Jesus.

Although the evangelists have thus in their way achieved an encounter with the total person in the individual scene, their method cannot be that of a new quest. For although the Church's kerygmatic vocabulary does not necessarily occur in such instances, they are none the less kerygmatized narratives, i.e. they reflect the Easter faith. But the question before us is whether this kerygmatic significance is also visible in an encounter with the total person mediated through modern historiography. Consequently the methods to be followed must be in terms of modern historical methodology.

B. THE CONTINUATION OF THE HISTORICAL-CRITICAL METHOD

In view of the emphasis which has been placed upon distinguishing the new quest from the original quest, it needs to be explicitly stated that a new quest cannot take place without the use of the objective philological, comparative-religious, and social-historical research indispensable for historical knowledge. Contemporary methodology has not discontinued these methods in its new understanding of history, but has merely shifted them more decidedly from ends to means. It is true that the 'explanation' of an event or viewpoint does not consist merely in showing its external causes or identifying the source from which an idea was borrowed. Much of what was once lauded as the 'truth' or 'reality' of history is now mocked by insight into the genetic fallacy. Yet despite all this, knowledge of the external cause or the detection of the source idea is often indispensable for understanding what was involved at the deeper level. Contemporary methodology consists precisely in the combination and interaction of objective analysis and existential openness, i.e. it seeks historical understanding precisely in the simultaneous interaction of phenomenological objectivity and existential 'objectivity'.[1]

[1]Twentieth-century historiography need not surrender the term 'objective' to nineteenth-century historiography. Scholarly objectivity does not reside simply in classifying the particular in categories with wider acceptance than one's own individual view, for such a procedure is blind to the twofold subjectivity residing in the categories of one's school of thought or day and age, and in the pervasive subjectivity of Western rationalism, which blunts true encounter into a merely outward stimulus for one's inner *a priori* faculties. Instead, objectivity resides in a complete openness to what the creative historical event has to say. This involves a willingness to listen for underlying intentions and the understanding of existence they convey, with an ear sharpened by one's own awareness of the problems of human existence, and a willingness to suspend one's own answers and one's own understanding of existence sufficiently to grasp as a real possibility what the other is saying. Thus one's historical involvement, not one's disinterestedness, is the instrument leading to objectivity, and it must be constantly observed that this 'subjective participation' of the historian consists precisely in the potential suspension of his own personal views, for the sake of hearing what the other has to tell him about his existence. Cf. Martin Heidegger *Sein und Zeit*, 1927, 395: 'The historical opening up of the "past" through fateful repetition is so little "subjective" that it alone assures the "objectivity" of history. For the objectivity of a science is primarily determined by whether it can bring to the understanding in uncovered fashion the thematically relevant beings in the basic form of their Being. In no science are the "universal validity" of the standards and the claims of "universality" which the impersonal "one" and its common sense requires, *less* possible criteria of "truth" than in authentic history.' Cf. further Bultmann, 'Ist voraussetzungslose Exegese möglich?', *TZ* XIII, 1957, 414 f.

The use of historical-critical method within modern historiography has met with opposition on theological grounds: would not two methods of studying history necessarily involve two classes of historical reality?[1] But this is not the case. The epistemological situation need no more lead to an ontological inference than it does in modern physics, where complementary methods produce either wave characteristics or particle characteristics, without a resultant inference that one has to do with two distinct sub-atomic worlds.[2] 'Every historical phenomenon is directed toward understanding, and belongs together with this [understanding, which is] its future. . . . The noetic possibility of considering the historical phenomenon with or without its future always prevails in principle within the one historical sphere of reality.'[3] As a matter of fact one can recognize, in the interaction of 'Jesus in the context of dead-and-gone first-century Judaism' and 'Jesus as a possible understanding of my existence', a formal analogy in terms of modern historiography to the *kerygma*'s identification of the Jesus of history with the heavenly Lord.

An analogous criticism has been made with regard to the self-hood of the participating historian: would not two methods of studying history necessarily involve two kinds of self-hood? If selfhood is constituted by the 'world' to which we give ourselves, and the objectified 'world' of critical scholarship is different from the existential 'world' of encounter, is not the subject in each case different? Is not the 'I' of an 'I-it' relationship necessarily different from the 'I' of an 'I-thou'

[1] This is the thesis of Heinrich Ott, *Geschichte und Heilsgeschichte in der Theologie Rudolf Bultmanns*, 1955, esp. Ch. I: 'Der doppelte Geschichtsbegriff', 8–57; of Hermann Diem, 'Die Kluft zwischen historischer und theologischer Fragestellung bei Rudolf Bultmann und der Versuch ihrer Überwindung durch das Kerygma', *Theologie* II, 114–26; and of René Marlé, *Bultmann et l'interprétation du Nouveau Testament*, 1956, 32. Cf. the criticisms of this position by Peter Biehl, 'Welchen Sinn hat es, von "theologischer Ontologie" zu reden?' *ZTK* LIII, 1956, 349–72, esp. 369–71 (to Ott), and 'Zur Frage nach dem historischen Jesus', *TR*, n.F. XXIV, 1957–8, 58–61 (to Diem); and by Bultmann, 'In eigener Sache', *TLZ* LXXXII, 1957, 242 (to Marlé). A mediating position is found in Fritz Lieb, ' "Geschichte und Heilsgeschichte in der Theologie Rudolf Bultmanns",' *EvTh* XV, 1955, 507–22 (on Ott's book).
[2] Cf. J. Robert Oppenheimer's Reith Lectures of 1953, *Science and the Common Understanding*.   [3] Peter Biehl, *ZTK* LIII, 1956, 369 f.

relationship?[1] To this we can begin by answering 'Yes'. But these two selfhoods do not correspond to the 'I' which encounters Jesus through a new quest and the 'I' which encounters him through the *kerygma*. For a new quest would not be confined to purely objective research, but would seek an existential encounter with his person, i.e. an 'I-thou' relation. For it is only where his existence speaks to me, i.e. it is only within an 'I-thou' relation, that the historical Jesus can be compared with the *kerygma*. Nor do I automatically exist in an 'I-thou' relation to the *kerygma*. For I must disengage the kerygmatic fragments from the New Testament before I can encounter them existentially. This is even true of human relations, where a certain degree of instinctive 'historical-critical' study is involved in becoming sufficiently acquainted with a person to lay hold of what his existence means to him. Hence this shifting selfhood is a dialectic inherent in the historicity of human existence.[2]

Nor is the dialectic permanently resolved in the encounter with God; rather it is accentuated by the addition of a further dimension, in which historical encounter becomes revelation. It would be *theologia gloriae,* a sophisticated form of perfectionism, to assume that the Christian is not called upon continually to confront the offence of Christianity when he encounters God. Grace continues to reside in judgement, life in death, revelation in historical ambiguity. It is in this dialectical movement from the old man to the new that one finds the distinctive characteristic of Christian existence (I Cor. 13.8–13), not in some other-worldly immediacy. One need merely recall Luther's definition of Christian existence: '*simul peccator et iustus, semper penitens.*'[3]

[1] I am indebted to Carl Michaelson for drawing my attention to this aspect of the problem. Cf. e.g. Martin Buber, *I and Thou*, 1937, 3, 62.

[2] Heidegger, *Sein und Zeit*, 1927, § 76, 'Der existenziale Ursprung der Historie aus der Geschichtlichkeit des Daseins', derives from the historicity of human existence the ontological basis of historical research, with all its detailed specialization, 'even down to its most unpretentious "handwork"' (394).

[3] *Vorlesung über den Römerbrief*, 1515–16, ed. J. Ficker, II, 108. Cf. also the first of the 95 theses: 'Dominus et magister noster Jesus Christus, dicendo: Poenitentiam agite etc. omnem vitam fidelium poenitentiam esse voluit.' Cf. Buber, *op. cit.*, 65: 'No man is pure person and no man pure individuality. None is wholly real and none wholly unreal. Every man lives in the twofold *I*.'

Still another criticism of the continued use of historical-critical method within a theologically relevant quest of the historical Jesus needs to be mentioned. For although it cannot lead to a suspension of that method, it does draw our attention to the basic problem[1] which it presents: 'According to our historical method employed thus far, we have before us apparently authentic material about Jesus in the tradition of the sayings of the Lord, only when the material can be understood neither [as derived] from primitive Christian preaching nor from Judaism. Accordingly, in the surest current way of getting on the track of Jesus' preaching, it is elevated to a methodological presupposition that everything which points toward the post-Easter *kerygma* cannot be considered for Jesus' preaching. Then what significance should the result of this research have for theology?'[2]

This criticism might lead one to suppose that such a method is valid only in terms of the original quest, which largely rejected the *kerygma* as a falsification of Jesus, and consequently set out to distinguish him sharply from that theological perversion. However on closer examination it is apparent that it is not the method, but only the absolutizing of its limited results, which results from the approach of the original quest. The effort to distinguish a historical event from later interpretation is a standard historical procedure, just as it is to question the historicity of such details in the tradition as clearly betray that later interpretation. As a matter of fact it is obvious that at least in some instances—one need think only of the Gospel of John—the *kerygma* was put into the mouth of Jesus by the evangelists. If it is a historical fact that this took place, it is a valid procedure for the historian to attempt to distinguish the 'authentic' from the 'unauthentic'[3] material.

[1]For a discussion of this cf. my article 'The Historical Jesus and the Church's Kerygma', *Religion in Life* XXVI, 1956, 393–409. [2]Biehl, *op. cit.*, 56.

[3]One may however observe that material regarded as wholly 'unauthentic' in terms of positivistic historiography may not seem nearly as 'unauthentic' in terms of modern historiography. For a saying which Jesus never spoke may well reflect accurately his historical significance, and in this sense be more 'historical' than many irrelevant things Jesus actually said. The hopeless ambiguity of the old term 'unauthentic' can be illustrated in terms of the essay of Erich Dinkler, 'Jesu Wort vom Kreuztragen', *Neutestamentliche Studien für Rudolf Bultmann*, 1954, 110–29. Dinkler maintains that the saying

The use of this method becomes illegitimate only when one fails to recognize its limitation. Although one may well assume that the founder of a sect has something in common with the sect he founds, this method is not able to reach whatever area of overlapping there may have been between Jesus and the Church. The method can affirm the historicity only of that part of Jesus in which he is least 'Christian'. For its 'historicity' depends upon the demonstration that it does not present the Church's view and consequently could not have originated there. Since the new quest of the historical Jesus is primarily concerned with investigating the area in which Jesus and the Church's *kerygma* overlap, the limitation of current methods for identifying historical material is apparent, and the resultant methodological difficulty must be recognized.

C. THE METHODOLOGICAL IMPASSE

The limitation inherent in traditional method cannot be adequately met by a supreme effort to solve the much-belaboured problems which these methodological considerations have rendered all but insoluble. The *kerygma* is to be found *expressis verbis* upon the lips of Jesus in the Gospels. Consequently the most obvious solution as to the relation of Jesus and the *kerygma* has always been that Jesus himself proclaimed the *kerygma*: he claimed

---

about taking up one's cross and following Jesus (Mark 8.34 parr.) is not, as has been usually assumed, 'unauthentic'. It was actually spoken by Jesus—only it did not originally refer to the cross. Instead Jesus was alluding to bearing God's seal or sign, so that one should translate σταυρὸς as 'Taw' or 'Chi' or 'X', rather than 'cross'. Hence according to Dinkler's interpretation the saying is 'authentic', i.e. spoken by Jesus, but the *meaning* it had for the evangelists and for Christians ever since, i.e. its allusion to Jesus' cross, is 'unauthentic'. Yet even here one must narrow the area of 'unauthenticity'. The traditional interpretation is, according to Dinkler's interpretation, only intellectually 'unauthentic', i.e. Jesus did not mean to refer to crucifixion when he spoke; but existentially the traditional interpretation is seen to be 'authentic', as soon as one recognizes that the existential meaning of the traditional Christian interpretation coincides with the existential meaning of the original saying: 'Surrender of self-assertion before God and surrender of the autonomous freedom which directs itself against God' (128). And in both instances this existential meaning is the meaning of *Jesus'* existence: In the traditional interpretation, I assume my cross as my union with the cross of Christ; in Dinkler's interpretation, I encounter an 'authentic' saying in which Jesus' existential selfhood finds expression.

for himself exalted titles and predicted his death and resurrection, just as the *kerygma* does. However it is precisely these most obviously kerygmatic sayings of Jesus whose historicity has been put indefinitely in suspension by current methodology. For these are the sayings which could most obviously have arisen within the Church as sayings of the heavenly Lord, and then, because of the unity of the heavenly Lord and the earthly Jesus, been automatically handed down with the 'rest' of the sayings of Jesus.

Perhaps the classical instance of such a problem has to do with the title 'Son of Man'. For it is the title to which Jesus most frequently makes claim in the Gospels, and with which the predictions of the passion are usually connected. Now the debate as to whether Jesus actually claimed this title for himself has been going on for nearly a century,[1] and is still not resolved. The classical presentation of the critical position[2] divides the 'Son of Man' sayings into three groups: apocalyptic sayings about the future 'Son of Man'; sayings in which Jesus' passion is spoken of as the passion of the 'Son of Man'; and miscellaneous sayings in which Jesus refers to himself during his public ministry as 'Son of Man'. The first group of apocalyptic sayings are conceded to be authentic, but in them Jesus does not explicitly identify himself with this future 'Son of Man'. The sayings in the second group connected with the passion are considered unauthentic *vaticinia ex eventu*. The sayings of the third group are looked upon as mistranslations of the Aramaic idiom, which means not only 'Son

[1] The history of this debate has been written by Erik Sjöberg, 'Ville Jesus vara Messias?, Bestridandet av Jesu messiasmedvetande i det sista seklets forskning' ('Did Jesus want to be Messiah? The Contesting of Jesus' Messianic Consciousness in the Research of the Last Century'), *Svensk Exegetisk Årsbok* X, 1945, 82–151.

[2] Although the argument is summarized in almost every discussion, perhaps the classic English presentation is that of F. J. Foakes Jackson and Kirsopp Lake in *The Beginnings of Christianity* I, 1920, 368–84. However their tabular presentation is in terms of sources, and the three groups which have become conventional are derived from Jean Héring, *Le royaume de Dieu et sa venue*, 1937, Ch. V, 'Jésus et le "fils de l'homme",' 88–100. This presentation can be found in John Knox, *Christ the Lord*, 1945, 30–44, or Rudolf Bultmann, *Theology of the New Testament* I, 30. The position has been reconfirmed in the unpublished Heidelberg dissertation by Gerhard Iber, *Überlieferungsgeschichtliche Untersuchungen zum Begriff des Menschensohnes im Neuen Testament* (1953), summarized in *TLZ* LXXX, 1955, 115 f.

of Man', but also simply 'man' or 'a man' (i.e. 'I', as in II Cor. 12.2 ff.); or as replacements for an original personal pronoun 'I'.[1] From this analysis of the 'Son of Man' sayings the conclusion is obvious: Jesus did not claim to be the 'Son of Man'. This position has been countered from the conservative side primarily with the argument that the term 'Son of Man' is not a christological title used by the primitive Church,[2] so could not have been attributed

[1]A. Meyer, *Jesu Muttersprache*, 1896, 95 ff., argued that since 'hahu gabra' ('this man') can be a circumlocution for 'I', the same would be true of 'hahu barnasha'. This interpretation has been generally accepted until Erik Sjöberg ('Litteratur till den bibliska kristologien', *STK* XVI, 1940, 294–305, esp. 299) protested that the conjectured idiom never occurs in Aramaic. Hence he (*Der verborgene Menschensohn in den Evangelien*, 1955, 239, n. 3) presented the alternate thesis: 'If the sayings are original, then one must reckon with the fact that Jesus simply said "I", which was then in the tradition replaced by "Son of Man", as in Matt. 16.13 over against Mark 8.27.' One can observe the effect of this shift upon the classical argument by noting the divergences in the presentations by John Knox from *Christ the Lord*, 1945, 30–44, to *The Death of Christ*, 1958, 86–102. Meanwhile however Matthew Black ('Unsolved New Testament Problems. The "Son of Man" in the Teaching of Jesus', *ExpT* LI, 1948–9, 32–36), while conceding that 'hahu barnasha' never occurs with the meaning 'I', has produced an instance of 'barnasha' meaning 'I' (34, n. 1): 'An exact parallel in Aramaic occurs in *Bereshith Rabba* (ed. J. Theodor, Berlin, 1927, Section 7, Beginning). A certain Rabbi Jacob of Nibburaya had been teaching that fish, as well as other living animals used for food, should be ritually slaughtered. R. Haggai "heard (of this), and (sent to him) and said, 'Come and receive your punishment' (as a false teacher). R. Jacob replied to him, 'A man (barnash) who has spoken a word according to Torah to be punished. Strange, indeed!' . . ." The reference is unambiguously to the speaker himself.'

[2]The absence of the term from the Church is not as complete as is usually assumed. For in addition to Acts 7.56, the term is reported by Hegesippus (in Eusebius, *Eccl. Hist.* II, 23) as used by James at his martyrdom: 'Why do you ask me about Jesus the Son of Man! He is now sitting in the heavens, on the right hand of the great Power, and is about to come on the clouds of heaven.' Cf. also Hippolytus, *Ref.* 5.26.30; Rev. 1.13; Justin, *Apol.* I, 51.9. Furthermore the title 'Son of Man' occurs in Heb. 2.5 ff., where Ps. 8.4–6 is interpreted christologically, and consequently the original anthropological meaning of the idiom has been replaced by the titular meaning. Jean Héring (*Die biblischen Grundlagen des christlichen Humanismus*, 1946, 5 ff.) has shown that here Ps. 8.4–6 has become a kerygmatic text on the pattern 'pre-existence, humiliation, exaltation', such as occurs in Phil. 2.6–11 and elsewhere. This further draws attention to the role which the concept, if not the term, played in the development of the *kerygma*. Cf. e.g. my 'Formal Analysis of Col. 1.15–20', *JBL* LXXVI, 1957, 270–87, esp. 277–80. Stauffer, *New Testament Theology*, n. 800, calls attention to an undeveloped tendency for the term itself to occur in the *kerygma*. The Pauline concept of the second Adam also belongs in this context. Furthermore even conservative scholarship concedes that the Church

to Jesus unless he had used it of himself.[1] Now of course there are variations in individual presentations on each side, and occasional concessions of specific points provide a certain fluidity to the debate. Furthermore new insights could conceivably provide new possibilities of solution.[2] Consequently research upon such classical

---

originated the use of the term in at least some of the sayings of Jesus (cf. e.g. Cullmann, *Die Christologie des Neuen Testaments*, 1957, 155-7, and Stauffer, *Novum Testamentum* I, 1956, 82). For the role of the 'Son of Man' in the Johannine tradition cf. Siegfried Schulz, *Untersuchungen zur Menschensohn-Christologie im Johannesevangelium*, 1957. Now Ernst Lohmeyer has clearly gone too far in postulating (*Galiläa und Jerusalem*, 1936, esp. 'Der Menschensohn-Glaube', 68-79) a Galilean branch of the primitive Church with a distinctively 'Son of Man christology' (in distinction to the Jerusalem church's 'Messiah christology'). But on the other hand the varied and imaginative ways in which the term and concept were used by the primitive Church weaken considerably the argument that the Church could not have initiated the identification of Jesus with the Son of Man whose coming he predicted.

[1]This position is well stated e.g. by Oscar Cullmann in his forthcoming *Christology of the New Testament* II, 2.2.

[2]Erik Sjöberg argues that the hiddenness of the 'Son of Man' is a constitutive aspect of the Jewish concept, and on this basis explains both Mark's 'messianic secret' and the absence of any clear identification of himself with the 'Son of Man' on the part of Jesus. Cf. *Der verborgene Menschensohn in den Evangelien*, 1955, and his earlier studies on the problem listed there. The traditional view of the title 'Son of Man' as presenting the 'ideal of humanity', 'the incorporation of the moral ideal in the person of Jesus', had been branded by Baldensperger as a modernization in terms of the humanistic ideal prevalent since the enlightenment. Cf. *Das Selbstbewusstsein Jesu im Lichte der messianischen Hoffnungen seiner Zeit*, 2nd ed., 1892, 178 f. However, when embedded in Jesus' eschatology and applied to his followers (and then, in the moment when all forsake him, to himself), this view has re-entered the discussion. Cf. T. W. Manson, *The Teaching of Jesus*, 1931, 211-34; 'The Son of Man in Daniel, Enoch and the Gospels', *Bulletin of the John Rylands Library* XXXII, 1950, 171-93; *The Servant-Messiah*, 1953, 72 ff., 80 f.; C. J. Cadoux, *The Historic Mission of Jesus*, 1941, 90-103; Vincent Taylor, *The Names of Jesus*, 1953, 25-35; *The Life and Ministry of Jesus*, 1955, 77-83. The increasing awareness in Bultmannian circles of the christology implicit in Jesus' eschatology has drawn attention to the incompatibility of this estimate of himself with the imminent expectation of some different 'Son of Man', and hence to the elimination of the whole 'Son of Man' complex from the sayings of Jesus, as a concept both distinct from and even incompatible with that of the kingdom of God. Cf. Käsemann, *ZTK* LI, 1954, 149 f.; Philipp Vielhauer, 'Gottesreich und Menschensohn in der Verkündigung Jesu', *Festschrift für Günther Dehn*, ed. W. Schneemelcher, 1957, 51-79; Hans Conzelmann, 'Gegenwart und Zukunft in der synoptischen Tradition', *ZTK* LIV, 1957, 281-3; *RGG*, 3rd ed., II, 1958, 668. A somewhat parallel position from a more conservative point of view is found in J. A. T. Robinson's *Jesus and his Coming* (1957), where the historicity of Jesus' prediction of the parousia of the Son of Man is denied, while his public ministry as that of the Son of

problems as the 'Son of Man' can meaningfully be continued. Yet scholarship cannot wait indefinitely on their solution, but must instead seek for completely new ways of bringing Jesus and the *kerygma* into comparison.

D. BASIC PROBLEMS OF A NEW QUEST

The historicity of those sayings of Jesus which are most like the *kerygma* has been put indefinitely in suspense by methodological considerations. Yet there is a considerable body of material about Jesus whose historicity tends to be generally accepted, on the basis of these same methods. This is material whose historicity is conceivable in terms of Jesus' Jewish, Palestinian background, and whose origin in the primitive Church is rendered unlikely by the absence of the distinctive views of the Church, or even by the presence of traits which the Church could tolerate but hardly initiate.[1]

Now the historical material which results from the rigorous application of these current methods is at first sight of little relevance to the purpose and problem of a new quest of the historical Jesus. For the tradition of Jesus' sayings has been purged of all traces of the Church's *kerygma,* and therefore could seem of little value in comparing Jesus with the *kerygma.* However this only appears to be the case; the much more important fact resulting from the application of these methods is that they do succeed in producing a body of material whose historicity seems relatively assured. The very objectivity of the methods used, objective precisely with regard to the *kerygma,* gives to this non-

---

Man is affirmed. It may prove to be relevant to the 'Son of Man' problem that the Similitudes of Enoch have not yet been identified as belonging to the Qumran library.

[1] These principal considerations are not of course the only tools for investigating the authenticity of material about Jesus, although most of the valid methods in current use merely implement them. For a more detailed presentation of methods cf. Joachim Jeremias, 'Kennzeichen der ipsissima vox Jesu', *Synoptische Studien,* 1953, 86–93, and 'Der gegenwärtige Stand der Debatte um das Problem des historischen Jesus', 168 f.; N. A. Dahl, 'Der historische Jesus als geschichtswissenschaftliches und theologisches Problem', *KuD* I, 1955, 104–32, esp. 144–22; and Franz Mussner, 'Der historische Jesus und der Christus des Glaubens', *BZ,* n.F. I, 1957, 224–52, esp. II: 'Kriterien für den historischen Jesus in den Evangelien', 227–30.

kerygmatic material an importance for comparing the historical Jesus and the *kerygma* which the more kerygmatic sayings never achieved, simply because their relation to the historical Jesus was never fully established. The material whose historicity *has* been established is sufficient in quality and quantity to make a historical encounter with Jesus possible. His action, the intention latent in it, the understanding of existence it implies, and thus his selfhood, can be encountered historically. And this can in turn be compared with the *kerygma,* once the meaning the *kerygma* conveys has begun to shine through the language in which it is communicated.

The kind of individual problems which arise from the purpose and focal problem of the new quest can be illustrated by an examination of some of the comparisons or contrasts which have been made between Jesus and the *kerygma.* Some of the contrasts which have been drawn are so basic that they would if valid tend to obviate even the possibility of a relevant comparison, and deserve therefore to be considered in first place.

One such contrast has been drawn by Käsemann himself:[1] the historical Jesus belongs to the past; only in the *kerygma* does Jesus encounter me in the present. 'In so far as one wishes to speak of a modification of faith before and after Easter, it can only be said that "once" became "once for all", the isolated encounter with Jesus limited by death became that presence of the exalted Lord such as the Fourth Gospel describes.' Yet, methodologically speaking,[2] the historical Jesus I encounter *via* historiography is just as really a possible understanding of my present existence as is the *kerygma* of the New Testament, whose 'contemporaneity' is equally problematic. And as a matter of fact this is the problem with which Käsemann is confronted. A new quest of the historical Jesus 'cannot replace the gospel, since historical remains

---

[1]*ZTK* LI, 1954, 139. Käsemann further (129) describes the kerygmatizing process as 'delivering the facts of the past from the possibility of being regarded as (just) curiosities and miracles', to which Heitsch (*ZTK* LIII, 1956, 204, n. 1) aptly comments: 'Can we say this? Was Jesus' action and language then [just] a remarkable occurrence whose reproduction would *not* have confronted one with decision (which after all resides in his words!)?'

[2]Cf. e.g. Rudolf Bultmann, 'The Problem of Hermeneutics', *Essays Philosophical and Theological,* 234–61.

are not able to assure us that those fragments of Jesus' message are still relevant to us today and attest to God's present action upon us. Only faith derived from Christian preaching is able to deduce the certainty of God acting upon us even from those fragments, which otherwise would remain only a small part of the history of ideas, and quite a problematic part at that.'[1] However all of this is equally true with regard to the New Testament *kerygma*. This parallel has been obscured by the fact that the term '*kerygma*' can ambiguously refer both to fragments of primitive Christian preaching embedded in the New Testament text, and to the word of God I encounter from the pulpit or in my neighbour today. But if it is true that the *kerygma* of the primitive Christians can become contemporaneous with me in my concrete historical encounters, then, in principle at least, this is equally true of the historical Jesus.

Bornkamm[2] has taken over Käsemann's basic distinction that Jesus' 'once' became at Easter 'once for all', but gives it a somewhat different explanation: The 'once' of 'Jesus' history' becomes the 'once for all' of 'God's history with the world'. Yet 'God's history with the world' is not only the interpretation put upon the history of Jesus by the *kerygma*, but is already the meaning residing in it for Jesus himself. Already for Jesus the 'once' of his historicity was the 'once for all' of God's saving event.[3] For Jesus conceived of his transcendent selfhood as constituted by God's intervention in history. And when one examines the nature of this

[1]'Zum Thema der Nichtobjektivierbarkeit', *EvTh* XII, 1952–3, 466.
[2]*Jesus von Nazareth*, 20.
[3]Joachim Jeremias, 'Der gegenwärtige Stand der Debatte um das Problem des historischen Jesus', 170, emphasizes this point even to the extent of minimizing the *kerygma*: 'The gospel of Jesus and the *kerygma* of the primitive Church may not be put on the same level; rather they are related to each other as call and reply. The life, work and death of Jesus, the authoritative word of the one who is able to say Abba, who in God's authority called sinners to his table and who went to the cross as Servant of God, is God's call. The believing witness of the primitive Church, the Spirit-led choir of a thousand tongues, is the reply to God's call. . . . It is effected by God's Spirit, but it does not stand equal to the call. The decisive thing is the call, not the reply.' Here full justice is hardly done to the primitive Church's conviction that their *kerygma* was not merely their Spirit-led reply to God's revelation in Jesus, but rather the heavenly Lord's revelation of himself.

selfhood, one sees that it was not a selfish selfhood, but by its very constitution a selfhood for others.

It was the content of this eschatological selfhood that Jesus should accept his death to the present evil aeon. This is the meaning of the paradoxical saying of Mark 8.35: 'For whoever would save his life will lose it, and whoever loses his life will save it.' In accepting his death he was free from the demonic power of the fear of death, and therein resided his transcendence. Yet the eschatological situation in which he found himself was not yet that of the final blessedness, but rather the 'last hour', in which forgiveness was offered to the penitent. This aspect of the situation was also constitutive of Jesus' selfhood. Hence his selfhood found its positive expression in his role as 'sign' of the eschatological situation to the world. He was finally put to death after persisting in this positive expression of his selfhood. Hence his death was seen as the realization of his eschatological selfhood: free from the demonic power of the fear of death, he was free to give his life for his neighbour. His selfhood was interpreted as *pro nobis* not first by the Church, but already by Jesus himself.

The distinction drawn by Käsemann and Bornkamm is in recognition of the distinctive significance of Easter. And as a matter of fact Easter *was* the revelation of Jesus' transcendent selfhood to his disciples. And yet what was revealed at Easter was the transcendent selfhood of *Jesus,* as the *kerygma* insists; i.e. the Easter experience, even though separated from Jesus' lifetime, was the culmination of their historical encounter with him.[1] And it was the selfhood of Jesus to which they witnessed in the *kerygma*. Hence to maintain that Jesus' transcendent selfhood can be encountered historically is not to minimize Easter, but rather to affirm its indispensable presupposition.

This basic problem as to whether the historical Jesus and the

[1]Cf. Bultmann, *Kerygma and Myth,* 207, n. 1: 'It goes without saying that this Word need not necessarily be uttered at the same moment of time in which it becomes a decisive word for me. It is possible for something I heard yesterday or even thirty years ago to become a decisive word for me now; then it begins (or perhaps begins once more) to be a word spoken to me, and is therefore shown to be a word addressed with reference to my present situation.'

kerygma are sufficiently commensurable to be subject to comparison can be posed in a different way. The *kerygma* proclaims an eschatological saving event of cosmic proportions. How can Jesus' understanding of himself, irrespective of what that understanding may have been, be subject to comparison with the *kerygma*'s understanding of the course of history or the condition of the cosmos? Now this would be a valid argument if one understood the self in terms of individual autonomy, so that one's understanding of one's self as subject would be quite distinct from one's understanding of the cosmic or historical situation one confronted as object. When however selfhood is envisaged on the basis of the historicity of the self, i.e. when it is recognized that selfhood is constituted in terms of a 'world' or 'context' to which one gives oneself, then it is apparent that one's understanding of one's self includes an understanding of the 'world' in which one exists.[1] In Jesus' case, his selfhood is eschatological, his life is lived out of transcendence, precisely because he has given himself to the eschatological situation introduced by John the Baptist. In his baptism he 'repents' of his former selfhood built upon a non-eschatological 'world', and in believing John's message of the eschatological situation assumes the eschatological selfhood which ultimately found expression in the title 'Son of Man'.

Yet this same criticism, that Jesus' understanding of his selfhood is incommensurate with the *kerygma*'s concept of a dramatic shift in the course of history or the cosmos, has been presented in still more radical fashion. Is not this whole assumption that Jesus was concerned with a new selfhood, irrespective of whether it be conceived individualistically or in terms of the historicity of human existence, based upon a false theologizing of the historical Jesus? Was he not much more like a Jewish prophet or Rabbi, concerned basically with moral reform? Did he not simply say what man should do, rather than presenting dramatic views of

[1]Cf. Rudolf Bultmann's remarks to this effect in *Kerygma and Myth,* 203 f. It is clearly not inherent in this approach that theology be reduced to anthropology, as in the case of Bultmann's presentation of Pauline theology (*Theology of the New Testament* I, 190 ff.). Such a consequence has been specifically repudiated by Ernst Käsemann, 'Neutestamentliche Fragen von heute', *ZTK* LIV, 1957, 13 f.

what God has done or will do? It is this contrast between Jesus and the Church which characterized scholarship at the turn of the century.

The sharpest formulation was that of William Wrede:[1] 'The teaching of Jesus is directed entirely to the individual personality. Man is to submit his soul to God and to God's will wholly and without reserve. Hence his preaching is for the most part imperative in character, if not in form. The central point for Paul is a divine and supernatural action manifested as a historical fact, or a complex of divine actions which open to mankind a salvation prepared for man. He who believes these divine acts—the incarnation, death, and resurrection of a divine being—can obtain salvation. This view is the essential point of Paul's religion, and is the solid framework without which his belief would collapse incontinently; was it a continuation or a further development of Jesus' gospel? Where, in this theory, can we find the "gospel" which Paul is said to have "understood". The point which was everything to Paul was nothing to Jesus.'

The very radicality of this quotation draws attention to its basic error: the Jesus of this antithesis is the modernized Jesus of the nineteenth-century biographies. He is of course incompatible with the Paul of the first century (whose unmodern credulity is somewhat overdrawn). For a moral reformer of the Victorian era is quite different from the message of divine salvation proclaimed by an eschatological sect of the Hellenistic world. But once one has come to see Jesus in his first-century context of Jewish eschatology, the basic antithesis tends to disappear. His eschatological message that the kingdom of God is already beginning to break into history is, like Paul's message, 'a divine and superhuman action manifested as a historical fact, or a complex of divine actions which open to mankind a salvation prepared for man': 'If it is by the finger of God that I cast out demons, then the kingdom of God has come upon you' (Luke 11.20). 'Woe to you, Chorazin! woe to you, Bethsaida! for if the mighty works

[1] *Paulus*, 1905. The quotation is the point of departure of Johannes Weiss' *Paul and Jesus*, 1909, 3.

done in you had been done in Tyre and Sidon, they would have repented long ago in sackcloth and ashes' (Matt. 11.21). It is this eschatological action of God in history which Jesus proclaimed, and which reached its final formulation in the *kerygma*.

But even if Jesus was, like the *kerygma*, proclaiming God's dramatic intervention in history, was not its significance for the hearer merely that of a call to moral reform? Had Jesus recognized it as a basic dilemma that man's selfhood has been determined by the 'present evil aeon', and that he is subsequently unable to free himself? Was for him the inbreaking of the kingdom of God the possibility of a 'new being', or was it merely the occasion for a sharpening of one's conscience in view of the impending judgement? Such a distinction has, as a matter of fact, been drawn by Ernst Fuchs:[1] 'What is still lacking for Jesus is now supplemented as a consequence of Jesus' cross: the problem of sin expands to the problem of death as a whole. The question: "What should I do (to become blessed)?" yields to the question, "How do I overcome the impotence, under death's sway, of my existence lost before God?" Rom.7.24.' However in this case it is Bultmann who sees no such distinction, but rather understands Jesus to be here existentially as radical as Paul. If for Paul the *kerygma* means 'pronouncing upon oneself the sentence of death and placing one's confidence not in oneself, but in God who raises the dead (II Cor. 1.9), then 'it is clear that *these explicit theological trains of thought are not present in Jesus*. But it appears to me to be equally clear that they are only explicating Jesus' thought in definite historical antitheses. . . . What Jesus does not at all express is this, that the only way it is *a priori* at all *possible* for the law to encounter the man who desires to secure himself by his own performance, is by becoming for him the παιδαγωγός. To be sure, no matter how foreign this theological idea may be to Jesus' preaching, factually his message implies it none the less.'[2] Hence Jesus' call for obedience in the eschatological situation logically presupposes an eschatological selfhood.

[1] *Festschrift Rudolf Bultmann*, 55.
[2] *GuV* I, 197 f. Italics by Bultmann.

This survey of basic problems for a new quest has not led to the conclusion that Jesus and the *kerygma* are basically incommensurate, a conclusion which would have made the positive solution of the central problem *a priori* impossible. Rather it has tended to reaffirm the working hypothesis of the new quest: if an encounter with the *kerygma* is an encounter with the meaning of Jesus, then an encounter with Jesus should be an encounter with the meaning of the *kerygma*. However no working hypothesis will long maintain its validity, unless one actually enters with it into the work itself. Therefore at least an initial attempt to work upon the central problem in terms of specific problems should be made.

E. TOWARD THE SOLUTION OF TYPICAL PROBLEMS

The typical formulation of the antithesis between Jesus and Paul around the turn of the century was to the effect that 'Jesus preached the kingdom but Paul preached Christ'. *'The Gospel, as Jesus proclaimed it, has to do with the Father only and not with the Son.'*[1] This distinction has been renewed by Ernst Heitsch as a basic incompatibility between Jesus and the *kerygma*.[2] However here too we may well inquire as to whether we are not dealing with a misunderstanding of both Jesus and the *kerygma*. Certainly Jesus did not teach a christology as the Church did. Yet nothing has been more characteristic of research in the past generation than the growing insight that 'Jesus' call to decision implies a christology'.[3] Nor has anything been more characteristic of recent

[1] Adolf Harnack, *What Is Christianity?* (1900), 144 of the 1957 edition. Italics by Harnack.

[2] *ZTK* LIII, 1956, 208 f.: 'Jesus does not point to his person . . .; rather he immediately retreats behind his words, in order to leave the hearer alone with them. . . . (The primitive Church) concerns itself less with acknowledging a commission to reveal God's will, in confrontation with the substance of Jesus' sentences . . .; rather is it concerned with understanding resurrection and redemption through Jesus as the resurrected Son of God. How little it thereby was able to do justice to the intention of the historical Jesus is nowhere more apparent than in the fact that at times it twisted his intention, and just at the decisive points, in that it intentionally or unintentionally changed the absolute freedom and unprotectedness of man under the claim of God, which Jesus taught, into the freedom merely of the Son of Man.'

[3] Rudolf Bultmann, *Theology of the New Testament* I, 43. Similarly Hans Conzelmann speaks of Jesus' 'indirect' christology (*RGG,* 3rd ed. II, 1958,

research than the gradual detection of early kerygmatic fragments in the New Testament, in which the original eschatological meaning of the christological titles used in the *kerygma* is still apparent, and is clearly distinct from their later metaphysical use: Jesus is 'exalted' to the rank of cosmocrator with the 'name that is above every name, . . . Lord Jesus Christ', in order to subjugate the universe (Phil. 2.9–11);[1] he is made 'Lord and Christ' as the inauguration of eschatological existence at Pentecost (Acts 2.36); in this sense he is 'appointed Son of God according to the Spirit of holiness by the resurrection of the dead' (Rom. 1.4).

Now Heitsch is correct in saying that the Church soon and repeatedly lost sight of the eschatological existence proclaimed originally by the *kerygma*. However this in no way affects its original meaning. If the existential decision originally called for by the *kerygma* corresponds to the existential decision called for by Jesus, then it is apparent that the *kerygma* continues Jesus' message; and if the decision called for by Jesus as well as by the *kerygma* was at the basis of his own selfhood, then it is apparent that his person corresponds to its christology.

---

667 f.): 'Jesus connected the hope of salvation with his person to the extent that he sees the kingdom effective in his acts and understands his preaching as the last word of God before the end.' Cf. also his forthcoming article there on 'Jesus Christus'.

[1] Cf. Ernst Käsemann, 'Kritische Analyse von Phil. 2.5–11', *ZTK* XLVII, 1950, 313–60, esp. 335, 340: 'The emphasis can no longer be placed upon the condition of the person of Christ in the different phases of his way, even though individual expressions may tempt us in this direction. When the divine glory of the pre-existent was mentioned, this was done only to bring clearly to light the miracle of the saving act. But in the following lines we always find primary mention of what Jesus did, not of what he was. This is not the least thing that distinguishes New Testament christology from the later viewpoint of the early Church. . . . All these statements are not intended to give a definition of essence in the sense of the christology of the early Church, but rather speak of events in a connected series: he emptied himself, took on the form of a servant, appeared as a being like a man; one could establish the fact that he had become man. It is not a question here of the identity of a person in various phases, but rather of the continuity of a miraculous occurrence.' Similarly Hans Conzelmann, 'Das Urchristentum', *Reformatio*, 1957, 564–73, esp. 568: 'From [Easter] on, faith included the relation to the person of Jesus as the Lord ruling today. Put differently, our relation to God and consequently to the world is constantly determined by him.'

This thesis has been carried through by Ernst Fuchs.[1] The existential meaning of the *kerygma* is still visible in the earliest written source, the Pauline epistles. 'Life means for [Paul] actually the joy which can unite a man with God (cf. also Rom. 14.17), and by "death" he understands the anxiety which must separate a man from God (cf. Rom. 7.24; 8.15, etc.). The man who believes in Jesus as Lord is free for such joy and free from this anxiety' (216). 'Obviously for Paul faith in Jesus comes down to the paradoxical truth that man has found refuge in the very God whom he otherwise flees or would have to flee. . . . It is just in the God of wrath that the God of grace purposes to be found—life in the place where death is, joy in the desert of anxiety. In this sense Paul appealed to the crucified Jesus as the resurrected Lord' (217). Now the crucial question is: 'What does all this have to do with the *historical Jesus?* . . . Is it not easily possible that Paul has placed something quite different or even his own concept of faith in the place of Jesus?'

An answer to this question is sought by Fuchs in a brief study of the historical Jesus: Jesus' parables of God's boundless mercy are in defence of Jesus' own conduct in receiving sinners. 'It is true, he means to say, that God has to be severe. But nevertheless God purposes to be gracious, when a sinful man flees to the very God from whom he would otherwise have to flee in fear of judgement.' Now since one's conduct reflects one's understanding of existence, and Jesus' message corresponds to his conduct, it is legitimate to look also in his message for a commentary on his existence.[2] Since Jesus' message centred in a call for decision, one

[1]'Die Frage nach dem historischen Jesus', *ZTK* LIII, 1956, 210–29.

[2]This methodological point, not mentioned by Fuchs, indicates the way in which Peter Biehl's question (*TR*, n.F. XXIV, 1957–8, 76) to Fuchs is to be answered: 'Wherein is the hermeneutical insight, that from what Jesus requires one can infer what he himself did, based *in terms of existentialistic analysis* ("*existential* begründet")?' Once this point has been clarified, i.e. once it has become permissible to deduce Jesus' decision from the decision for which he called, then it is possible to arrive at his historical factuality in terms of existentialistic analysis. Cf. Martin Heidegger, *Sein und Zeit,* 394: 'If Dasein is "actually" only real in existence, then its "factuality" constitutes itself precisely as a determined casting in terms of some chosen possibility of Being. Then what has "factually" really been, is the existential possibility,

may assume that 'this requirement is simply the echo of the decision which Jesus himself made'. 'So when Jesus directs the sinner through death to the God of grace he knows that he must suffer. Committing himself to God's grace, he also commits himself to suffering. His threats and woes, as well as the severity of his requirement, all stem from his stern will to suffer. For in all this Jesus exposes himself to his enemies, although he has the violent death of the Baptist before his eyes' (224).[1]

Once we have grasped the decision in terms of which Jesus' self-hood is constituted, the repetition of his decision involves the accepting of his selfhood as one's own. Hence making the decision for which Jesus called, corresponds to accepting him as Lord. Jesus confronted his hearer with the question: *'Does God intend us to feel so free towards him that we appeal directly to him* over against the well-grounded fear of his judgement which we all have long since secretly known? That is exactly what the decision of the historical Jesus affirms. That is why he said to the sinner: "Follow me" (Mark 2.14), and gave sinners precedence over the righteous. Thus for the man who hears and follows, Jesus is *indeed* the Lord' (228).

Now since Paul understands the *kerygma* as calling for basically

---

in which fate, chance, and world-history were actually determined. Since existence is cast only as actual, historical study will open up the quiet power of the possible all the more penetratingly, the more simply and concretely it understands and "merely" presents what has been in the world in terms of its possibility.'

[1]Fuchs (222) looks upon the death of the Baptist as a significant factor in constituting Jesus' selfhood: it radicalizes for him the Baptist's call to submit to judgement. Bultmann (*ZTK* LIV, 1957, 254, n. 1) considers this an attempt to prove 'through biographical psychological argumentation' Fuchs' correct insight that 'Jesus' relation to God presupposed suffering from the very beginning' (224). Bultmann's view is: 'Surely one may only say that Jesus' understanding of God's will contains the possibility of having to suffer.' However if it is true, as it seems to be (cf. Mark 1.14; Dibelius, *Jesus,* 1951, 57), that the Baptist's death played such a role in Jesus' thought, it would seem to be a dogmatic limitation of research on the part of Bultmann to maintain that one may not say it. Hence Heitsch is correct, even if one-sided, in detecting this theological limitation of historical research on the part of Bultmann (*ZTK* LIII, 1956, 196–203); and Biehl goes too far in his defence of Bultmann, in denying that this prejudice ever occurs (*TR,* n.F. XXIV, 1956–7, 62).

the same decision as did the historical Jesus, it would seem that faith in the heavenly Lord not only coincides with commitment to the selfhood of the historical Jesus, but also involves a positive response to his message. 'Certainly (for the Church) repetition of Jesus' decision was something new to the extent that it automatically involved taking a position toward Jesus. Jesus' enemies had seen to that. But it none the less remained the old decision, since it had to claim for itself anew God's will and name. To be sure, Jesus' person now became the content of faith. But that took place completely in the name of the God who had acted upon and in Jesus, and who in the future was to act with Jesus even more, as is apparent in the confessions, their Pauline interpretation, and later the Gospels' (227). It is the role of preaching to restore to christology this existential meaning originally inherent in the *kerygma.*

In this presentation Fuchs has clearly worked out, in terms of the decision constituting selfhood, the basic parallelism between the selfhood of the earthly Jesus and the heavenly Lord, and the correlative parallel between the decision called for by Jesus and the decision called for by the *kerygma.* Thus he has not only contributed a solution to a typical problem of the new quest, but has also illustrated in exemplary fashion the formal pattern in terms of which a solution to the focal problem can be sought.

In view of the current concept of the historicity of the self, it is not surprising that the most characteristic distinction between Jesus and Paul during recent years has been in terms of the differing situations in which they found themselves. Bultmann has made the shift in aeons the decisive factor distinguishing Jesus from Paul: 'Jesus looks into the future, toward the coming reign of God, although to be sure toward the reign *now* coming or dawning. But Paul looks back: *The shift of the aeons has already taken place.* . . . Paul regards what for Jesus was future as present, i.e. a presence which dawned in the past. . . . Since Jesus only stands in anticipation, his message discloses the situation of man in anticipation, while Paul discloses the situation of man receiving, although to be sure also awaiting; for unless one understands awaiting, one cannot understand receiving.'[1] However Bultmann himself[2] has subsequently modified this position to some extent: 'To be sure it is also true of him, that he knew himself to be between the times. He knows that the power of Satan is at an end, for he saw him fall from heaven like lightning (Luke 10.18); and in the power of God's Spirit he drives out the demons (Matt. 12.28; Luke 11.20), since the reign of Satan is broken already (Mark 3.27). . . . Thus his present activity stands in an "interim".' This recognition of Jesus' present as the interim has led Bornkamm[3] to accentuate Jesus' present as the time of salvation, so that Bornkamm's presentation of Jesus' situation comes to equal Bultmann's original presentation of Paul's situation: 'Unmediated presence is always the characteristic of Jesus' words, appearance and action, within a world which . . . had lost the present, since it lived . . . between past and future, between traditions and promises or threats.' Thus the basic distinction between Jesus and Paul in terms of their situations would seem to disappear.

Yet Bultmann[4] still remains reluctant to interpret Jesus' present as based upon historical encounter: 'This judgement of his about his present comes from his own consciousness of vocation; thus he creates it out of himself; and it is not, as was later the case in his Church, based upon looking back upon an event decisive for him. It is of course possible that the coming of the Baptist and his preaching gave him the initial stimulus as one of the signs of the time which he called upon his hearers to observe (Luke 12.54–56). If Matt. 11.11–14 has at its root a genuine saying of Jesus, and if the passage is not completely created by the Church, then Jesus did in fact see in the coming of the Baptist the shift of the aeons. But he does not look back upon him as the Church later looked back upon Jesus, as the figure through whom the old aeon had been brought to its end and the new aeon had been introduced.' Here Bultmann attempts to avoid the conclusion that John is

[1] *GuV* I, 200 f.
[2] 'Der Mensch zwischen den Zeiten,' *Man in God's Design*, 1953, 44.
[3] *Jesus of Nazareth*, 75.
[4] 'Der Mensch zwischen den Zeiten', *Man in God's Design*, 44.

the shift of the aeons, by casting doubt upon the authenticity of the relevant sayings. However this position is untenable, both because Bultmann himself has not provided sufficient grounds for considering the sayings unauthentic,[1] and because there stand arrayed against him the outstanding treatments of John the Baptist written in the present century.[2] Consequently one must

[1] In *Die Geschichte der synoptischen Tradition* (3rd ed. 1957), 177 f., Bultmann concedes that Matt. 11.7–11a is 'perhaps an authentic saying of Jesus', but doubts the authenticity of the rest. His argument is that both the positive and negative sayings about John could derive from the Church; 'for both points of view were given in the anti-Jewish and anti-Baptist polemic respectively'. Now on form-critical grounds this is certainly a less valid approach than that of Martin Dibelius, who introduced form criticism (*Die urchristliche Überlieferung von Johannes dem Täufer*, 1911) with the position that the Church, in its polemics against the Baptist sect, progressively played down the high positive significance Jesus attributed to the Baptist. Hence the *Sitz im Leben* of the material playing John down is much more apparent than the *Sitz im Leben* of the material speaking highly of John. Bultmann's conjecture that the *Sitz im Leben* of the positive material could be anti-Jewish polemics is nowhere attested in the sources, whereas Dibelius succeeds in documenting the polemical use of the tradition about John in the debate between Christians and Baptists. Hence the authenticity of the positive statements about the Baptist (Bultmann lists: Matt. 11.7–11a, 16–19; 21.32; Mark 11.27–30) cannot on form-critical grounds be put in question to the same degree as that of the negative sayings. Bultmann considers Matt. 11.12 f. as belonging among those sayings in which John is played down, and consequently as clearly unauthentic. For this interpretation he appeals to Goguel (*Au seuil de l'évangile; Jean-Baptiste*, 1928, 65–69), who whoever maintains the authenticity of the saying on the basis of Luke's effort to make some sense out of it: 'The tradition would not have created a declaration whose meaning it had not grasped.' Bultmann further appeals to Hans Windisch, 'Die Sprüche vom Eingehen in das Reich Gottes', *ZNTW* XXVII, 1928, 168 f., who however bases his whole position upon v. 11b, whose unauthenticity is conceded by most (including Bultmann). Windisch does not refer to v. 12. Once v. 12 is removed from the context of v. 11b, the positive exegesis of the saying, and hence its authenticity, become more apparent. Cf. Ernst Percy, *Die Botschaft Jesu*, 1953, 5, 198 ff., and the resultant non-committal position of the 'Ergänzungsheft' to the 3rd ed. of Bultmann's *Geschichte der synoptischen Tradition*.

[2] Martin Dibelius, *Die urchristliche Überlieferung von Johannes dem Täufer*, 1911, concedes the authenticity of: Matt. 11.12 f. (23 ff.: 'the time of John's appearance forms the frontier'); Matt. 21.32 (20 f.: 'Jesus seems to feel himself here in solidarity with John'); Mark 11.27–30 (21 f.: this 'paradigm' is 'a further proof that Jesus felt himself in content kin to John'). Dibelius' position is (29) as a consequence the reverse of that of Bultmann: 'Since the days of John the kingdom of God exists, even though under pressure by the "violent". Therefore the new time begins with John. . . . He introduces the first period in the earthly history of this kingdom. Hence there must at least be recognized in his activity a factor which supported the coming of the kingdom. . . . The Baptist's appearance has a material significance for

simply carry through the logic which Bultmann conceded but
hesitated to follow. Since Matt. 11.11–14 has at its root a genuine
saying of Jesus, and since the passage is not completely created by
the Church, then Jesus did in fact see in the coming of the Baptist
the shift of the aeons. Hence to this extent Jesus did look back
upon him as the Church later looked back upon Jesus,[1] as the

---

Jesus. . . . In the activity of John, Jesus detected the nearness of the kingdom of God, the kingdom which he felt called to preach.' Nor did Bultmann's
subsequent form-critical research alter Dibelius' view. In his *Jesus* (1949), he
says (56 f.): 'Jesus (by his baptism) affirmed what he certified later through
his praise of the Baptist as the greatest of all those born of women, viz., that
in John's call to repentance and in his command to be baptized God had
spoken to the nation. . . . We know with certainty only this: the Baptist
movement was taken by Jesus as the sign that God's kingdom was in fact
drawing near.' Similarly Ernst Lohmeyer, *Das Urchristentum*, I. *Johannes der
Täufer*, 1932, 20, 113: 'With the Baptist the dividing-line and the shift of
the times is there. The law and the prophets are no longer the last thing which
gave meaning and existence to the past. Events are there where formerly
prophecies prevailed.' 'What formerly was an object of promise and hope
has moved into the stage of action, through and since John.' This is also the
view of Carl H. Kraeling, *John the Baptist*, 1951, 156 f.: Matt. 11.12 f. is
authentic, and speaks of 'a period of violence that begins with John', who
'stands at the dividing line between the period of anticipation and the period
in which the kingdom is present but in conflict.'

[1]There is as a matter of fact in Jesus' 'clear confession' to John (Lohmeyer,
Johannes der Täufer, 20) something analogous to the Church's *kerygma*. Therefore one may reasonably inquire as to whether there occur in the primitive
Church any echoes of Jesus' identification of John as the turning-point.
Traces of such a pattern may be found in the tradition Luke uses in Acts 1.22
to support his concept of an apostle, but whose grammatical structure suggests it originated apart from that usage (cf. Dibelius, *Studies in the Acts of the
Apostles*, 1956, 111, n. 5, and *Jesus*, 1951, 50). Now this formula seems to be
presupposed in Acts 10.37: 'beginning from Galilee after the baptism which
John preached', although it has been subordinated to the formula from Luke
23.5: 'beginning from Galilee even to this place (Jerusalem)'. The latter half
of the original formula may not have referred to the ascension, as Luke uses
it (Acts 1.2), but rather to the ascent to Jerusalem. For the corresponding
Aramaic and Syriac expression is used interchangeably of the pilgrimage to
Jerusalem and of the ascent of the soul to heaven. Cf. Dirk Plooij, 'The
Ascension in the "Western" Textual Tradition', *Mededeelingen der Koninklijke
Akademie van Wetenschappen*, Afdeeling Letterkunde, Deel 67, Serie A, No. 2
(39–58), 1929, especially the additional note (55–56) by A. J. Wensinck. This
original significance may still be reflected in Luke 9.51: 'when the days drew
near for his ascent, he set his face to go to Jerusalem.' Cf. also Mark 10.32;
John 2.13; 5.1; 7.8. The possibility of such a Semitic origin of the formula
is strengthened when one observes that the opening of the expression ('beginning from . . .') is classified by C. C. Torrey (*The Composition and Date
of Acts*, 1916, 6, 23, 25, 36) and de Zwaan (*The Beginnings of Christianity* II,

figure through whom the old aeon had been brought to its end and the new aeon had been introduced. It is therefore not surprising that Käsemann[1] emphasizes: 'The Baptist introduced (the kingdom of God), i.e. brought about the shift of aeons.' Similarly Bornkamm[2] says of the Baptist: 'He is no longer only the proclaimer of the future, but belongs himself already within the time of fulfilled promise', 'the sentinel at the frontier between the aeons'. Consequently the existence of a historical event at the shift in the aeons seems not to be a factor distinguishing Jesus' situation from that of the Church.[3] Both Jesus and the Church look upon their existence in terms of a situation created by divine intervention in the form of historical occurrence.[4]

A further consequence was inherent in Bultmann's original distinction between Jesus and Paul in terms of the shift of the aeons: 'It could also be expressed as follows: Jesus preaches law and promise, Paul preaches the gospel in its relation to law.'[5]

1922, 50) as a clear indication of translation. The emphasis upon the *terminus ad quem* of this formula at Jerusalem and the cross could have led to the disappearance of the *terminus a quo,* just as in the case of the Church's normal *kerygma* the same emphasis upon the cross often led to the disappearance of the *parousia*. Vestiges of the turning-point at John may be preserved in the earliest concept of a Gospel: not only Mark and John begin with the Baptist, but, to whatever extent one can speak with assurance concerning them, also 'Q' and 'Proto-Luke' (note that the famous synchronization of Luke 3.1 f. is for the purpose of dati. g John's ministry). And traces of John as a turning-point occur in the sermons of Acts (10.37; 13.24 f.) and the credal formula of Ignatius, *Smyrn.* 1.1. John seems in fact to have been the 'beginning of the gospel of Jesus Christ' (Mark 1.1).

[1] *ZTK* LI, 1954, 149.

[2] *Jesus of Nazareth,* 51. It is not clear what Bornkamm has in mind when he states (67) that there is the difference between John and Jesus 'as between the eleventh and the twelfth hour'.

[3] Lieb (*Antwort,* 589, 592) also recognizes this crucial significance of John the Baptist. Biehl (*TR,* n.F. XXIV, 1957-8, 73) refers to this position as too 'rigid', apparently in dependence on Fuchs (*ZTK* LIII, 1956, 221), who does not wish to build his interpretation of Jesus upon Matt. 11.12 f., for: 'We would have to emphasize Jesus' conduct so strongly that one would have to ask oneself why Jesus also teaches anything.' Even if the saying necessarily raised this problem, this would be no valid reason for neglecting such an important saying, whose authenticity Biehl (73) concedes.

[4] Cf. already my argument for a historical *terminus a quo* of the situation presupposed in Jesus' parables: 'Jesus' Understanding of History', *The Journal of Bible and Religion* XXIII, 1955, 17-24.

[5] *GuV* I, 201.

However Käsemann[1] also drew the inference from his own divergent position: 'Jesus did not come to proclaim general religious and moral truths, but rather to say how things stand with the kingdom that has dawned, namely that God has drawn near man in grace and requirement. He brought and lived the freedom of the children of God, who remain children and free only so long as they find in the Father their Lord.' And, as we have already seen, Bultmann[2] has subsequently adopted Fuchs' insight to the effect that Jesus received all at his table, as an action reflecting God's grace: 'The one who proclaims the radical requirement of God at the same time speaks the word of grace.' Jesus' calls for decision with regard to his person in Matt. 11.6, Luke 12.8 f., are, like the *kerygma*'s call for decision with regard to his person, 'at the same time words of promise, of grace: at this very moment the gift of freedom is offered the hearer'. Hence the classical Protestant distinction between law and grace no longer seems necessarily to separate Jesus from the Church's *kerygma*.

It has been an integral part of the method employed in all these comparisons of Jesus and the *kerygma,* that we operate below the terminological level, within the deeper level of meaning. For on the one hand we have recognized that the language of the *kerygma* must become transparent, if an interpretation of Jesus is to be seen through it. And on the other hand the historical Jesus cannot for methodological reasons be approached in terms of sayings where kerygmatic language occurs, but only in terms of sayings diverging from the language of the *kerygma*. However we may well wonder how long an agreement on the deeper level of meaning can continue without at some point producing a similarity of terminology.[3] If it cannot be argued that the Church's *kerygma* provides such a terminological parallel to Jesus' message, because of the uncertainty as to whether he used that language, we must then inquire as to whether the terminology which the historical Jesus is known to have used did not at some

[1] *ZTK* LI, 1954, 151.
[2] 'Allgemeine Wahrheit und christliche Verkündigung', *ZTK* LIV, 254.
[3] Rudolf Otto's *Mysticism East and West* (1932) presents an interesting instance of similar positions producing similar terminology.

point at least come to be used·by the primitive Church as synonymous with its own *kerygma*. Hence we wish finally to confront
the most typical terminology of Jesus' message with the most
typical formulations of the *kerygma*, to investigate what underlying unity of meaning may exist, and then to inquire as to whether
this meaning ever came to be expressed in a union of the two
terminologies. Thus the solution of *this* typical problem of a new
quest of the historical Jesus should consist in a demonstration
ad oculos.

The essential content of Jesus' message was: 'Repent, for the
kingdom of God is near.' The dramatic future coming of the
kingdom has drawn so near that its coming already looms over
the present, calling for a radical break with the present evil aeon
and an equally radical commitment to God's coming kingdom.
Hence Jesus' thought centres in a call to the present on the basis
of the eschatological event of the near future. He pronounces
divine judgement and blessing, and explains God's other mighty
acts which he does (such as exorcism), on the basis of the nearness
of the kingdom. This call to the present in terms of the nearness
of the kingdom is so central a theme as to produce something
approaching a formal pattern,[1] to which many of Jesus' sayings
conform, and of which the following are typical instances: Matt.
4.17; Luke 6.20 f., 24 f.; Matt. 21.31; 18.3; Luke 11.20.

Repent,	for the kingdom of God is near.
Blessed are you poor,	for yours is the kingdom of God.
Blessed are you that hunger now,	for you shall be satisfied.
Blessed are you that weep now,	for you shall laugh.
But woe to you that are rich,	for you have received your con-solation.
Woe to you that are full now,	for you shall hunger.
Woe to you that laugh now,	for you shall mourn and weep.
The tax collectors and the harlots	go into the kingdom of God be-fore you.
Unless you turn and become like children,	you will never enter the kingdom of heaven.

[1] I have tried to show in a forthcoming article, 'The Formal Pattern of
Jesus' Message', that this pattern permeates Jesus' whole message and provides the norm for interpreting it. Hence the sayings here compared with the
kerygma are not chosen at random, but are just as central to Jesus' message
as the *kerygma* was to the primitive Church.

If it is by the finger of God that I cast out demons,	then the kingdom of God has come upon you.

Now the essential content of the *kerygma* was equally clear, and therefore also tended to give rise to a pattern of death and resurrection, suffering and glory, humiliation and exaltation.[1]

That Christ died for our sins according to the Scriptures,	And that he was raised on the third day according to the Scriptures,
And that he was buried,	And that he was seen by Cephas, then by the twelve.
That the Christ should suffer these things	And enter into his glory.
The sufferings of Christ	And the subsequent glory.
The one come by the seed of David according to the flesh,	The one appointed Son of God according to the Spirit of holiness by the resurrection of the dead.
Put to death in the flesh	But made alive in the Spirit.
Who was revealed in the flesh,	Vindicated in the Spirit,
Preached in the nations,	Seen by angels,
Believed on in the world,	Taken into glory.[2]

Now when one compares these typical instances of Jesus' message and the Church's *kerygma,* one can readily observe that there is a complete separation in terminology, and even in doctrine: Jesus' message is eschatological, the Church's *kerygma* is christological. Jesus called upon his hearer to break radically with the present evil aeon, and to rebuild his life in commitment to the inbreaking kingdom. Paul called upon his hearer to die and rise with Christ. Yet when one moves beyond such an initial comparison to the deeper level of meaning, the underlying similarity becomes increasingly clear. To break categorically with the present evil aeon is to cut the ground from under one's feet, to open oneself physically to death by breaking with the power structure of an evil society, and to open oneself spiritually to death by renouncing self-seeking as a motivation and giving

[1] I Cor. 15.3-5; Luke 24.26; I Peter 1.11; Rom. 1.3 f.; I Peter 3.18; I Tim. 3.16.
[2] Eduard Schweizer has shown that I Tim. 3.16 is built throughout upon the 'humiliation–exaltation' pattern, but with one irregularity, so as to produce the outline A B B A A B. Cf. *Erniedrigung und Erhöhung bei Jesus und seinen Nachfolgern,* 1955, 63-66, and *TWNT* VI, 414.

oneself radically to the needs of one's neighbour, as one's real freedom and love. To do this because of faith in the inbreaking kingdom is to do it in faith that such total death is ultimately meaningful; in it lies transcendence, resurrection. Thus the deeper meaning of Jesus' message is: in accepting one's death there is life for others; in suffering, there is glory; in submitting to judgement, one finds grace; in accepting one's finitude resides the only transcendence. It is this existential meaning latent in Jesus' message which is constitutive of his selfhood, expresses itself in his action, and is finally codified in the Church's *kerygma*.

The extent to which the *kerygma* continues to reveal the existential meaning of Jesus can be illustrated from an interesting Pauline passage, I Cor. 4.8–13, which describes Christian existence first in eschatological terms such as Jesus used, and then in Paul's more typical language of union with Christ.

Jesus spoke eschatological 'woes' as well as beatitudes, according to the 'Q' version of the 'Sermon on the Mount' (Luke 6.24 f.):

> Woe to you that are *rich*, for you have received your consolation.
> Woe to you that are *full now*, for you *shall* hunger.
> Woe you that that laugh *now*, for you *shall* mourn and weep.

Clearly these woes are pronounced upon those who are out of step with God. They prosper now, in the present evil aeon; hence they will not prosper then, in the kingdom of God. This same eschatological message, in much the same language, is presented by Paul:

> *Already* you are *filled!*
> *Already* you have become *rich!*
> Without us you reign!

Here the Corinthians are reproached not simply for prosperity, but rather for prosperity already now, before God's reign comes. They are reigning in the present evil aeon, but Paul longs to reign in God's reign: 'And would that you did reign, so that we might reign with you!' But before God's reign comes, i.e. within the present evil aeon, eschatological existence consists in suffering.

Jesus' beatitudes in the 'Q' version retain also their original eschatological orientation (Luke 6.20–23):

Blessed are you poor, for yours is the *reign* of God.
Blessed are you that *hunger now*, for you *shall* be satisfied.
Blessed are you that weep *now*, for you *shall* laugh.
Blessed are you when men hate you, and when they exclude you and revile you, and cast out your name as evil, on account of the Son of Man. Rejoice in that day, and leap for joy, for behold, your reward is great in heaven.

Now Paul describes himself, in contrast to the Corinthians, in terms of this same eschatological understanding of existence:

For I think that God has exhibited us apostles as last of all, like men sentenced to death; because we have become a spectacle to the world, to angels and to men. We are fools for Christ's sake, but you are wise in Christ. We are weak, but you are strong. You are held in honour, but we in disrepute. *To the present hour* we *hunger* and thirst, we are ill-clad and buffeted and homeless, and we labour, working with our own hands. . . . We have become as the refuse of the world, the offscouring of all things, *until now*.

Thus Paul has described first non-Christian existence, and then Christian existence, in much the same eschatological language which Jesus used. But in the midst of his eschatological description of Christian existence Paul introduces a few phrases which express the existential meaning of the *kerygma*. The identity in existential meaning between Jesus' eschatological message and the Church's *kerygma* could not be made more apparent:

When reviled,	we bless.
When persecuted,	we endure.
When slandered,	we try to conciliate.

As Paul says (v. 17), these are his 'ways in Christ' which he teaches in every church, so that one should not be surprised to find this pattern recurring frequently, e.g. II Cor. 6.8–10:

We are treated as impostors,	and yet are true;
as unknown,	and yet well known;
as *dying*,	and behold we *live*;
as punished,	and yet not killed;
as sorrowful,	yet always rejoicing;
as poor,	yet making many rich;
as having nothing,	and yet possessing everything.

Now this message of life in death is clearly intended as the existential appropriation of the *kerygma*, as becomes increasingly apparent in other instances of this pattern (II Cor. 4.8–12; 1.8 f.; 13.4):

We are afflicted in every way,	but not crushed;
perplexed,	but not driven to despair;
persecuted,	but not forsaken;
struck down,	but not destroyed;
always carrying in the body the *death of Jesus*,	so that the *life of Jesus* may also be manifested in our bodies.
For while we live we are always being given up to *death* for Jesus' sake,	so that the *life of Jesus* may be manifested in our mortal flesh.
So *death* is at work in us,	but *life* in you.
We do not want you to be ignorant, brethren, of the affliction we experienced in Asia; for we were so utterly, unbearably crushed that we despaired of life itself. Why, we felt that we had received the sentence of *death*;	but that was to make us rely not on ourselves, but on God who *raises* the dead.
He was crucified in *weakness*,	but *lives by the power of God*.
We are *weak in him*,	but shall *live with him by the power of God* toward you.

Thus Paul's description of his Christian existence is rooted in the *kerygma*, in which Jesus' transcendent selfhood is proclaimed. It is no coincidence that it is precisely in this context (I Cor. 4.16) that Paul can call upon the Corinthians to 'be imitators of me', for the implication is clear: 'Be imitators of me, as I am of Christ' (I Cor. 11.1). Paul's transcendent existence is one with the selfhood of Jesus proclaimed by the *kerygma*.

It is in this sense that one can detect the existential significance of Paul's mystic language: 'Christ is our life' (Col. 3.4). 'It is no longer I who live, but Christ who lives in me' (Gal. 2.20). Our 'life' which is 'hid with Christ in God' (Col. 3.3) is the transcendent selfhood created by Jesus, and made available to us by him. In this way the line of continuity from the historical Jesus to the Second Adam of Pauline speculation is apparent. And, although we today no longer use these speculative categories, the selfhood of Jesus is equally available to us—apparently both *via* historical research and *via* the *kerygma*—as a possible understanding of our existence.

PART TWO

Other Essays on the New Quest

VI

THE FORMAL STRUCTURE OF JESUS' MESSAGE

I

One of the most significant trends in theology today is the new quest of the historical Jesus undertaken in Germany in the past few years.[1] The task of this new quest does not consist simply in the restudy of previous methods and the search for new methods of disengaging the historically authentic material in the Gospels. The role of the new quest in the broader theological undertaking, and thus the theologically relevant scope of the new inquiry, needs also to be clarified.

Instigated by the kerygma's reference to Jesus' person, research has been directed to the question of the continuity between Jesus' person and the kerygma, i.e., to the question as to the legitimacy of the kerygma's claim to be rooted in the person of Jesus. This focus is to be distinguished from one having as its ultimate objective Jesus' personality or his teachings, which would be of ultimate interest to the religious psychologist or to the historian of ideas but would leave the original theological question unanswered. Rather, research is directed toward identifying that which is constitutive of his person, in order to verify the right of the kerygma to appeal to him.

It is this interest in the relation of Jesus to the kerygma that is new and fruitful from a methodological point of view in the efforts

---

[1]The discussion through the first part of 1958 is reported in *A New Quest of the Historical Jesus* reprinted above. The discussion up to early 1960 is reported in the revised and enlarged German edition *Kerygma und historischer Jesus* (1960), and up to early 1965 in a second revised and enlarged German edition (1967). The German editions also include an additional chapter in which my own initial contribution to the new quest, only suggested at the end of the English edition, is more fully developed. The present essay is intended to make the substance of this supplement available in English.

of Gerhard Ebeling[2] and Ernst Fuchs[3] to establish Jesus' understanding of faith. However, their approach has encountered various difficulties which have limited the extent to which it has gained acceptance. The terminology employed has at times been too reminiscent of the psychological orientation at the end of the nineteenth century, whereas in Germany one is expected to maintain a clear distinction of one's position from that which ended so abruptly half a century ago.[4] Furthermore this approach, largely instigated by the newly awakened interest in the philosophic and theological significance of the phenomenon of language as a key dimension of existence,[5] all too hastily sought in the term "faith" the linguistic actualization of an understanding of existence shared by Jesus and primitive Christianity.[6] This has proved to be too small a basis, especially since Ernst Käsemann had attributed the faith formulas

---

[2]"Jesus und Glaube," *ZTK*, 55 (1958), 64–110, reprinted in *Wort und Glaube*, I (1960), pp. 203–54, ET *Word and Faith* (1963), pp. 201–46. Cf. also *Was heisst Glauben? SgV* (1958), p. 216.

[3]"Glaube und Geschichte im Blick auf die Frage nach dem historischen Jesus. Eine Auseinandersetzung mit G. Bornkamms Buch über Jesus von Nazareth," *ZTK*, 54 (1957), 117–56. "Jesus und der Glaube," *ZTK*, 55 (1958), 170–85, both reprinted in *Zur Frage nach dem historischen Jesus, Gesammelte Aufsätze* II (1960), pp. 168–218, 238–57, ET of the second only, *Studies of the Historical Jesus*, SBT, 42 (1964), pp. 48–64.

[4]The need for this distinction has been stressed with regard to the position of Ebeling and Fuchs by Hans Conzelmann, *ZTK*, 56 (1959), Beiheft 1, pp. 6–9.

[5]Cf. Ernst Fuchs, *Zum hermeneutischen Problem in der Theologie* (1959), especially "Das Sprachereignis in der Verkündigung Jesu," pp. 281–305, and Gerhard Ebeling, *Das Wesen des christlichen Glaubens* (1960), especially the appendix on "Wort Gottes und Sprache," pp. 243–56, ET *The Nature of Faith* (1961), with the appendix "The Word of God and Language," pp. 182–91. The Evangelischer Theologentag, May 27–31, 1958, dealt with the problem; cf. the volume of addresses published by Wilhelm Schneemelcher in 1959 under the title *Das Problem der Sprache in Theologie und Kirche*. Cf. further the volume of addresses published by the Wissenschaftliche Buchgesellschaft in 1959 entitled *Die Sprache*, with contributions by Romano Guardini, Carl Friedrich von Weizsäcker, Friedrich Georg Jünger, Thrasculos Georgiades, Martin Heidegger, and Walter F. Otto; the chapter on "Die Sprache als Vermittler von Mensch und Welt" in Karl Löwith's *Gesammelte Abhandlungen* (1960), pp. 208–27; and the chapter on "Die Sprache" in Heinrich Ott's *Denken und Sein* (1959), pp. 176ff.

[6]This was especially true of Ebeling's essay "Jesus und Glaube," *ZTK*, 55 (1968), 64–110, reprinted in *Wort und Glaube*, I (1960), pp. 203–54, ET *Word and Faith* (1963), pp. 201–46. It is significant that Ebeling bases his argument largely upon detailed research in Bultmann's article on faith in *TWNT*, VI, 174ff., ET *TDNT*, VI, 174ff., and yet disagrees with Bultmann's unwillingness to speak of the concept of the faith of the historical Jesus. Günther Bornkamm in his *Jesus von Nazareth*, (1956; ET *Jesus of Nazareth*, 1960) had already devoted a section of his chapter on "The Will of God" to "Faith and Prayer."

in the healing narratives to the institution of exorcism in the primitive church.[7]

To be sure, the question as to the linguistic expression of materially similar positions cannot be avoided.[8] Yet this interest will have to take account of the basic methodological insight that by and large, at least at first, whatever terminology may have been common to Jesus and the primitive church must be left out of the discussion, and that the question as to continuity must consequently be approached below the surface of terminological divergence: on the basis of underlying intention. For, on the one hand, the demythologization discussion has drawn attention to the fact that it is less the terminology of the kerygma than its intention which points to Jesus. The terminology is more often derived from the cultural environment than from Jesus, and even there was often only mythological, whereas the kerygma uses this terminology to express the significance of the historical person Jesus. And, on the other hand, there is widespread agreement that the terminology of Jesus must be distinguished from kerygmatic elements before it can provide a historically reliable basis for a comparison with the kerygma. For the current criteria for establishing the authenticity of sayings make it hardly possible to establish the authenticity of those areas in which the terminology of the historical Jesus and the primitive church overlap.[9] Therefore it is advisable to put to one side, for the time being, specific terminological agreements and to turn one's attention to those logia which are generally held to be probably authentic, precisely because of the absence in them of kerygmatic terminology. It is they which are to be investigated as to their

---

[7]RGG (3d. ed.), II, 995. Cf. also the criticism by Fuchs, "Jesus und der Glaube," *ZTK*, 55 (1958), 180, reprinted in *Zur Frage nach dem historichen Jesus* (1960), p. 251, ET "Jesus and Faith," *Studies of the Historical Jesus* (1964), p. 59, and Ebeling's implicit retraction, "Die Frage nach dem historischen Jesus und das Problem der Christologie," *ZTK*, 56 (1959), Beiheft 1, p. 21, reprinted in *Wort und Glaube*, I (1960), p. 308, ET "The Question of the Historical Jesus and the Problem of Christology," *Word and Faith* (1963), p. 296.

[8]Already Rudolf Otto in his *Westöstliche Mystik*, (1926; ET *Mysticism East and West*, 1932) presents an interesting illustration of the extent to which similar positions lead, independently of each other, to similar linguistic expression.

[9]Cf. my essay "The Historical Jesus and the Church's Kerygma," *Religion in Life*, 26 (1956), 40–49. It is largely for this reason that the problem of Jesus' "messianic consciousness" has remained a moot question.

underlying intention. Only when in a broader complex of such logia that gives expression to Jesus' understanding of his situation, in commitment to which his existence and thus his person is constituted, is one in a position to move on to inquire into the continuity of Jesus' person with the kerygma of primitive Christianity.

Herbert Braun[10] has put Jesus' understanding of existence in the center of his argument. Since a person's understanding of existence is implied in all he does, such an investigation can be carried through even when one recognizes that Jesus did not present an explicit Christology. Braun's thesis is: In a comparison between the preaching of the historical Jesus and the various phases in the development of the primitive Christian kerygma, "anthropology is the constant, Christology the variable."[11] Although the initial point of departure in Jesus' understanding of existence is valid, the development of the argument in terms of anthropology is at least open to misunderstanding. To be sure, one can hardly argue that Braun's distinction between anthropology and Christology amounts to eliminating the person of Jesus in favor of some general concept of humanity. For by anthropology Braun means "Christology as exhortation," in distinction from an "explicit Christology."[12] Thus his "anthropology" remains a matter of the understanding of existence involved in the person of Jesus and the kerygma. The danger in the terminological identification of "understanding of existence" and "anthropology" consists rather in the probability that many persons will not sense in the term "anthropology" the historicity of humans involved in the term "existence," in which the legitimacy of this term for our purposes resides. When one inquires as to the existence of a person, it is presupposed that the person is not to be understood individualistically or naturalistically as an isolated person. Rather, it is recognized that one must investigate, as constitutive for a person, that from which one lives, the "world" in which the person is at home, the history which orients the person. Hence

---

[10]"Der Sinn der neutestamentlichen Christologie," *ZTK*, 54, (1957), 341–77. In this essay Braun develops the Christological implications of his two-volume *Spätjüdisch-häretischer und frühchristlicher Radikalismus: Jesus von Nazareth und die essenische Qumransekte* (1957).

[11]"Der Sinn der neutestamentlichen Christologie," p. 368.

[12]"Der Sinn der neutestamentlichen Christologie," p. 344.

the term "existence" implies an understanding of the world, of history, or even of God.

To be sure, the concept of existence has, up to the present, been used largely to express an anthropology (in which, of course, humans have been understood historically). The advantage of this preliminary concentration on an understanding of humanity should not be overlooked. It consists in the connection thereby made possible with the theology of modern times, which, since the Enlightenment, has been increasingly anchored in one or the other kind of anthropology. The widespread effect of the theologies of Schleiermacher and Bultmann among the intelligentsia of their day has made this obvious. It stems not from an apologetic or a popularizing simplification of theology but rather from the factor that modern people, whether one likes it or not, find relevance from an anthropological perspective. People can assume a theological position most readily if the alternatives are in terms of a theological anthropology.

This advantage of an anthropological concentration is, however, at the same time its disadvantage. For the anthropological narrowness of modern thought is not only a given in our spiritual situation but also our fate, from whose power the gospel is to free us, just as it is to free us from every form which fate assumes (Gal. 4.4–9). Admittedly the Bible's language about God, the world, and history is often colored by mythological traits (as is incidentally also its language about humanity). Hence demythologizing is an unavoidable task of interpretation. But in carrying through this task one may not take a point of departure in a concept of myth derived from the mystical theology of the *religionsgeschichtliche Schule,* according to which religious language has by definition no interest in the world or history. For it would then be unavoidable to end in a mystical-individualistic theology. When the Bible talks, e.g., about the world, one cannot assume a priori that the mythically thinking author was—in what he said about the world—merely expressing in world-ly terms something basically *unworldly.* Rather one must first consider whether such a mode of expression is not intended to bring to assertion a certain understanding of the *world.*[13]

[13]Cf. my essay "The Biblical View of the World. A Theological Evaluation," *Encounter,* 20 (1959), 470–83.

It might well involve a *metabasis eis allo genos,* if without further ado one transposed the New Testament understanding of God, history, and the world into an understanding of humanity. In such a procedure something essential could be lost. This does not imply that demythologizing can be altogether avoided. Rather the task of demythologizing must be more precisely clarified. The current concentration on anthropology must be understood as a defensible, but preliminary, point of departure, which made possible a relevant normative discussion in the modern world but is to be regarded in the long run as a transition stage.[14]

The present status of theological thought makes it imperative that the broader meaning of the term "existence" be brought into the foreground. Existence is, formally speaking, always rooted *extra nos,* for better or worse, for existence takes place in historical decision, which always implies an understanding of the world or history. Thus far, this implicit understanding of the world or history has hardly been explicated, since it could all too easily be confused with an objectively provable *Weltanschauung* (supposedly based, e.g., on natural science or objective historiography)—or with a mythological world-view. But the greater danger just now seems rather to reside in the possibility that our renunciation of the task of working out an understanding of the world could be confused with the Gnostic repudiation of the world. Thus, the reflection of contemporary theology has reached a point analogous to the point biblical scholarship reached with its conclusion that renouncing the question of the historical Jesus and the Christology implicit in his message and action—legitimate though this renunciation seemed in antithesis to the defects of the traditional quest of the historical

[14]In much the same way Bultmann defends himself against the criticism of Karl Barth, *GuV,* 2 (1959), 234, ET *Essays Philosophical and Theological* (1955), pp. 259–60: "Existence is not the 'inner life of humans,' which can be caught sight of while ignoring what is distinct from humans and encounters humans (be it environment, fellow-humans or God)—for example, what can be caught sight of from the point of view of the psychology of religion, but not from an existential point of view. For the latter proposes to catch sight of and understand the real (historical) existence of humans, who exist only in one's living relationship with what is 'separate' from oneself, that is, who exist only in encounters. Existentialistic analysis is concerned with the fitting terminology in which this can take place." In discussion, Bultmann reacted positively to my suggestion of such a second phase of demythologization.

Jesus—was gradually leading to a docetic Christology, which could only be avoided by a reopening of the quest of the historical Jesus. The convergence of these two lines in the present defines the point of departure of our investigation: In order to take up the question as to the historical Jesus in view of the kerygma's constant allusion to him, the understanding of existence constitutive of Jesus' person should be investigated; and thus the term "understanding of existence" should not be understood anthropologically but rather as the meeting-point of an understanding of humanity with a correlative understanding of God, history, and the world.

The definition of the term "existence" here envisaged corresponds formally to the exegetical situation with regard to the preaching of the historical Jesus and the kergyma of the primitive church. The historical Jesus is concerned, first of all, with an eschatological message which gives expression to the present situation of humanity in our world and history *sub specie dei*. The kerygma is concerned with the exaltation of Jesus to the rank of Cosmocrator, the shift of aeons, existence in the interim. Hence, neither the preaching of the historical Jesus nor the primitive Christian kerygma has an individualistic interest in the person Jesus, but rather is concerned with him as the middle of the eschatological saving action of God having to do with the world and history at large. This theological position of the person Jesus in the world-encompassing saving event can, without formal difficulties, find its expression in the concept "existence" as defined above.

Lest this attempt to clarify more fully the task of a new quest of the historical Jesus remain purely theoretical, we wish to illustrate it at the beginning of the new period of research, on the basis of the results of the preceding period. For although the last generation's work did not center on the quest of the historical Jesus, it nonetheless worked on it indirectly and achieved results which can be used at the beginning of the new period of research for a preliminary orientation. Certainly the status of research at the beginning of a period should not determine the outcome of this research. On the contrary, one must expect that the new research will gradually alter the current picture. Otherwise the new research would not be necessary. But precisely because the research will lead into unknown territory, one cannot make use of its imagined results in advance to explicate the task. One must in all humility and tentativeness make the initial probe with the help of what results are already available. These insights provided by the scholarly tradition consist, on the one hand, in the disengaging of a certain complex of probably authentic logia and, on the other hand, in a certain consensus as to the general direction and meaning of the message of Jesus. By combining these two aspects of the antecedent situation of scholarly research one can attempt to work out the historical Jesus' understanding of existence.

In the question of authenticity there is widespread agreement upon two points. First, there are the parables, whose distinctive character has been sufficiently recognized to make it possible to differentiate the original form from the allegorizing alteration in the primitive church and to lend support by and large to their authenticity. Hence, on this point such scholars as Joachim Jeremias and Ernst Fuchs, notwithstanding the considerable difference in theological position, reach common conclusions.[15] Second, this general agreement has to do with the individual logia, whose authenticity was basically shaken neither by literary nor by form-critical research. Although views vary as to the synoptic material to be considered authentic on the basis of form criticism, there is nonetheless a minimum[16] of authentic tradition which by and large determines the contemporary understanding of the historical Jesus. This material provides a point of departure which is especially reliable from a historical point of view when one does not base the discussion on details of the wording or on single logia or a single stream of tradition but—as in the following discussion—investigates the common structure of various logia; particularly to the

---

[15]Cf. for example, Joachim Jeremias, *Die Gleichnisse Jesu* (6th ed., 1962), p. 227, n. 1, ET *The Parables of Jesus*, rev. ed. (1963), p. 230, n. 1: "I can only welcome with hearty approval the determination with which Fuchs catches sight of hidden Christological testimonies of the historical Jesus to himself in the parables." Similarly *Das Problem des historischen Jesus*, Calwer Hefte, 32 (1960), p. 21, ET *The Problem of the Historical Jesus*, Facet Books, Biblical Series (1964), p. 21.

[16]In practical terms this means that—as in the following discussion—one confines oneself to the material which Bultmann in his *Geschichte der synoptischen Tradition* (3d ed., 1958; ET *The History of the Synoptic Tradition*, 1963) hold to be the oldest layer and hence probably authentic.

point is the fact that this structure, as can be shown, is not confined to *one* stream of tradition but occurs in the different streams of tradition in which the same logion is transmitted.

If the prevailing character of the parables can be related to the dominant consensus as to the basic direction of Jesus' message, and this convergence can be identified and traced as a structuring tendency through the individual logia sifted by form criticism, probably as high a degree of historical reliability will have been attained as can be expected at the beginning of a new period of research.[17]

In the broad scope of New Testament research there is an unmistakable movement toward a consensus as to the basic direction of Jesus' message. Since Albrecht Ritschl one knows that Jesus' message gravitates around the concept "kingdom of God," and since the turn of the century one has recognized that this concept must be interpreted eschatologically. But only in recent years has there arisen a consensus as to *how* Jesus understood his situation as eschatological. For, on the one hand, C. H. Dodd has modified his concept "realized eschatology"[18] in favor of the formulation by Ernst Haenchen, who speaks of "eschatology in the process of being realized."[19] And, on the other hand, Rudolf Bultmann has modified his understanding of the situation of Jesus as a time of decision in favor of an emphasis upon the inbreaking of the grace of God in Jesus' "conduct."[20] This means that the extremes in the scholarly situation have met in a middle position. And it may be no coincidence that for both New Testament scholars the shift took place in view of research on the parables, in Dodd's case with allusion to Joachim Jeremias' book on *The Parables of Jesus,* in Bultmann's case

---

[17]In this definition of the point of departure I welcome the support of Hans Conzelmann, in his article "Jesus Christus," *RGG* (3d ed.), III, 643, ET *Jesus* (1973), p. 74; "Zur Methode der Leben-Jesu-Forschung," *ZTK,* 56 (1959), Beiheft 1, p. 9, ET "The Method of the Life-of-Jesus Research," in *The Historical Jesus and the Kerygmatic Christ: Essays on the New Quest of the Historical Jesus,* ed. by Carl E. Braaten and Roy A. Harrisville, 1964, pp. 63–64.

[18]Cf. *The Parables of the Kingdom* (1935), p. 49, n. 1.

[19]Cf. Dodd, *The Interpretation of the Fourth Gospel* (1953), p. 477, n. 1, where the new expression is attributed to Joachim Jeremias. The latter, in turn, in *Die Gleichnisse Jesu* (6th ed., 1962), p. 227, n. 3, ET *The Parables of Jesus,* p. 230, n. 3, ascribes it to Haenchen.

[20]"Allgemeine Wahrheiten und christliche Verkündigung," *ZTK,* 54 (1957), 224, reprinted in *GuV,* 3 (1960), 176f.

in connection with the parable theory of Ernst Fuchs. For one can express formally the fundamental direction of the parables,[21] as well as the recent consensus, in the general and tentative statement that the message of Jesus consists basically in a pronouncement to the present in view of the imminent eschatological future. It is precisely this polarity in the message of Jesus that can be detected as a structuring tendency in the individual logia. One gradually catches sight of a structure in terms of two members, which can be related to the Jewish apocalyptic doctrine of two aeons as its *religionsge-schichtliche* background. The first member, the pronouncement to the present, is related primarily to the "present evil aeon"; the second member, the allusion to the near future, looks to the "aeon to come."

Of course only rarely do the logia occur without the presence of other structuring factors in addition to this eschatological polarity. For Jesus made use of various forms of discourse current in Judaism, of which the parable is merely the best known. But the very fact that the eschatological polarity occurs as a structuring tendency in sayings belonging to various given forms of discourse lessens the danger that the logia reflecting the structuring influence of the eschatological polarity have a common setting in the primitive church[22] which could itself, rather than Jesus, be the origin of the

[21]Since the form of the parables is bound by their own character as parables and by the story to be narrated, the structuring tendency inherent in the eschatological polarity central to Jesus' message cannot express itself here fully. Nonetheless, this polarity has been identified by the decisive advances in parable research in the past generation. On the one hand, a correct understanding of the rabbinic idiom employed has separated the *tertium comparationis* from the first-mentioned object or person (cf. Jeremias, *Die Gleichnisse Jesu*, pp. 99ff., ET *The Parables of Jesus*, pp. 100ff.) and has transposed it to the end of the story—by identifying the eschatological character of the symbols employed (harvest, banquet), or by observing the sharply marked contrast to present conditions. Thus the futurity of the kingdom of God at the outcome of the stories in the parables has been safeguarded. On the other hand, one no longer understands the parables, as did Jülicher, as illustrations of eternal ethical maxims, but rather as comforting or warning exhortation to those in a particular (namely, an eschatological) situation in the present. Cf. the summary of Hans Conzelmann in the article "Formen und Gattungen II. im NT" in *Evangelisches Kirchenlexikon*, 1 (1956), 1310ff.

[22]Such an assumption would be questionable in view of the fact that the various logia which come under consideration reflect varying settings. For example, the saying about the children in Matt. 18.3 was early (Mark 10.15) used as a baptism formula, as Joachim Jeremias has shown, *Die Kindertaufe in den ersten vier Jahrhunderten* (1958), pp. 61–68, ET *Infant Baptism in the First Four Centuries* (1962), pp.

structure we are primarily considering. Rather the logia in question reflect, e.g., the style of the legal pronouncement,[23] the wisdom saying,[24] the beatitude.[25] The structuring tendency in the eschatological polarity of Jesus' message expresses itself as a special accentuation or a further development of such traditional forms. For these genres refer chiefly to matters in this aeon. An eschatological accent is not inherent in them and occurs only peripherally, e.g., when influenced by apocalypticism. Hence the detection of the common eschatological structure of the various logia will provide a

48–55; cf. also his article "Mc. 10, 13–16 Parr. und die Übung der Kindertaufe in der Urkirche," *ZNW*, 60 (1941), 243–45. This relation to baptism need not put in question the authenticity of the original logion (Matt. 18.3), where a relation to baptism is not apparent. And one cannot identify such a relation to baptism in the other logia which reflect the formal structure. For example, the logion Luke 22.16, 18; Mark 14.25; Matthew 26, 29 obviously has its setting in the Eucharist. Therefore, the assumption of a common setting for all logia with the same formal structure becomes increasingly difficult.

[23]For the legal style cf. Albrecht Alt, *Kleine Schriften zur Geschichte des Volkes Israel*, Vol. I (2d ed., 1959), especially the essay "Die Ursprünge des israelitischen Rechts," pp. 278–332, but also the essays "Zur Talionsformel," pp. 341–44, and "Das Verbot des Diebstahls im Dekalog," pp. 333–40. Already in the process of the literary fixation of the Pentateuch the various genres of legal usage lose their profile, and the LXX seems to lack sensitivity for these genres. This has rendered difficult the stimulating attempt of Ernst Käsemann, "Sätze heiligen Rechtes im NT," *NTS*, 1 (1954–55), 248–60, reprinted in *EVB*, II (1964), 69–82, ET "Sentences of Holy Law in the New Testament," in *New Testament Questions of Today* (1969), pp. 66–81, to identify traces of a primitive Christian prophetism which exercised eschatological justice. For he sought to identify in the New Testament a style of casuistic law making use of the *jus talionis*, from which one could then infer the setting of the logia built in this style. This attempt is made all the more difficult by the fact that casuistic law was originally profane, not sacred, that the *jus talionis* belongs, in terms of genre, not to casuistic but to apodictic justice, that the multiplication of conditions in the first member, so characteristic of casuistic law, is missing; and that the holy, apodictic law is built according to quite different formal characteristics. Only exceptionally, by coincidence or owing to the freedom of the LXX in translating, does one find parallels in the Old Testament to the legal style discussed by Käsemann, e.g., in Exod. 21.12:

Whoever strikes a man so that he dies	shall be put to death.

But here it is not a matter of the *jus talionis*, but rather of a fixed death penalty, which is announced in the second member equally clearly irrespective of whether the first member deals with an instance of death or not (cf. v. 15–17). On this *mōt jūmat* series as a mixed form cf. Hartmut Gese, "Beobachtungen zum Stil alttestamentlicher Rechtssätze," *TLZ*, 85 (1960), 147–50.

[24]One cannot explain the formal structure of the sayings of Jesus from the wisdom sayings. Although a few sayings, which Bultmann (*Geschichte der synoptischen Tradition*, pp. 78ff., ET *The History of the Synoptic Tradition*, pp. 74ff.) lists among the "personally formulated" wisdom sayings, display the formal structure under consideration, this structure is not constitutive for this type of wisdom saying. To be sure, there are a few rabbinic wisdom sayings (Bultmann, *Geschichte,*

means for tracing through the individual logia the eschatological polarity of Jesus' message which has already been worked out in the parables. This in turn will make it possible to follow through the distinctive accentuation within the eschatological tension of Jesus' message. The implication is not that Jesus' eschatology is itself the new or essential element in his message. Rather the tracing of the eschatological thread through his message is of primary relevance for our undertaking only since the movement of his eschatology tends toward an understanding of existence characteristic of Jesus.

The formal structure derived from the eschatological polarity of Jesus' message serves as a common ground upon which the tendency or the movement within Jesus' eschatology can be detected. For when one follows this formal structure through the various logia, one arrives at the negative conclusion that here—as is also true of the parables—the eschatological polarity is not centrally determined by a temporal sequence. The characteristic which holds the two members of the formal structure apart is not limited to the temporal distinction between present and near future. The temporal distinc-

---

p. 75, *History*, p. 71) which move in the direction of the formal structure of Jesus' sayings, yet without an eschatological accentuation: Erubin 13 b (Strack-Billerbeck, *Kommentar zum Neuen Testament,* II [1928], p. 402):

The person who humbles oneself	the Holy One, blessed be He, raises up,
and the person who exalts oneself	the Holy One, blessed be He, humbles;
from the person who seeks greatness,	greatness flees
but the person who flees from greatness,	greatness follows;
the person who forces time	is forced back by time,
but the person who yields to time	finds time helping that person.

Shabbat 127 a (Strack-Billerbeck, I, 441):

The person who judges one's neighbor in the scale of merit	is oneself judged (by God) favorably.

[25]To the style of the beatitudes cf. Augustin George, "La 'forme' des Beatitudes jusqu'à Jésus," *Mélanges bibliques rédigés en l'honneur d'André Robert* (ca. 1955), pp. 398–403. On the basis of this analysis, it is apparent that the eschatological orientation and the two-member form are basically foreign to the beatitude. Only under apocalyptic influence does one detect steps toward an orientation in terms of the "splendeurs eschatologiques," with which the form of Jesus' beatitudes could be related, such as, for example, Tob. 13.15b–16 (LXX; 13.14 RSV):

How blessed are those who love you!	They will rejoice in your peace.
Blessed are those who grieved over all your afflictions;	for they will rejoice for you upon seeing all your glory, and they will be made glad for ever.

tion tends to lose importance in favor of a material antithesis, so that a dialectic relation of tension between the two members results, just as in general Jesus' eschatology reflects an overlapping of present and future due to the inbreaking of God's reign into the present. The decisive scope of Jesus' eschatology reveals its positive content in terms of an understanding of existence, when this movement is followed through within the formal structure of the logia. For the material antithesis, which not only occurs there but even overshadows the temporal distinction, is itself a first attempt to give expression to the understanding of existence implicit at the center of Jesus' message. Here repudiating the powers of this world and holding out in the resultant hardship is related dialectically to God's inbreaking presence, which makes possible the liberation from the powers of the "present evil aeon" and gives to one's lot its meaning. Hence the existential meaning of the kingdom's futurity, a concept Jesus apparently retained, seems to consist, in substance, in the recognition that the kingdom's nearness, as the effective intervention of God, takes place beyond our control and hidden in the midst of the continuing evil aeon, i.e., that the historical form of the kingdom becomes and remains freedom within lowliness. When thus the eschatological future as God's coming breaks into the present, it is apparent that the eschatological message of Jesus is directed to an eschatological understanding of existence in the present. This understanding of the present toward which Jesus' message moves is the context of his existence, in terms of which his existence actualizes itself. As the illumination of his existence, this understanding of the present can be designated his understanding of existence. The eschatological coming of God in his action is the act in which his existence consists. That God does not even fail him at his death is attested by the Easter faith that the act in which his existence consists still takes place. Thus one can speak nonmythologically of the presence of the resurrected Lord. Here is provided the critical norm for evaluating the kerygma, whose reference to the person Jesus is only then legitimate when this understanding of existence constitutive of Jesus' person is retained, i.e., only when the act of faith in the kerygma is understood as the act of God in human life in which Jesus' existence consists, and hence as "union with Christ."

II

The eschatological polarity of Jesus' message, which consisted in a proclamation to the present in view of the near future, finds expression sometimes in a form not highly or fully developed. In the simplest sentence structure the subject characterizes persons whom the predicate confronts directly with the kingdom of God. Thus the present is brought clearly into the glare of the eschaton, i.e., the shift in aeons becomes the turning point in the fate of the individual actualized in the present, as, e.g., in Matthew 21.31b: "The tax collectors and the harlots go into the kingdom of God instead of you." Just as this confrontation of present and future not only means comfort for the outcasts but is also intended as a warning to the insiders ("you"!), the wealthy, the subject of the logion Mark 10.23, the wealthy, are placed by the predicate over against the eschatological future: "How hard it will be for those who have riches to enter the kingdom of God!" How readily this confrontation expressed in the most common sentence construction can be connected with other forms of discourse is apparent in the comparison with a camel which occurs in the same context and has the same general meaning, Mark 10.25: "It is easier for a camel to go through the eye of a needle than for a rich man to enter the kingdom of God." Similarly the logion in Luke 9.62 describes an attitude in the present which is given its significance from the eschatological future: "No one who puts his hand to the plow and looks back is fit for the kingdom of God."

In the comparison with the children in Matthew 18.3[26] the proclamation to the present in view of the imminent future achieves a full, two-member structure, which marks out sharply the confrontation of present and future:

[26]Cf. also Mark 10.14, 15:

| Let the children come to me, do not hinder them; | for to such belongs the kingdom of God. |
| Whoever does not receive the kingdom of God like a child | shall not enter it. |

The fact that the Matthean variant is the older form of the saying, which in Mark has become a baptismal formula, is apparent, on the one hand, in that "Matthew displays the strongest Semitic coloring in language" (Jeremias, *Die Kindertaufe in den ersten vier Jahrhunderten,* p. 64, ET *Infant Baptism in the First Four Centuries,* p. 52), and, on the other hand, in that this is the form presupposed in the streams of tradition reflected in John 3.2, 5 and Justin, Apol. I.61, 4.

| Unless you turn and become like children, | you will never enter the kingdom of heaven. |

This structure composed of two members recurs in various logia, which, when compared, make it possible, on the basis of their common structure, to trace the apparent trend, namely, a certain accentuation or pointing up of the content. On the basis of the logia already cited one senses that the language about entering the kingdom is not intended simply as a prediction of what will take place in the future. For reflections are hardly made specifically about the future entering of the kingdom itself.[27] Rather this language about the future entering of the kingdom gives direction to the present: the future kingdom is active now in the present and determines it—whether the inbreaking of the eschatological judgment into the present is announced in the indicative, and the separation of the sheep from the goats is carried through now, or the necessity of orienting one's present action toward the future is expressed more imperatively as a warning or exhortation.

Jesus let his own conduct be determined by the imminent kingdom, as the variously transmitted saying in Luke 22.16, 18, and Mark 14.25 shows:

I shall never eat it again	until it is fulfilled in the kingdom of God.
From now on I shall not drink of the fruit of the vine	until the kingdom of God comes.
I shall not drink again of the fruit of the vine	until the day when I drink it new in the kingdom of God.

The fact that Jesus' action was determined by the imminent kingdom comes to particularly impressive expression in the logion on exorcism in Luke 11.20:

| But if it is by the finger of God that I cast out demons, | then the kingdom of God has come upon you. |

The relation of the statement about the kingdom to the present, which was already sensed in the unmediated confrontation of the two members of the formal structure, is made especially clear in the

[27]The *proagein* in the first logion Matt. 21.31b seems, on first glance, to betray an interest in the sequence of future events. But Joachim Jeremias (*Die Gleichnisse Jesu*, p. 126, n. 2, ET *The Parables of Jesus*, p. 125, n. 48) has shown that the Aramaic that lies behind it may be understood exclusively, not temporally. Cf. Hans Windisch, "Die Sprüche vom Eingehen in das Reich Gottes," *ZNW*, 27 (1928), 166.

logion on exorcism. The accentuation consists partly in directing the second member about the kingdom awaited in the near future to the present by the expression "has come upon you." But the superimposing of the future on the present is even further emphasized in that the first member, whose content deals normally with the difficult condition of holding out in the present evil aeon, is dialectically enlarged through the express mentioning of the present form of the kingdom. For "by the finger of God" designates even in the first member the inbreaking of the kingdom of God into the present, which the second member expresses with its "has come upon you."[28] In this twofold way the logion on exorcism expresses the dialectic understanding of the present toward which this formal structure in Jesus' message tends, even though the doctrine of the two aeons in Jewish apocalypticism as the *religionsgeschichtlich* background of the two-member structure would suggest a temporal separation, rather than overlapping, of present and future.

This tendency within the formal structure is visible in the beatitudes and woes, for example, in the collection in Luke 6.20–21, 24–25:

Blessed are you poor,	for yours is the kingdom of God.
Blessed are you that hunger now,	for you shall be satisfied.
Blessed are you that weep now,	for you shall laugh.
But woe to you that are rich,	for you have received your consolation.
Woe to you that are full now,	for you shall hunger.
Woe to you that laugh now,	for you shall mourn and weep.

One finds here, first of all, the same formal structure, in which the content of the first member addresses the outcasts or those at ease in Zion in the present evil aeon in view of the kingdom announced in the second member. But just as the logion on exorcism expressed the inbreaking of the future into the present in the first member, here too the future blessing or curse expressed in the second member is already realized in the first member by the term "blessed" or "woe." Thus, the two-member structure externally related to apoc-

---

[28]This connection of "by the finger of God" to the "kingdom of God" is especially emphasized by the interpretation in Matthew ("by the Spirit of God"). For "Spirit" is in primitive Christianity a technical term for the present manifestation of the kingdom, as is indicated by the designation of the Spirit as "firstfruits" (Rom. 8.23) or "guarantee" (II Cor. 1.22).

alypticism serves in the beatitudes and woes as a means of expression for an eschatological understanding of the present toward which the tendency within the formal structure moves.[29] Here the movement within the formal structure is carried a step farther. For the allusion to the kingdom, which has in the other instances been characteristic of the second member, is replaced in the second and third beatitude and woe by terms chosen to express the antithesis of the designations used in the first member. The element distinguishing the two members is thereby shifted decisively from the temporal factor to the material antithesis of the two members, that is, the weight shifts from the temporal distinction derived from the doctrine of two aeons onto the material antithesis of the two aeons. For although in the formal structure the *religionsgeschichtlich* context of the imminent expectation is retained, the temporal distinction is replaced by the material contrast as the determinative distinguishing characteristic which controls dialectically the opposing and relating of the two members. This provides content to the tendency which we have formally described as the imposing of the statement about the eschatological future in the second member upon the first member dealing with the present. The picture of the finger of God which intervenes in the existence of the demoniac, i.e., the coming of God into this demonic world, or the eschatological judgment which already takes place as blessing or curse, is now given content in antithetic verbs designating an existential dialectic: "hunger"/"be satisfied," "weep"/"laugh," "be full"/"hunger," "laugh"/"mourn and weep."

This existential dialectic which thus becomes the material characteristic of the formal structure, and which can consequently serve as a guiding line for an existentialistic interpretation of the eschatological message of Jesus, recurs in other logia. In Mark 8.35, Matthew 10.39, and Luke 17.33 (cf. also John 12.25) one finds it in the pair of terms "save" (or "find" or "gain" or "preserve")/ "lose":

For whoever would save one's life	will lose it,
and whoever loses one's life (. . .)	will save it.
The person who finds one's life	will lose it,
and the person who loses one's life (. . .)	will find it.

[29]Thus the beatitudes and woes present an exposition of what could only be suspected in a preliminary way in the logia about "the tax collectors and the harlots" (Matt. 21.31b) and the rich (Mark 10.23, 25).

Whoever seeks to gain one's life	will lose it,
but whoever loses one's life	will preserve it.

The pair of terms "exalt"/"humble," already anticipated in the Old Testament,[30] illustrates the same existential dialectic in the logion Matthew 23.12:[31]

Whoever exalts oneself	shall be humbled
and whoever humbles oneself	shall be exalted.

and Luke 14.11 (18.14):

But every one who exalts oneself	will be humbled,
and the person who humbles oneself	will be exalted.

Still a further logion uses the antithesis "first"/"last." In Luke 13.30 the temporal separation of the two members is still in place:

And behold, some are last	who will be first,
and some are first	who will be last.

But how little the temporal distinction still provides the real basis of the separation of the two members is evident from Matthew 20.16 and Mark 10.31. Here the future verb has been removed from its normal position in the second member and has been placed before the first member, so that the antithetic terms confront each other directly.[32]

So will be	the last	first,
	and the first	last.
But there will be many	first	last,
	and the last	first.

These variants illustrate the logical outcome of the tendency within the formal structure which we have traced: The eschatological mes-

[30]Cf. Job 22.29; Prov. 29.23; Ezek. 21.26b.
[31]Cf. the variant in Luke 16.15, where the temporal element is completely lacking:

What is exalted among men	is an abomination in the sight of God.

In Matt. 18.4 the language of the logion enters into a combination with the saying about the children (Matt. 18.3), so as to provide Matthew with an answer to the question of 18.1 as to "who is the greatest in the kingdom of heaven" (cf. Gunther Bornkamm, *Überlieferung und Auslegung im Matthäus-Evangelium* [1960], p. 17, ET *Tradition and Interpretation in Matthew* [1963], p. 20). In this case too the material dialectic receives the emphasis rather than the temporal distinction:

Whoever humbles himself like this child,	he is the greatest in the kingdom of heaven.

[32]In Mark 9.35 the logion is connected with the paraenetic saying Mark 10.43f;

sage of Jesus, which is rooted *religionsgeschichtlich* in Jewish apocalypticism's doctrine of two aeons, whose polarity leads to a two-member structure in many sayings of Jesus, was directed so consistently to the present that an existential dialectic became visible. It gave expression to Jesus' understanding of the present and thus became the content of Jesus' understanding of existence. For this eschatologically qualified present, this coming of God, is the context, the source, the constitutive ingredient of believing existence. Jesus' action consists in the actualization of this existence. His message consists in bringing this understanding of existence to expression.

III

God forgives the tax collectors and prostitutes; he breaks the security of the wealthy. The childlike are saved. The possessed are freed by the finger of God. Within poverty is God's reign, within hunger fullness, among tears joy, whereas the full starve, and laughter becomes weeping and wailing. The self-saving life loses itself, while the person who opens oneself without reserve even to the extent of death lives all the while from God. Those who puff themselves up are brought down hard, but the lowly are borne by God. For he counts the first last and the last first. In this eschatological occurrence, taking place in Jesus' present, his existence is constituted. This existence finds expression in various ways, but within the variety of expression there is a consistent interpretation of existence.

To be sure, one cannot preserve this understanding of the existence of Jesus simply by transmitting it as doctrine. For Jesus' understanding of existence consists essentially in that Jesus saw his existence determined not primarily by humans but by God and by the eschatological situation given by God. Hence, it would be inappropriate to assume this existence could be actualized without a continuation of God's intervention in the world. Such a consideration makes it clear that a Christian understanding of existence

---

Matthew 23.11, where again the temporal tension yields to the material antithesis. For the *estai* in the second member is not meant as a future tense, but rather is imperative in meaning ("he must be . . ."). Cf. Blass-Debrunner, *Grammatik des neutestamentlichen Griechisch*, Abschnitt 362, ET *A Greek Grammar of the New Testament and Other Early Christian Literature*, tr. by Robert W. Funk (1961), Section 362, p. 183.

always involves a certain understanding of God, the world, and history. Hence, Christian existence is not possible without Easter, that is, without the installation of Jesus' existence as that of the Cosmocrator. For the kerygma's proclamation of Jesus as Cosmocrator brings ontologically to expression what happened ontically in Jesus. In the Easter event, that is, in the Cosmocrator, resides the basis of Christian preaching, but in the unity of the Cosmocrator with the existence of Jesus resides the norm for the critical question as to the theological legitimacy of such preaching. This critical question has to test whether Christian preaching proclaims only formally the name of Jesus, or whether it implies, also materially, his understanding of existence. For only when and if the act in which Jesus' existence consists happens in the Christian's life, as one commits oneself to Jesus' understanding of existence in one's act of faith—only then can one say theologically the person is actually united with Christ and a participant in his new life. For here resides the "mystical union" with Christ which is neither mystical nor mythological, but existential reality. The question as to whether Christian preaching and believing correspond to this reality of Jesus' person or only bear his name—that is, the normative theological question—cannot be pursued simply by inquiring whether the message of Jesus has been accurately transmitted even to the *ipsissima verba* themselves, or by inquiring whether the primitive Christian kerygma has been preserved without subsequent doctrinal contamination—neither of which is, of course the case. Rather the critical question is whether, in each transformation of the sayings of Jesus and in each subsequent development of christological conceptualizations, Jesus' understanding of existence, and, hence, that which constitutes his person, has been faithfully proclaimed and believed.

This critical question has already been illustrated elsewhere[33] with regard to the primitive Christian kerygma. It is now to be illustrated with regard to another form of early Christian proclamation, namely, the transmission of sayings of Jesus as authoritative messages of the heavenly Lord. For this purpose one may use the saying of Jesus about the children already cited from Matthew 18.3, which soon became a baptismal formula and hence occurs frequently in the early church. Just as the kerygma repeatedly refers to Jesus, this logion is almost always cited expressly as a saying of the Lord.

[33]*A New Quest of the Historical Jesus,* above, pp. 122–25.

But just as in the case of the kerygma, the decisive question here is whether, with the express attribution of the saying to Jesus, only his name or also the understanding of existence constitutive of his person is retained. The simple transmission of the logion as a saying of Jesus denotes, in and of itself, relatively little. For a different understanding of existence could be read into the saying, which would then lose its material relation to Jesus' person. Or the saying could lose its original scope directed to an understanding of the present and of existence in that present, and could be reduced to an apocalyptic prediction of future occurrence or to a Gnostic speculation about securing the path of the soul in its ascent at death into heaven. In this case, too, Jesus' understanding of existence is basic to the saying in its original intention, and, hence, the legitimacy of its citation as a saying of the Lord would be lost.

Baptism, as the setting of the saying, explains how the logion soon appears expressed in terms of regeneration rather than in terms of a simple comparison with children.[34] The following instances may be cited: John 3.3, 5:

Unless one is born from above	one cannot see the kingdom of God.
Unless one is born from water and the Spirit,	one cannot enter the kingdom of God.

Justin, Apol. I. 61, 4:

Unless you are born again,	you will not enter the kingdom of heaven.

Pseudo-Clementine Homily XI, 26.2:

Unless you are born anew with living water, in the name of the Father, the Son, the Holy Spirit,	you will not enter the kingdom of heaven.

Clement of Alexandria, Coh. ad Gr. IX, 82.4:

"For unless you become again as the children and are born anew," as Scripture says, [i.e., unless] you receive him who is truly the Father,	"you will never enter the kingdom of heaven."

[34]Cf. my article on "Regeneration" in *The Interpreter's Dictionary of the Bible,* IV (1962), pp. 24–29.

The question as to the legitimacy of such an alteration of the original logion cannot be decided simply by pointing out that in the process of transmission the *ipsissima verba* of Jesus were replaced by the theological conceptualizations of a later time and a different environment. Rather one must inquire whether the understanding of existence expressed in the terms of Jesus is retained in the new terminology. If the baptismal water were here understood magically, e.g., as water filled with Spirit because it was running ("living") water,[35] or as water whose substance was purified by Jesus' baptism, which then, like the eucharistic elements, worked mechanically as a "medicine of immortality" (compare Ignatius, Eph. 18.2 with 20.2), and which, hence, was at the disposal and in the power of the ecclesiastical authorities, then in fact one would suspect that Jesus' understanding of existence had been replaced by the security and hubris of a massive sacramentalism[36] and an equally massive clericalism.[37] Then to designate a logion so materially falsified as a saying of the Lord would be illegitimate. On the other hand, the repudiation of the regeneration terminology would not, as such, authenticate the use of the logion as a saying of the Lord. For one would then have to inquire, e.g., as to whether a moralizing interpretation as the alternative does not move toward works righteousness, and, thus, via opposed conceptualizations, also end in a

[35]The "living water" in the Pseudo-Clementine Homily XI, 26.2 is, in view of the presence also of the members of the Trinity in the logion, doubtless due to the influence of Didache 7.1: "Concerning baptism, baptize thus: Having said all these things, baptize in the name of the Father and of the Son and of the Holy Spirit in living water." But the discussion in Didache 7.2–3 of the other methods of baptism, which, though not put in first place, are at least permitted, indicates that running water was not an indispensable prerequisite to legitimate baptism. This would indicate that the magical implications latent in the preference for running water were not emphasized.

[36]The version of the logion occurring in the Apostolic Constitutions VI, 15.5 may be open to this sacramentalistic interpretation: "But also a person who out of contempt does not wish to be baptized is to be considered as an unbeliever and reproached as one without grace and without knowledge. For the Lord says:

'Unless one is baptized from water   one will not enter the kingdom of
and the Spirit   heaven.'

And again: 'A person who believes and is baptized will be saved, but a person who does not believe will be condemned.'"

[37]The interpretation of the logion in Clement of Alexandria, Coh. ad. Gr. IX 82.4, is open to such an interpretation: "Come, come, my young men. 'For unless you become again as the children and are born anew,' as Scripture says, (that is,

self-secured understanding of existence, incompatible with that of Jesus.[38] When the regeneration terminology is understood in the sense of Johannine theology, the introduction of the logion as a saying of the Lord is legitimate to the extent that here Jesus' understanding of existence finds expression in a different terminology.[39]

The logion occurs further in Gnostic documents, e.g., the Martyrium Petri 9.[40] The use of the logion by a martyr—here, of course, a literary fiction—would involve a shift in the setting, which would be easy in view of the interpretation of martyrdom as equivalent to baptism, that is, as blood baptism. Since baptism had already, as regeneration, been associated with union with the primal human who bears the image of God (cf. Col. 3.10), it took only a bit of Gnostic fantasy to see in the tradition of Peter's crucifixion upside down the deeper meaning of representing the head-down flight of the primal human from heaven to earth. Now in such an upside-down position the right side becomes the left side, the left side the right, etc.; and the "profound" spirit sees in all this the hint of a complete reversal of directions or values, which incidentally leaves the door wide open for further speculation. This train of

---

unless) you receive him who is truly the Father, 'you will never enter the kingdom of heaven.' For how is it permitted to the stranger to enter? But if, I suppose, one is enrolled and has citizenship and receives the Father, then one will be 'in the Father's house,' then one will be counted worthy to inherit, then one will share the paternal kingdom in the true (Son), the 'beloved.'"

[38]Clement of Alexandria brings in Paed. I, 5.12 an interpretation which is opposed to the idea of regeneration and finds its point of departure in the simplicity of the child: "The Lord himself makes clear the intention of what was said, when he says:

'Unless you turn and become as   you will not enter the kingdom of
these children,   heaven.'

Here he is not speaking allegorically of regeneration, but is commending to us for imitation the simplicity in children." Here there is the danger of a moralistic self-assurance which in its way would miss Jesus' understanding of existence, as the development of this interpretation in the Shepherd of Hermas, Sim. IX 29.1–3, suggests.

[39]Such an interpretation of the development in John 3.5 seems suggested, on the one hand, by the emphasis on baptism by the Spirit and, on the other, by the Johannine formulation of the logion in John 3.3 (for example, *anōthen*, which relates regeneration to John's Christology; cf. 3.13, 31, 36).

[40]Lipsius-Bonnet, *Acta Apostolorum Apocrypha*, I, 94.

thought provides the introduction to the logion,[41] and provides also the explanation for the drastic alterations in the wording of the logion.[42]

Unless you make the right as   you will not know the kingdom.
the left
and the left as the right
and the above as the below
and the behind as the before,

It is not surprising, in view of the fertility of such imaginations and the open invitation to further speculation in this reversal of all values, that the logion is still further transformed, this time in the service of sexual asceticism. When one considers that repudiation of sex was a condition to admission to some Gnostic groups, somewhat as baptism was a condition of admission into the church at large, it is not too difficult to see how a logion whose original setting was baptism could be taken over and remolded in the analogous setting of admission to the sect. This particular development would also be facilitated by the view of baptismal regeneration (or Peter's blood baptism) as a mystical union with the primal human,

[41]The introduction concludes: ". . . whereby he showed the right (to be) the left and the left the right, and he changed all the signs of their nature, to apprehend the beautiful as that which is not beautiful and the good as that which is actually bad, concerning which the Lord says in a mystery: . . ."

[42]In the *Acta Philippi* 34 (Lipsius-Bonnet, II, 2.74f.) the same form of the logion occurs. According to the Gamma text the logion runs:

Unless you make your below the   you will not enter my kingdom.
above and the left the right,

In the Theta text one senses some awareness for the reversal of values originally involved in the logion:

Unless you make the left right and   you will not be able to enter the
consider the dishonorable honor-   kingdom of heaven.
able,

But in the Delta text one senses hardly more than the pedantic completion of the metaphors of reversal:

Unless you turn the below into the   you will not enter the kingdom of
above   God.
and the above into the below
and the right into the left
and the left into the right,

In all these textual traditions the second member retains the allusion to entering the kingdom which in the Martyrium Petri 9 had been "improved" from a Gnostic point of view to read "*know* the kingdom."

whose bisexuality was a common idea.[43] The result of this development upon the logion can be seen in logion 22 of the Gospel of Thomas:[44] "Jesus saw infants being suckled. He said to His disciples,

'These infants being suckled are like those who enter the Kingdom.'
They said to Him: 'Shall we then, as children, enter the Kingdom?' Jesus said to them,
'When you make the two one,
and when you make the inside like the outside
and the outside like the inside,
and the above like the below,
and when you make the male and the female
one and the same,
so that the male not be male
nor the female female;
and when you fashion eyes in place of an eye,
and a hand in place of a hand,
and a foot in place of a foot,
and a likeness in place of a likeness,
then will you enter
[the Kingdom].'"

The logion begins with a sufficiently neutral statement of the reversal of all values ("when you make the two one")[45] as to invite a

[43]Cf. the bibliography to the concept *arrenothēlus* in A. D. Nock and A.-J. Festugière, *Corpus Hermeticum* (1945), Vol. I, p. 20, n. 24, and p. 22, n. 43.

[44]*The Nag Hammadi Library in English* (1977), p. 121.

[45]This line seems merely to suggest the principle of the reversal of all relations in logion 106 of the Gospel of Thomas: "Jesus said.

When you make the two one,   you will become the sons of man,
and when you say, 'Mountain, move   it will be moved."
  away,'

Yet Puech, *Neutestamentliche Apokryphen*, ed. by Wilhelm Schneemelcher (3d ed., 1959), I, 215 suggests the possibility that this line could be meant sexually: "Werdet ihr Söhne des Menschen (des Männlichen?) werden." The ET, *New Testament Apocrypha*, I (1953), 299, does not present this option: "You shall become sons of Man." This sexual interpretation is clear in the quotation from the Docetist Julius Cassianus on celibacy or on being a eunuch, cited by Clement of Alexandria, *Stromata* III, Ch. XIII, 92.2, who derives the saying ultimately from the Gospel of the Egyptians (cf. Schneemelcher, *op. cit.*, pp. 110f., ET, p. 168): "When Salome asked when one would know that concerning which she had asked, the Lord said:

When you will tread your feet
  on the clothes of your shame
and when the two will become one
and the male with the female
  (will be) neither male nor female."

The fact that this passage must have originally stood in connection with the saying

collection of various alternate versions,[46] yet all brought together at the end by the reminder that this is the metamorphosis involved in regeneration, when one receives "a likeness (*eikōn*) in the place of a likeness." The result is a logion all but transformed beyond recognition, were it not that the hint provided by the basic structure is confirmed by the introduction, in which it becomes clear that the logion grew out of the saying about the children. For it is this insight into the history of the transmission of the logion which is given pictorial presentation in the scene where Jesus' remark about the children is "clarified" by Jesus himself, in the terms of the final form which the logion has assumed at that time.

Even when a logion is thus transformed until it is beyond rec-

---

about the kingdom is made clear by II Clement. Here one reads in 11.7:

| If therefore we do righteousness be- | we will come into his |
| fore God | kingdom. . . . |

Then there follows in 12.1 the exhortation, in view of the uncertainty as to the date of the eschaton, to "await the kingdom of God in love and righteousness." For, 12.2: "When the Lord himself was asked by someone when his kingdom would come. he said:

> When the two will be one,
> and the outside as the inside
> and the male with the female
> neither male nor female."

After a moralistic interpretation, clearly secondary to the original meaning which gave rise to this form of the saying, one finds in 12.6 the summary:

| "If you do these things," he said, | "the kingdom of my Father will |
| | come." |

The relation between the sexual interpretation of the first member and the entrance into the kingdom as the second member is also attested in logion 114 of the Gospel of Thomas: "Simon Peter said to them, 'Let Mary leave us, for women are not worthy of Life.' Jesus said, 'I myself shall lead her in order to make her male, so that she too may become a living spirit, resembling you males.

| For every woman who will make | will enter the Kingdom of Heaven.' " |
| herself male | |

[46]The fact that we have to deal here with a collection of various traditions is supported by the way in which the beginning of the logion recurs three times (in addition to the opening line), thus grouping the appended material into three parts according to the theme involved: (1) inside and outside, above and below (cf. the Martyrium Petri 9, etc.); (2) male and female (cf. the Gospel of the Egyptians, etc., n. 45 above); (3) eye, hand, foot (cf. Mark 9.43, 45, 57?). The fact that (1) and (3) begin with *hotan* (though only implicitly carried over from the opening line), while (2) begins with *hina,* increases the probability that we have a collection of originally separate traditions. This latter distinction was ignored in the translation quoted, but was observed, e.g., by Johannes Leipoldt (*TLZ,* 53 [1958], 481–96), who translated "und wenn . . . , und dass . . . , wenn . . . ."

ognition,[47] one still cannot repudiate such a drastic attempt to
"bring it up to date" (theologically spoken: one cannot deny that
it is spoken authoritatively to the situation by the heavenly Lord)
simply by calling attention to the strangeness of its cultural context
and conceptualizations in comparison to those of Jesus (or of the
world today). On the other hand, the legitimacy of such a development is not strengthened by the Gospel of Thomas's rooting its
logion in Jesus' saying about the children. For this is merely an
observation (probably valid) as to the history of the transmission of
the logion, but not a theological justification. The material justification for such a development of the original logion could be
provided only if it could be shown that, throughout the alteration
of cultural and conceptual contexts, an understanding of existence
was proclaimed consisting in the same act of God in human action
in which Jesus' existence consists. Only then would the saying be
theologically rooted in the person of Jesus and, hence, suitable for
authoritative Christian proclamation as the word of the heavenly
Lord, in which the believer comes into union with him. For in the
occurrence of the act which the original saying of Jesus proclaims,
there would be actualized the existence which is Jesus' existence,
that is, Christian existence would be actualized—in the paradoxical
form (Gal. 2.20) necessitated by its paradoxical content (for example, Mark 8.35 discussed above).

[47]For example, the logion Ib of the Oxyrhynchus Papyrus 655 seems to lack
any connection with the saying about the children with which we are concerned:
"'Who could add to your life span? He himself will give you your clothing.' His
disciples say to him: 'When wilt Thou be revealed to us and when will we see
Thee?' He says: 'When you disrobe and are not ashamed! . . .'" But now the
logion in its entirety has become available in the Gospel of Thomas, logion 37:
"His disciples said, 'When will You become revealed to us and when will we see
You?' Jesus said,

'When you disrobe without being ashamed and take up your gar-
ments and place them under your feet like little children and tread
on them, then (will you see) the Son of the Living One and you will not be afraid.'"

Here one discovers that the saying did not grow out of the context of Matt. 6.27ff.
into which the Oxyrhynchus Papyrus put it. Instead the tenuous connection of the
original saying of Jesus about the children, with the logion from the Gospel of the
Egyptians about treading on one's clothes (cf. n. 45 above), suddenly becomes
visible for a moment through the remarkable occurrence of the original phrase
"like little children." This instance should provide a final illustration of the insight
that the *ipsissima verba* do not automatically preserve with them Jesus' understanding of existence.

VII

THE RECENT DEBATE ON THE "NEW QUEST"

I have been asked to analyze the development of the new quest of the historical Jesus since 1959, to bring up to date the presentation in my book, *A New Quest of the Historical Jesus*. Since at the time of the second impression of that book in 1961 it was not possible even to include the additional material found in the German edition of 1960, such an updating of the material is highly necessary. The quantity of literature which has appeared since 1959 exceeds considerably what had appeared prior to that date. And, although much of this added material has been repetitious and has hardly advanced the debate, some significant developments have taken place. They have their focus in the emergence of an opposition which had hardly become visible by 1959.

I

In spite of various inadequacies in my publication of 1959, it has served its major purpose of calling forth an American discussion of a new trend in German theology at a time when the German discussion was still in a formative stage, and with the result that the discussion could become a two-way affair. The very fact that the National Association of Biblical Instructors is presenting a symposium on this topic in 1961, only seven years after the publication of Ernst Käsemann's programmatic essay,[1] whereas the NABI symposium on demythologizing in 1957 came sixteen years after Rudolf Bultmann's proposal of 1941, is symptomatic of the increasing synchronization of the two theological traditions which should be an

---

[1] "Das Problem des historischen Jesus," *ZTK*, LI (1954), 123–53, reprinted in *EVB* (Göttingen: Vandenhoeck und Ruprecht, I [1960]), 187–214, ET "The Problem of the Historical Jesus," *Essays on New Testament Themes*, Studies in Biblical Theology 41, London: SCM Press, 1964, 15–47.

attainable objective in our day.[2] A series of symposia to that end published under the title, *New Frontiers in Theology: Discussions Among Continental and American Theologians,* consists of volumes entitled *The Later Heidegger and Theology, The New Hermeneutics* and *Theology as History.*[3]

The extent to which the new quest of the historical Jesus has become a two-way conversation is symbolized by the fact that Rudolf Bultmann's reply to his students before the Heidelberg Academy of Sciences[4] not only included critiques of my book as well as of his German students, but also was able to appeal for support to letters from Edwin M. Good of Stanford University and Van A. Harvey of Southern Methodist University, and to a review by R. H. Fuller of Seabury-Western Theological Seminary. Accordingly, one of the significant new aspects of the discussion with which we can appropriately begin is the American participation and the particular role it plays.

Since the original quest of the historical Jesus never really ended in America, we sense very acutely that the basic issue regarding the new quest is whether it can be anything other than a revival of the old quest with all its weaknesses, that is, whether it can be genuinely post-Bultmannian in retaining Bultmann's valid criticisms of the old quest. To be sure, the very persistence of the original quest at the grass roots means that the new one can count on a grassroots receptivity. Indeed, one may expect a blurring of the distinction between the original quest and the new one—a setback I sought to avoid by devoting the first half of my book to a presentation of Bultmann's valid argument that the original quest was historically

---

[2]Lest one project this graph into the past in terms of a concept of straight-line progress, and in a way that discredits the past, it should be noted that Shirley Jackson Case's *The Historicity of Jesus* appeared in 1912, analyzing a German debate which, though begun somewhat earlier, at least had been brought to its peak by Arthur Drews' *Die Christusmythe* of 1909 and the latter's debate with Hermann von Soden before the *Monistenbund* of Jan. 31 and Feb. 1, 1910 (cf. 39f., note 2 in Case's presentation).

[3]Edited by James M. Robinson and John B. Cobb, Jr. (New York, Evanston, and London: Harper and Row, 1963, 1964, 1967).

[4]*Das Verhältnis der urchristlichen Christusbotschaft zum historischen Jesus,* presented July 25, 1959, published in the *Sitzungsberichte der Heidelberger Akademie der Wissenschaften, Philosophisch-historische Klasse,* Jg. 1960, 3. Abh., 27 pp., ET "The Primitive Christian Kerygma and the Historical Jesus," in *The Historical Jesus and the Kerygmatic Christ,* ed. by Carl E. Braaten and Roy A. Harrisville (New York and Nashville: Abingdon, 1964), 15–42.

impossible and theologically illegitimate. Of course, it is also possible that one will change with the changing times. Thus, Ernest Cadman Colwell, speaking before this association in 1959 on prospects for New Testament scholarship during the next fifty years, was able to refer to the new quest as typical of the research of the future, not simply because he as a student of Shirley Jackson Case was convinced that Christianity must build upon the historical Jesus, but also because he believed that the socio-historical method of Case must be replaced or at least supplemented by the new methods he had found exemplified in Powicke and Bloch and which are usually associated with the names of Dilthey and Collingwood.[5]

The issue involved in this unbroken continuity with the original quest, which is for better or worse the American setting of the new quest, becomes quite visible in a recent American life of Jesus, Morton Scott Enslin's *The Prophet from Nazareth*.[6] In this volume, form criticism and its kerygmatic theology are brushed aside with the standard caricature: "In place of the historical Jesus, whom they assume it is impossible to discover, and thus for whom further search is an unwarranted waste of time, they set the figure of the Eternal Christ and his part in the all-central epic of salvation—the technical term is *Heilsgeschichte*—which comprise the one and only important chapter of all cosmic history."[7] By thus presenting form criticism as maintaining the obviously absurd position that we can know nothing of Jesus, the original questers seek to eliminate their critics and to continue their quest as if nothing had happened. It is no surprise that in such a situation a young and vigorous Bultmannian systematician, Schubert M. Ogden, should take a first look at the new quest and complain, "But it still remains a fair question whether the extent of the alleged 'newness' may not depend entirely too much upon seeing it against the background of a highly oversimplified and even false impression of Bultmann's own position."[8] When Ogden then comments in a footnote that "this question is

[5]"New Testament Scholarship in Prospect," *JBR* 28 (1960), 199–203, esp. 202f.

[6]New York: McGraw-Hill, 1961. See the review-article by James M. Robinson, "The Prophet from Nazareth," *JBR* 30 (1962), 46–48.

[7]Enslin, *The Prophet from Nazareth*, 5.

[8]In the introduction to a collection of Bultmann's shorter writings published as *Existence and Faith*, ed. Ogden (New York: Meridian Books, 1960), 12. Cf., similarly, Ogden, *Christ without Myth* (New York: Harper & Brothers, 1961), 81.

even raised, though no doubt unintentionally, by Robinson himself," I would merely respond that I quite intentionally questioned the caricature of Bultmann's position and even went to the trouble of collecting a long footnote of quotations from Bultmann to disprove the caricature. However, in spite of all that we can do, the caricature persists as a foil for the continuing quest of the "compelling personality" and "unflinching bravery" of Jesus.[9]

It is as just one more instance of this well-known tradition that the talk of a new quest of the historical Jesus strikes many ears. The younger generation, for whom that well-known tradition is anathema, is therefore tempted to react to the new quest by rejecting it out of hand. Paul W. Meyer puts the matter bluntly: "In form, this [new quest] parallels perfectly the older liberal understanding of faith as the reproduction, in my religious experience, of Jesus' feeling of Sonship in relation to God—and it is like the other totally dependent on historical familiarity with Jesus' person. We seem to have here a complete capitulation to the heirs of Schweitzer."[10] And, significantly enough, Meyer alludes to Walter Bell Denny's *The Career and Significance of Jesus* (1934) as "an extreme example"—as if to say, bad company corrupts good manners. Hence, if any advocate of the new quest is to make one's point in the present situation, one must go to great pains to argue that the new quest does *not* "parallel perfectly" the old. The new quest does not attempt to discover how Jesus felt, for the records tell us not how he felt but what his significance was. Jesus' understanding of existence was not his stream of consciousness, but the understanding of existence which emerged in history from his words and deeds. It is this, not his personality or the alleged specifics of his biography, which is his historic person. Neither is faith to be regarded as the imitating reproduction of a human stance. Faith is a response to God, to the same eschatological act of God which the kerygma proclaims as one with the event of Jesus. Faith is not totally dependent on historical familiarity with Jesus' person, for that eschatological act of God is proclaimed in the kerygma. Indeed, it is as a result of faith in the kerygma—which itself points to Jesus as the

[9]Enslin, *The Prophet from Nazareth*, 212, 214f.
[10]Paul W. Meyer, "The Problem of the Messianic Self-Consciousness of Jesus," *Novum Testamentum*, IV (1960), 133.

locus of God's action—that the *fides quaerens intellectum* as theological reflection enters upon the new quest. Hence, the new quest need not and should not be "a complete capitulation to the heirs of Schweitzer" and, in fact, I conclude my review-article of *The Prophet from Nazareth* with the statement, "The critical reader of this book is compelled to become a Bultmannian."

This issue of the new quest's situation within the context of the old is present within systematic theology as well as in the New Testament aspect of the debate. Thus, John Macquarrie welcomes the new quest as support for his insistence that the historian should provide the kerygma with an "empirical anchor," a "minimal core of factuality." What Macquarrie has in mind is suggested by his criticism that a demythologizing interpretation of the stilling of the storm denies "any objective reference in the story," i.e., denies "that Christ had in fact stilled a storm on the lake." Over against this, Macquarrie affirms, "the minimal assertion is that 'the Word became flesh and dwelt among us.'"[11] But anyone who expects such a statement as this last from a *historian* simply does not understand the limits set on the historian's trade. And, indeed, Macquarrie's contention is more reminiscent of the positivistic program of Ethelbert Stauffer, roundly rejected by all involved in the new quest, than of the new quest itself. To be sure, Macquarrie states his "minimal core" in language much like that of the new quest: "Simply that there was someone who once exhibited in history the possibility of existence which the kerygma proclaims."[12] He apparently means by this that the reality proclaimed by the kerygma is to be proven historically to have taken place in the case of Jesus. But again, this reality is God's eschatological, saving action, and, as such, it simply cannot be proven historically. This act of God is *faith's* "fact" and that is why no "minimal core" of this kind of "factuality" can ever be provided by the historian. To be sure, Bultmann rightly identifies the gospel as consisting for Paul in the having-happenedness of the eschatological event once and for all, and it is that message which is directed to me as the proclamation that it is happening in my life. But this does not mean that the

---

[11]John Macquarrie, *The Scope of Demythologizing: Bultmann and His Critics* (New York: Harper & Brothers, 1960), 18, 19, 91ff., 245ff.

[12]Macquarrie, *The Scope of Demythologizing*, 93.

gospel is to be proved in the one case and believed in the other, but rather that I believe it to have happened once and for all when I believe that it happens now to me. This is the way the Christian understands his or her existence. But to prove that this understanding of existence emerges from the historical Jesus is not to prove that such an understanding is true, that is, it does not prove that God has acted or does act. Nor can the desire for a "minimal core" of proven security be the motive for inquiring after Jesus' understanding of existence. The real motive lies within the context of *fides quaerens intellectum*, of theology reflecting upon its faith; it does not lie outside faith in a realm that supposedly furnishes a proven access into faith. Hence, Carl Michalson is correct in his criticism of Macquarrie: "This positivistic drive leads Macquarrie to misinterpret the purpose of the current revival of the question of the historical Jesus."[13]

II

The most significant thing that has taken place in the discussion within German circles since 1959 is not the endless flood of publications. (These are often more impressive in quantity than quality; the 710-page symposium, *Der historische Jesus und der kerygmatische Christus,* published in East Berlin, is a most glaring instance.[14]) Of primary significance instead is the emergence of an opposition in Germany, paralleling that in the United States and emerging for much the same reason. For previously the surprise caused by a Bultmannian proposing a new quest was only equalled by the way in which the new quest at first swept everything before it. The "hefty debate" originally predicted by Käsemann has only now begun to emerge—although not quite as he expected. For he probably

[13]Carl Michalson, "A Misunderstanding of Bultmann," *Interpretation,* 15 (1961), 491–96, esp. 494.
[14]Ed. Helmut Ristow and Karl Matthiae (Berlin: Evangelische Verlagsanstalt, 1960). Its contributors are K. Adam, P. Althaus, E. Barnikol, G. Bornkamm, H. Braun, E. Brunner, R. Bultmann, F. Buri, M. Burrows, H. Conzelmann, O. Cullmann, N. A. Dahl, J. Daniélou, G. Delling, H. Diem, E. Fascher, J. de Fraine, E. Fuchs, H. Gollwitzer, L. Goppelt, W. Grundmann, O. Haendler, E. Heitsch, I. Henderson, R. Hermann, J. L. Hromádka, J. Jeremias, H. Jursch, K. Karner, W. G. Kümmel, J. Leipoldt, R. Marlé, W. Michaelis, O. Michel, W. Nagel, B. Reicke, H. Riesenfeld, B. Rigaux, R. Schnackenburg, J. Schneider, H. J. Schoeps, E. Schott, H. Schürmann, E. Schweizer, E. Stauffer, H. Urner, K. Weiss, and M. Werner. Several of the essays are reprints of earlier publications.

did not anticipate that he would himself be pushed more and more toward the opposition by the way in which his main competitor for the mantle of leadership in Bultmannian circles, Ernst Fuchs, would be combining the new quest with a revival of nineteenth-century theology.[15] Käsemann himself has most recently identified the fanatical apocalypticism emerging from the Easter experience—not from any imminent expectation in Jesus' eschatology—as the "matrix of Christian theology."[16] Hence, *Heilsgeschichte,* rather than the new quest, seems a better way to express the primitive Christian concern for history.

In a somewhat parallel way Hans Conzelmann, as long as he was at Zürich with Gerhard Ebeling, was willing to share in the new quest, merely warning against potential dangers in the position of Fuchs and Ebeling. But when he went to Göttingen, where an unbroken continuity with the original quest was—in the person of Joachim Jeremias—most ably represented in Germany, Conzelmann withdrew from the new quest by arguing that although one was free to inquire as to the historical Jesus the matter was irrelevant to Christian faith.[17]

[15]Cf. Fuchs' collected essays on the topic, *Zur Frage nach dem historischen Jesus, Gesammelte Aufsätze,* Vol. II (Tübingen: J. C. B. Mohr, 1960), ET of most of them, *Studies of the Historical Jesus,* Studies in Biblical Theology, 42 (London: SCM Press, 1964). Cf. also his subsequent essays, "Muss man an Jesus glauben, wenn man an Gott glauben will?" *ZTK* LVIII (1961), 45–67, and "Das Neue Testament und das hermeneutische Problem," *ibid.,* 198–226, both reprinted in *Glaube und Erfahrung, Gesammelte Aufsätze,* Vol. III (Tübingen: Mohr, 1965), 249–79, 136–73, ET "Must One Believe in Jesus if He wants to Believe in God? Preliminary Reflections on the Interpretation of 1 Cor. 15:1–11," in *The Bultmann School of Biblical Interpretation: New Directions? Journal for Theology and Church,* I (1965), 147–68; "The New Testament and the Hermeneutical Problem," in *The New Hermeneutic,* New Frontiers in Theology 2 (1964), 111–45; *Jesus Wort und Tat* (Tübingen: J. C. B. Mohr [Paul Siebeck], 1971).

[16]"Die Anfänge christlicher Theologie," *ZTK,* LVII (1960), 162–85, ET "The Beginnings of Christian Theology," in *New Testament Questions of Today* (Philadelphia: Fortress Press, 1969), 82–107. Cf. the critical replies by Gerhard Ebeling, "Der Grund christlicher Theologie," *ZTK,* LVIII (1961), 227–44, and Ernst Fuchs, "Über das Aufgabe einer christlichen Theologie," *ZTK,* LVIII (1961), 245–67. All three essays are brought together in English translation in *Apocalypticism, Journal for Theology and the Church,* VI (1969): "The Beginnings of Christian Theology," 17–46; "The Ground of Christian Theology," 47–68; "On the Task of a Christian Theology," 69–98. See also Rudolf Bultmann, "Ist die Apokalyptik die Mutter der christlichen Theologie? Eine Auseinandersetzung mit Ernst Käsemann," *Apophoreta* (Haenchen Festschrift, BZNW 30 [1964], 64–69).

[17]This is the substance of Conzelmann's inaugural address at Göttingen, which he does not plan to publish, since its delivery coincided with the publication of Bultmann's address which Conzelmann regards as stating adequately his own po-

A New Quest of the Historical Jesus

The emergence of critical reservations concerning the new quest is not confined to such more-sensed-than-fully-documented feathers in the wind. For Bultmann's reply to his own students, first expressed in personal correspondence, was made public in an address before the Heidelberg Academy of Sciences on July 25, 1959 and was published in December, 1960.[18]

Bultmann begins his reply by distinguishing the question of the historical continuity between Jesus and the kerygma from the question of their material relation to each other. With respect to the question of historical continuity, first, he points out that his position does not deny a historical continuity. Such continuity is affirmed in his very insistence upon the *"dass"* rather than the *"was,"* his insistence that the kerygma, while not interested in historical information about Jesus, was centrally concerned to affirm *that* the heavenly Lord was one with Jesus of Nazareth. Had there been no Jesus, there would have been no kerygma.[19] Secondly, Bultmann investigates current attempts to demonstrate a material relation that goes beyond this *"dass."* Some have sought to do this by arguing that the kerygma includes a picture of the historical Jesus and his work. But Bultmann points out that kerygmatic traditions prior to the gospels do not contain such a picture. Hence, the debate boils down to whether the gospels, as one form of the kerygma, can be regarded as a kerygmatic tradition which included a picture of the historical Jesus. Bultmann first argues the point, which by now is hardly contested, that the gospels do not have the kind and amount of historical information needed for a biography. To be sure, some historical information can be inferred from the Synoptics, information which Bultmann summarizes. He senses, however, that the great difficulty in working out a picture of the historical Jesus is that one cannot know how Jesus faced his death. The predictions of the passion are *vaticinia ex eventu,* and the psychological argument by Fuchs emphasizing the impact of John the Baptist's death is not convincing, since Jesus did not understand himself as being at one

---

sition. Cf. also Conzelmann's essay, "Jesus von Nazareth und der Glaube an den Auferstandenen," in *Der historische Jesus und der kerygmatische Christus,* ed. Ristow and Matthiae, 188–199.

[18]*Das Verhältnis der urchristlichen Christusbotschaft. . . .* ET "The Primitive Christian Kerygma. . . ."

[19]*Ibid.,* 8; ET 18.

with John. Furthermore, while we do not really know much about Jesus' last twenty-four hours, we must reckon with the possibility that he was convinced that he was to be killed for the wrong reason, and hence that he looked ahead to his coming death as a meaningless failure.

Now, worthwhile though such information about Jesus' death might be to someone writing a biography or a personality sketch, Jesus' relation to his death is theologically relevant at only one point: When the kerygma speaks of Jesus giving up his life and accepting his death, is this talk about Jesus of Nazareth or, despite the use of his name, talk not about him but about, e.g., a nonhistorical death-resurrection myth? If the former, it is not a matter of how he did or did not interpret what was going on in his final twenty-four hours; it is not a matter of his psychological processes, his stream of consciousness, at any given time. It is a matter of the emergence from Jesus of Nazareth of an understanding of existence consisting in the renunciation of the present evil aeon in order to live, instead, out of the inbreaking kingdom of God as expressed, e.g., in the saying that he who loses his life saves it, and he who saves his life loses it. Bultmann refers to my "avoiding" the problem of our ignorance of how Jesus felt on Good Friday, in that I appeal to the acceptance of death, which emerges pervasively as Jesus' understanding of existence.[20] As a matter of fact my point is one Bultmann himself once made, in asserting that Paul's understanding of existence is implicit in Jesus' thought.[21] I am merely arguing that it is the implicitness of the kerygma in Jesus' understanding of existence that is required by the kerygma's reference to Jesus, if that reference is in fact a fitting one. Since this problem can be met without recourse to the insoluble question of how Jesus felt in his final twenty-four hours, it is methodologically sound to avoid the *cul de sac.*

Bultmann's basic objection to the appeal to the Synoptics is that it involves a "perversion" of the actual situation with regard to those sources. "The combination of historical report and kerygmatic christology in the synoptics is not intended to legitimize the ke-

---

[20]*Ibid.,* 11, n. 18. ET 23, n. 17.
[21]*Glauben und Verstehen* (Tübingen: Mohr, 1933), Vol. I, 196ff.; ET *Faith and Understanding* (London: SCM, and New York: Harper & Row, 1969), Vol. I, 228ff.

rygma of Christ by means of history, but the other way around, to legitimize so-to-speak the history of Jesus as messianic, by putting it in the light of the kerygmatic christology."[22] Bultmann appeals in this connection to Hans Conzelmann's presentation of the messianic secret.[23] Now the view of the messianic secret originally held by Wrede and Bultmann does support Bultmann's present position: Unmessianic stories became acceptable only with the help of the excuse that Jesus kept his messiahship secret; i.e., the historical Jesus was acceptable only when he no longer posed a threat to Christology, but had been brought indirectly into conformity with Christology. But Bultmann has not revised his use of the messianic secret to conform to Conzelmann's view of the messianic secret, which is explicitly a reversal of the traditional interpretation of Wrede and Bultmann. Prior to Mark, the oral tradition had already become messianic or Christological. Mark's work consists in superimposing upon this Christological tradition his own paradoxical understanding of the kerygma, explicated in terms of the secretness of the messiahship. Thus, two kerygmatizing phases are involved. The congregation made use of the Jesus tradition to present its Christology. But this Christology seemed inadequately kerygmatic to Mark. So, rather than returning to the Pauline alternative of proclaiming only the cross, Mark accepted the principle that the Jesus tradition must itself present the true kerygma. Accordingly, he corrected the Jesus tradition to bring it into line with the true kerygma, thereby producing the *genre* "gospel." If thus the Jesus tradition was corrected by the kerygma, that tradition was already of such theological relevance that the question of whether it conformed to the kerygma was crucial not only for it but also for the kerygma.[24]

This emergence of the Jesus tradition into the light of history in Mark had a background in primitive Christian debate, to which

---

[22]*Das Verhältnis* . . ., 13. ET 24–25.

[23]"Gegenwart und Zukunft in der synoptischen Tradition," *ZTK*, LIV (1957), 293–95, ET "Present and Future in the Synoptic Tradition," in *God and Christ: Existence and Providence, Journal for Theology and the Church*, V (1968), 26–44.

[24]Cf. the similar but independent argument by Gerhard Ebeling, *Theologie und Verkündigung: Ein Gespräch mit Rudolf Bultmann, Hermeneutische Untersuchungen zur Theologie*, Vol. I, 1962, Appendix 7, "Die Frage nach dem theologischen Motiv der Evangelienbildung," 125–27; ET *Theology and Proclamation: Dialogue with Bultmann* (Philadelphia: Fortress Press, 1962), Appendix 7, "The question of the theological motive behind the formation of the Gospels," 130–33.

recent research has drawn our attention. Since Bultmann has taught us that believing the kerygma involves committing ourselves to a specific understanding of existence, we are now in a position to correlate debates about Christian existence with Christological developments, and out of this combination to reconstruct meaningful segments of primitive Christian history previously only vaguely sensed. There emerged in Paul's Corinthian congregation, as can be inferred from First Corinthians, a protognostic perception of existence, according to which the baptized are already in glory and thus are beyond historical existence with all its temptations and suffering.[25] According to this view, one is united with the resurrected Lord, not with the earthly Jesus; indeed, Jesus can even be anathematized (I Cor. 12:3).[26] Paul's letter insists upon the cross "side" of the kerygma as the position where the Christian in this life is to be located, i.e., he insists that the kerygma proclaims the understanding of existence involved in taking up one's cross. Our resurrection must wait its turn, which is not yet but at the end. The power of the resurrection is in this life paradoxical, that is, it is revealed by our suffering, since that power is the power to persist and endure in temptation and suffering. So Paul argues in terms of the cross, rather than in terms of the historical Jesus, although he does repudiate the anathematizing of Jesus.

If First Corinthians succeeded in its objective, Paul's procedure in this case is an instance of Bultmann's oft-repeated appeal to Paul (and John) as evidence that faith does not need the historical Jesus. But the plot thickens when one observes a new heresy being brought into Corinth by wandering evangelists, against whose position Second Corinthians is directed.[27] This new heresy, rather than anathematizing Jesus, preaches "another Jesus" (II Cor. 11:4), and on the basis of this position the evangelists claim to be in a particular way "Christ's" (II Cor. 10:7). If one may infer from their view of a superior apostle their view of Jesus' superiority, the latter view seems to have consisted in regarding Jesus as an impressive, power-

[25]Cf. the summary by Heinrich Schlier, "Über das Hauptanliegen des 1. Briefes an die Korinther," *EvTh*, XI (1948/49), 462–73.
[26]Cf. Walter Schmithals, *Die Gnosis in Korinth*, (Göttingen: Vandenhoeck und Ruprecht, 1956), 45ff., 2d rev. ed. 1965, 117ff., ET *Gnosticism in Corinth*, 1971, 124ff, also Dieter Georgi's review of this work, *VuF* (1958/59), 1960, 91.
[27]Cf. Dieter Georgi, *Die Gegner des Paulus im 2. Korintherbrief*, Wissenschaftliche Monographien zum Alten und Neuen Testament, Vol. XI, 1964.

wielding, miracle-working θεῖος ἀνήρ. In this new heresy much the same understanding of existence is advanced as had previously been advocated in Corinth by appeal to union with the heavenly Lord, except that now the appeal is made to a Jesus tradition. The way that this invasion by a Jesus tradition into the Pauline congregation threatens to sweep everything before it is reflected by the violence of Paul's "tearful letter" (II Corinthians 10–13) and by the extreme anxiety he expresses over how the mission of Titus to Corinth to deliver that letter will turn out (II Cor. 2:12–13; 7:5ff.). It is in this situation that Paul makes his dramatic statement against knowing Christ according to the flesh (II Cor. 5:16), a statement to which Bultmann so often appeals. In sharp contrast to such a fleshly understanding of Jesus and its resultant understanding of existence as a whole, Paul presents in Second Corinthians as in First Corinthians the understanding of existence which he identifies in the kerygma.

If by a supreme effort, yet merely by use of the kerygma and without recourse to a Jesus tradition, Paul thus succeeded in reasserting his authority in Corinth against the "superlative apostles," this solution was to prove increasingly difficult to maintain, as the Jesus tradition continued to circulate. Hence, by the time of Mark, what had been possible for Paul was no longer possible, and Mark had to meet the θεῖος ἀνήρ Jesus tradition on its own ground. His solution was the messianic secret (as interpreted for us today by Conzelmann). Mark's problem, resulting in his messianic secret, was not to impose messiahship upon a non-messianic tradition, but to superimpose upon a θεῖος ἀνήρ Jesus tradition the paradox of Christian existence, the theology of the cross.[28]

It follows that Bultmann's incessant appeal to Paul and John for justification that the historical Jesus is not necessary is valid only in a certain situation and not in another. For it was impossible to worship a heavenly Lord in terms of one understanding of existence and then to identify that Lord with a Jesus tradition expressing a reverse understanding of Jesus' existence. Once such a Jesus tradition had gained common acceptance, it was in terms of that concrete

[28]This thesis has been carried out in detail by Johannes Schreiber, "Die Christologie des Markusevangeliums," *ZTK*, LVIII (1961), 154–83.

situation that the gospel had to be proclaimed. (In every day and age, the gospel must be addressed to concrete situations.) Hence, the question concerning the necessity of a new quest can be relevantly answered not in the abstract, as Bultmann does, but only in the concrete, in the situation in which we find ourselves. And the truth is that our situation is one where hero worship is much more widespread than the acceptance of the kerygma as a norm of existence, where the endless spawning of lives of Jesus is one of the facts of life, and where a church that cannot claim Jesus for its message is in a very awkward position. Although we will not, I hope, turn our backs on the kerygma in another back-to-Jesus movement, but will instead proclaim the kerygma in our situation, we must nevertheless implement the kerygma's claim to be proclaiming a Lord who is one with Jesus, and we must do this by critical participation in the discussion of the Jesus tradition of our day. To this extent, our situation reproduces that of the Synoptics rather than that of Paul.[29] When Bultmann then asks me whether the evangelists' interest in emphasizing the significance of history for faith goes beyond merely affirming the *"dass,"* the fact that the Lord was a historical person,[30] I must reply: In the situation in which the synoptic authors found themselves, one could no longer maintain, as Paul could, the *"dass,"* the historicalness of the worshipped Lord, merely by repeated assertion of the fact of his historicalness. In their situation—and ours—an emphasis upon the *"dass,"* indispensable as it is for the kerygma and for Bultmann, could only be made in terms of the Jesus tradition and not by ignoring that tradition through an exclusive proclamation of the Easter gospel. In their situation, the synoptic writers could retain

[29]To be sure, the synoptics do not use an objective, historical Jesus tradition, but rather the Jesus tradition current in the church of their day. Yet, once we recognize that our historical reconstructions are themselves historically conditioned by our own situation, the actual distinction between our critical-historical reconstruction of Jesus and the kerygmatized Jesus tradition of the Synoptics is relativized. (Indeed, the heroic courage and impressive personality of Jesus proclaimed in the current lives of Jesus are materially not too different from the divine-man Christology visible at times in the oral tradition!) Bultmann tacitly recognizes this when he builds his argument upon the fact that Paul only rarely cites sayings of the Lord and that John does not operate like the Synoptics—points which suggest that Pauline citations and the Synoptic Gospels might to an extent be comparable to the modern quest of the historical Jesus.

[30]*Das Verhältnis* . . ., 13, n. 24, ET 25, n. 23.

the "*dass*" only by maintaining a position on the "*was*," that is, only by making corrective use of the Jesus tradition, by replacing the un-Christian understanding of existence, which had invaded the Jesus tradition, with a Christian understanding of existence. This is the setting, the tendency, which accounts for and justifies the practice of the Synoptics, so different from early kerygmatic texts and from Paul, and which also authenticates the Gospels as canonical and, with them, the validity and necessity of the new quest in our situation.

III

Bultmann then turns to investigate the other way of handling the material relation between Jesus and the kerygma. If the first approach, typified by Althaus, has looked within the kerygma for details of the historical Jesus, the second approach, typified by the new quest, seeks an implicit kerygma in Jesus' deeds and words. This latter can be done either in terms of the traditional historical-critical method, which views the past objectively, or by supplementing that method through understanding history in terms of an existential relation to history ("existentialist interpretation"). From the standpoint of the historical-critical method alone, one can say that Jesus understood himself as an eschatological phenomenon, and that his call for a decision concerning his message implied a Christology, which was explicated in the Christology of the primitive church.[31] Thus, the historical continuity from Jesus the proclaimer to Jesus Christ the proclaimed is made intelligible. But this demonstration of continuity does not answer the question of a material unity of Jesus' words and deeds with the kerygma. Nor can this explanation of historical phenomena of the past "mediate" an eschatological self-understanding to us today, in the way that the kerygma does.

It is the second alternative of "existentialist interpretation" which Bultmann's students have primarily followed and which seems more congenial to Bultmann himself. Accordingly, he commends my "methodological reflections" and the execution of this program by Herbert Braun.[32] But he argues that Ernst Fuchs has not carried

[31]*Ibid.*, 15–17, ET 27–30.
[32]*Ibid.*, 18, ET 31.

through existentialist interpretation consistently and has, indeed, given up that method.[33] For the focus of Fuchs upon Jesus' conduct slides into a historical-psychological interpretation, through considering that conduct perceptible to an objectifying view. Jesus' self-understanding and his decision are treated by Fuchs as phenomena observable to the objectifying historian, that is, Jesus' self-understanding is assumed to be self-conscious. Furthermore, the arguments by Fuchs that Jesus' parables defend his conduct and that he himself had made the same decision as he summoned others to make are regarded as psychological observations irrelevant to the understanding of existence implicit in Jesus' message. Rather than affirming that existentialist interpretation leads to our being called upon to believe, Fuchs reflects upon Jesus' faith and his prayer life. The guiding question of a material continuity between Jesus and the kerygma should rather have raised the question of whether those who hearkened to Jesus before Easter had the equivalent to faith in the kerygma.

There is an odd parallel between this criticism of Fuchs and a common criticism of Bultmann. According to this criticism, Bultmann's insistence upon the necessity of the unique event of the past is held to be inconsistent with, or at least unnecessary to, the self-understanding involved in the kerygma. For, according to Bultmann, the self-understanding involved in the kerygma consists materially in understanding oneself as dependent for one's Christian existence on that once-for-all saving event. It seems inconsistent, therefore, that in investigating the self-understanding involved in Jesus' message, Bultmann should ignore this possibility and sense only the psychologizing overtones in the treatment by Fuchs. Fuchs has most recently shifted his terminology from Jesus' self-understanding to his time-understanding, which may clarify the distinction between psychological observations falling outside an existentialist interpretation and structures relevant to an existentialist interpretation.[34]

[33]*Ibid.*, 18–20, ET 31–33.
[34]Cf. "Das Zeitverständnis Jesu," a lecture course of 1959–60, published in *Zur Frage nach dem historischen Jesus*, 304–76. In *Kerygma und historischer Jesus* (160, 2d ed., 224), I attempt to achieve this goal in the presentation of my own position by replacing the term "self-understanding" with "understanding of existence," which is in turn defined in terms of Jesus' eschatological "understanding of the

Bultmann criticizes similarly Ebeling,[35] Bornkamm, and Käsemann for not distinguishing clearly between an existentialist interpretation and an objectifying view.[36] On the other hand, he identifies Herbert Braun as the most consistent user of the existentialist method.[37] Braun does not ask about historical continuity but about the material consistency between the self-understanding in the proclamation of Jesus and the self-understanding in the proclamation of the church. By going behind the terminology to the latent intention, Braun succeeds in showing the material unity of the kerygma about Christ with the preaching of Jesus. Bultmann concedes that I, by "raising programmatically the requirement of existentialistic interpretation," attain the same goal. He accepts my formulations of this understanding of existence, but then questions whether, in my analysis of the formal structure of Jesus' sayings, I have succeeded in identifying in Jesus the existentialist dialectic of believing existence which he finds first emerging explicitly in Paul and John.[38]

I am indebted to Schubert M. Ogden at this point for having called Bultmann's attention to statements of his own which are in substance the same as mine. Bultmann has replied to this that in his statements equivalent to mine, he had in mind the existentialist meaning of Jesus' message, while in his statements denying the dialectic in Jesus, he had in mind Jesus' self-consciousness. Bultmann concedes that Jesus was conscious of a chronological "betweenness" with respect to the old and the new aeons. But Jesus was not conscious of the fact that his message of his chronological

---

present." In Fuchs' essay, "Das Neue Testament und das hermeneutische Problem," *ZTK*, LVIII (1961), 198–226, which he considers an indirect reply to Bultmann's criticism, he presents Jesus' message in terms of such an "understanding of time."

[35]Cf. Ebeling's detailed reply to Bultmann, *Theologie und Verkündigung. Ein Gespräch mit Rudolf Bultmann*, ET *Theology and Proclamation: Dialogue with Bultmann*, esp. chap. 3, "Kerygma and the historical Jesus," 32–81, which not only in its title but also in its argument has much in common with my position with regard to Bultmann. Unfortunately this work appears too late (end of April, 1962) to be included in the present paper other than in such a note as this added at the time of proofreading. See my *Kerygma und historischer Jesus*, 2d ed., 1967, esp. 72–78.

[36]*Das Verhältnis* . . ., 19–21. ET 33–35.

[37]*Ibid.*, 21–22. ET 35–36.

[38]*Ibid.*, 22; 23, n. 72. ET 36; 38, n. 72.

interim served to place his hearers in a paradoxical, material "be-tweenness," with which my existentialist interpretation has to do, and which was to become conscious in Paul and John. Thus, a distinction is again made between "implicit" and "explicit," be-tween "self-understanding" and "self-consciousness." Since my case does not depend on whether Jesus' self-understanding emerged into his self-consciousness, the material distinction between my position and Bultmann's tends to disappear. R. H. Fuller's argument that there is a "greater degree" of fulfillment in the kerygma than in Jesus, a view which Bultmann follows in criticizing the new quest,[39] thus becomes a distinction only on the conscious level of formula-tion, not at the existential level of meaning.

However, Bultmann adds that there is a material difference be-tween Jesus and the kerygma, in that the kerygma not only presents the paradox of future and present as a possibility for understanding one's existence, but also calls for faith in Jesus Christ. Here is the point at issue between Bultmann and myself in our understandings of Jesus: I have argued that implicit in Jesus' message there is a structure corresponding to the kerygma's reference to the once-for-all event of cross and resurrection. I do not have in mind predictions of the passion or messianic claims, against which Bultmann rightly but one-sidedly protests, but rather the presupposition, upon which Jesus' ministry was built, of divine intervention in the last hour. Thus, the debate over whether we should study Jesus historically depends to some extent upon the outcome of such study—a fact which need embarrass not those who maintain the theological rel-evance of such study, but only those who deny it.

Yet the question of the material relationship between Jesus and the kerygma does not rest simply upon whether there is a consis-tency in the respective understandings of existence. For the "matter" involved in these understandings of existence is not simply or even primarily a human stance, but rather an understanding of God's action as the context of one's existence. It is this action of God as the "matter" or "content" of Jesus' understanding of existence that cannot be carried over into the present by historical research. Bult-mann asks critically:

[39] *Ibid.,* 27. ET 42.

Does Jesus' eschatological consciousness mediate an eschatological self-understanding to the person who perceives it as a historical phenomenon? But that is precisely what the kerygma intends, which as kerygma claims to be an eschatological occurrence (2 Cor. 5:18–20; John 5:24; etc.), which as direct address grants death and life (2 Cor. 2:15f.). Does Jesus' claim of authority, perceived as a historical phenomenon, reach beyond the time of his earthly activity? Does the exhortation and reassurance of the historical Jesus, in its "unmediatedness," reach later generations? But it is precisely that which happens in the kerygma, in which it is not the *historical* Jesus but the *Exalted* who says: "All power has been given me." The Christ of the kerygma has so-to-speak pushed the historical Jesus to one side and now addresses with authority the hearer—every hearer. How then can one speak of a likeness of Jesus' activity with the kerygma in the sense that in Jesus' deed and word the kerygma is already contained *in nuce?*[40]

This argument seems to me to rest upon a failure on Bultmann's part to make a distinction between two meanings of the word kerygma. For "kerygma" is used to mean both the content of primitive Christian preaching and the act of preaching then and now. One can perhaps say that the English term, as popularized by C. H. Dodd, is most commonly used to refer to the content of primitive Christian preaching, whereas Bultmann normally has in mind the authoritative act of preaching. I would agree with Bultmann that the encounter with God does not take place in the modern historian's existentialist interpretation, but rather in the confrontation with the proclamation of the church (in the broadest sense). But the use of the same word, kerygma, both for the church's act of preaching and for the content of the Easter message of cross and resurrection obscures the fact that the problem of Jesus' message as against that of the modern preacher is no different from the problem of primitive Christianity's message as against that of the modern preacher. A historian's reconstruction, for example, of the pre-Pauline kerygma is just as non-kerygmatic as is the historian's reconstruction of Jesus. Yet since the rise of historical-critical method, the historical kerygma has been a legitimate and necessary subject of inquiry—not to replace the minister's preaching, but to improve it. The denial of the relevance of the historical study of Jesus can be separated only in an arbitrary way from a denial of the relevance

[40]*Ibid.*, 17. ET 30.

of historical-critical and existentialist exegesis of the New Testament text. Just as one can say that historical-critical and existentialist interpretation of the New Testament is not of the *esse* of preaching, but belongs to the *bene esse* of preaching, so one can say that in our situation the historical study of Jesus is not of the *esse* of preaching, but belongs to its *bene esse*. Thus, the basic refutation of Bultmann's position on the relevance of the historical Jesus is that if carried to its ultimate consequence it would prove too much. It would bring to an end the scholarly study of the Bible and historical scholarship in general as having any function for the church. At stake ultimately is the relevance of biblical and historical scholarship for the church, a point which is by no means always conceded by the church but upon which we at least should be of one mind.

VIII

ALBERT SCHWEITZER'S *QUEST OF THE HISTORICAL JESUS* TODAY

A. THE NATURE OF SCHWEITZER'S ACHIEVEMENT

The search for the Jesus of history—as an activity distinct from faith in Jesus Christ—is a phenomenon of modern times. It began with the Enlightenment, toward the end of the eighteenth century, and dominated critical theology throughout the nineteenth century. The debate about the historical Jesus in the twentieth century is a debate with that mainstream of nineteenth-century theology. Yet few have read the massive and inaccessible tomes from that period. Hence it is fortunate indeed that one of the truly great human beings of our century has provided us with a classic that brilliantly analyzed this period of research. A study of it is prerequisite to a relevant participation in the debate with which the present volume is concerned. Hence we present a critical analysis of Schweitzer's masterpiece, designed to bring into focus the issues he identified as they bear upon the discussion today.

Schweitzer's book was entitled in German *From Reimarus to Wrede: A History of Research on the Life of Jesus*.[1] As this title indicates, the book belongs to the *genre* of scholarly reports on a period of research

---

[1]The first edition appeared in 1906 under the title *Von Reimarus zu Wrede: Eine Geschichte der Leben-Jesu-Forschung.* The second enlarged edition of 1913 was entitled simply *Geschichte der Leben-Jesu-Forschung.* It has been reprinted unaltered; the sixth edition, 1951, included a new Introduction by Schweitzer. The most recent, seventh edition, in two-volume paperback format, 1966, contains the present essay as an Introduction; the references here to the German original are to that edition. The ET of the first edition by W. Montgomery was entitled *The Quest of the Historical Jesus: A Critical Study of its Progress from Reimarus to Wrede.* It appeared in 1910, and has been subsequently reprinted, supplemented (only in the third, British edition, 1954) by Schweitzer's Introduction to the sixth German edition, and by the present essay in the first Macmillan paperback edition of 1961, to which reference is made in the notes that follow. The revisions and new chapters added in the second German edition are not available in English; yet they tend to be laborious and today outdated, in distinction from the first edition, which presents in classical form the permanently relevant material.

about a given problem. The kind of reading usually encountered in this *genre* of literature can be rather laborious, even in such thoroughly competent and informative instances as occur in journals specializing in this kind of thing, such as the *Theologische Rundschau* or the *Philosophische Rundschau*. Hence one is hardly prepared for the creative potentialities of this *genre* actualized in unsurpassable form by Schweitzer. Perhaps one might put beside it Karl Barth's *Protestant Thought: From Rousseau to Ritschl*.[2]

A less famous but nonetheless impressive further instance of the creative potentiality lurking in this *genre* of literature characterizes the *genre's* scope as follows: "In conformity with its objective of presenting the history of a problem, it concentrates on just those phenomena in the history of theology that actualize most decisively one after the other the possibilities that are given in the structure of the problem."[3] Schweitzer, himself deeply involved in research about the historical Jesus, was the first to grasp the structure of the problem and its possibilities as these had emerged in the course of the history of research. He summarized this structure in terms of three basic either/or decisions through which research of necessity had passed: "Strauss posed the first: Either purely historical or purely supernatural. The Tübingen School and Holtzmann worked out the second: Either Synoptic or Johannine. Now we have the third: Either eschatological or uneschatological!"[4] This is the distilled quintessence of the quest of the historical Jesus.

There were to be sure minor inaccuracies and omissions in Schweitzer's book,[5] and there are other and more recent reports on

---

[2]ET (1959) of *Die protestantische Theologie im 19. Jahrhundert: Ihre Vorgeschichte und ihre Geschichte*, 1947, based upon lecture courses at the University of Bonn in 1932–1933.

[3]Christian Hartlich and Walter Sachs, *Der Ursprung des Mythosbegriffes in der modernen Bibelwissenschaft (Schriften der Studiengemeinschaft der Evangelischen Akademien* 2), 1952, 1.

[4]*Geschichte*, 254, *Quest*, 238.

[5]The confusion of Wilhelm Ferdinand Wilke with Christian Gottlob Wilke (*Quest*, 112, n. 1) was noted by Julius Wellhausen and corrected already in the second German edition. Cf. *Geschichte*, 147, n. 26. The omission of English language material was largely rectified with the help of Burkitt in the second German edition. Cf. *Geschichte*, 29. Schweitzer has also been reproached for omitting mention of Martin Kähler's work of 1892, *Der sogenannte historische Jesus und der geschichtliche, biblische Christus*, ET *The So-Called Historical Jesus and the Historic Biblical Christ*, 1964. Yet this is a work that first came into prominence with the rise of Form Criticism (cf. the reprints of 1928, 1953, 1961). Its omission by Schweitzer was at that time not surprising, and was not a material defect, in that reference

research in this area that supplement it.[6] But if one has read them, one is all the more amazed at the undistracted persistence with which Schweitzer worked out a brilliant thesis as he worked his way through enormous masses of literature. Some of the works he treats extended to thousands of pages. Yet he worked with such intellectual concentration that he emerged with a thesis that brought to the surface what had really transpired, what was of real relevance to the core of the problem. Rarely have the basic decisions responsible for major advances in research been more clearly disengaged from the mass of literature in which they might seem to have been floundering without apparent direction. Schweitzer grasped the three creative epochs in the quest of the historical Jesus—the Thirties, Sixties, and Nineties of the last century—each at its decisive point. Thus he lets us participate in the decisions that are the inner life of the history of that research. It is his achievement that this history still confronts us today, not just as interesting (or boring) background material, but as laying an intellectual claim upon us as we for our part confront the problem of the historical Jesus. It is this intellectual claim that is now to be laid out.

B. THE EITHER/OR DECISIONS OF NINETEENTH-CENTURY RESEARCH

To be sure the first either/or is oddly formulated: "Either purely historical or purely supernatural." For in his presentation of Strauss, Schweitzer had emphasized the fact that Strauss overcame this an-

---

to it would have simply been further documentation for the path from David Friedrich Strauss to William Wrede, a path Schweitzer presented with full clarity. Cf. his comments on the materially parallel position of Georg Wobbermin in the second German edition, 521. To be sure, one difference is that with Kähler the kerygmatic nature of the Gospels had a conservative rather than a radical twist. Perhaps the most interesting omission from Schweitzer's presentation is the scissors-and-paste effort of Thomas Jefferson to reconstruct from the canonical gospels a historically valid biography, published by the U.S. government in 1904 under the title *The Life and Morals of Jesus of Nazareth.*

[6]E.g. the first chapter of Maurice Goguel's *Vie de Jésus,* 1932, second edition entitled *Jésus,* 1950, ET *The Life of Jesus,* 1933; C. C. McCown, *The Search for the Real Jesus: A Century of Historical Study,* 1940. Pedantic treatments of the French and English language literature are found in C. H. Hoffmann, *Les vies de Jésus et le Jésus de l'histoire,* 1947, and Otto A. Piper, "Das Problem des Lebens Jesu seit Schweitzer," *Verbum Dei manet in aeternum* (Otto Schmitz Festschrift), 1953, 73–93. Cf. also the anthology ed. by Harvey K. McArthur, *In Search of the Historical Jesus,* 1969. German bibliography is found in Dieter Georgi, "Leben-Jesu-Theologie," *RGG,* third edition, IV (1960), 249f.

tithesis, dominant in the antecedent period, and replaced it with something new: "The supernatural explanation of the events of Jesus' life had been followed by the rational [historical] explanation. It was as presumptuous as had been its predecessor, which interpreted everything supernaturally, in that it now presumed to make everything intelligible as natural occurrence. Both have said everything they had to say. Out of their struggle was born the new solution, the mythical interpretation."[7] But the emergence of the new from this struggle is hardly made clear by posing the issue as that of a choice between the old alternatives. The structure of the problem is further complicated by referring to it at times as a creative "dialectic" rather than an either/or. In fact Schweitzer here replaced his basic thesis of an either/or choice with the Hegelian pattern of a synthesis: "It [sc. the mythical interpretation] is, according to Hegelian method, the synthesis of the thesis, represented by the supernatural explanation, with the antithesis, represented by the rationalistic interpretation."[8]

In any case, the mythical position advocated by Strauss could not itself be validated by Hegelian philosophy. Rather, as Schweitzer quotes Strauss, "the decision can be confidently entrusted to historical criticism."[9] Yet Schweitzer understood Strauss only as a Hegelian, as indeed he has usually been understood—and all the more readily dismissed. It was first the research survey of 1952 alluded to above, tracing *The Origin of the Concept of Myth in Modern Biblical Research,* that brought to light the real background of Strauss' point of departure: the "Mythical School." The Oxford scholar and Anglican Bishop of the eighteenth century, Robert Lowth, had understood myth as *stilus parabolicus,* which the Göttingen classicist C. G. Heyne interpreted as *sermo mythicus.* It was this understanding of the mythical that the "Mythical School" applied to biblical studies: J. G. Eichhorn and J. P. Gabler[10] toward the end of the eighteenth century were the first biblical scholars to make use of the category of the mythical, understanding it as a form of expression historically necessary during the infancy of the human race *(aetas mythica).* W. M. L. de Wette—and, following

---

[7]*Geschichte,* 117, *Quest,* 80.
[8]*Geschichte,* 117, *Quest,* 80.
[9]*Geschichte,* 149, *Quest,* 114.
[10]Mentioned *Geschichte,* 115, *Quest,* 78.

him, Strauss—used it as a philosophy-of-religion category in the sense of a necessary form of expression for religious feeling in general. It is in this context that we are to understand the "historical criticism" that Strauss applied to the life of Jesus. For it is only in these terms that the surprising tendency and the short-range outcome of his criticism become intelligible. "The supernatural interpretation, as that which at least respects the wording of the text, comes off much better than does the rational interpretation, whose underhanded dealing is mercilessly exposed on all sides."[11]

Schweitzer adds: "Thus the terrain was prepared on which research today operates." One would think he had in mind his own solution, which declares the supernatural (understood not as miraculous, but as impractical, fanatical) to be historical. Such a synthetic position could indeed seem to correspond with that of Strauss, when the latter's position is regarded as the synthesis within a dialectic movement rather than as an either/or choice. Yet the synthesis would not be the same in the two cases. In Strauss's case it would be between rationalism's rejection of the historicity of the supernatural and supernaturalism's affirmation that the text has the supernatural in mind, the result of which is a mythical reading of the text—whereas the synthesis in the case of Schweitzer's solution would be between rationalism's insistence upon the nonmiraculous historicity of the narrative and supernaturalism's insistence upon the impossibility of explaining the given text in terms of normal human pragmatism and psychology, the result of which is the eschatological explanation of Jesus' odd history. Thus when one analyzes the nature of the continuity Schweitzer suggests between Strauss and his own position, one sees that they actually fall on opposite sides of the debate. This is true both when the issue is cast in the dialectic terms of a synthesis and when it is posed in the either/or terms for which Schweitzer's basic schematism calls. In passing Schweitzer does use such a formulation: "Myth or history."[12] When the supernaturalism of traditional orthodoxy is thus replaced by the concept of myth engendered by the Mythical School, Strauss' position emerges as a real alternative to that of Schweitzer. Hence Schweitzer is obliged to obscure for his own time

[11]*Geschichte*, 120, *Quest*, 84.
[12]*Geschichte*, 148, *Quest*, 113.

the decision of the 1830s that fell according to Schweitzer's own assessment in favor of the supernatural, or, more exactly, in favor of the mythical: "Strauss' *Life of Jesus* is for modern theology something different from what it was for his contemporaries. For them it was the work that cleared away historical faith in miracles and vindicated the mythical interpretation. But we discover in it also what is historically positive, in that the historical personality that towers above the myth was a Jewish Messianic pretender who lived in a purely eschatological world of thought. Strauss is not only a destroyer of untenable solutions, but also the prophet of a scholarship to come."[13]

In spite of the truth of this statement, the more direct inference from the first either/or decision in the quest of the historical Jesus is not the position of Schweitzer himself, but rather that of his opponent William Wrede. In Schweitzer's day this may not have been as obvious as it is now in retrospect. For the "offense that the term myth aroused, in that the recollection of pagan mythology shrouded it in ambiguity," was not only a "major difficulty" in Strauss' time,[14] but in Schweitzer's time as well. The chapters Schweitzer added to the second German edition of his work on "The Most Recent Contestation of the Historicity of Jesus" and "The Discussion of the Historicity of Jesus" make this quite clear. For "myth" implied skepticism as to historicity, with debunking overtones. In this connotation Schweitzer himself could not accept Strauss' side of the first either/or. Hence he retreated to the ambivalence of the antecedent term "supernaturalism," by which Strauss meant (unhistorical) myth but Schweitzer (historical) apocalypticism. But then Schweitzer added a fourth either/or, in which he rejected the bypassed ingredient in Strauss' mythical solution, namely historical skepticism. Thus Schweitzer in effect sided against Strauss, while claiming credit for carrying through to its ultimate consequence Strauss' solution.

The second either/or was: "Either Synoptic or Johannine." Of course the question of the sources was already implicit in the first either/or, even though it was only rarely grasped in the debate with Strauss. "The only person who understood what was at stake was

[13]*Geschichte*, 131, *Quest*, 95.
[14]*Geschichte*, 115, *Quest*, 78.

[the fundamentalist] Hengstenberg. He alone saw what it implied that scholarly theology, which had first acknowledged the mythical to be in the Old Testament, and then in the infancy and resurrection stories of the Synoptics (for which reason it felt obliged to surrender the first three Gospels and retain only the fourth Gospel), was now besieged by Strauss in its last stronghold."[15] The new answer to the question of the sources was the so-called Two-Document Hypothesis, to the effect that the traditions shared by Matthew and Luke were derived from two relatively old and reliable sources they both used: The Gospel of Mark and a collection of sayings today called Q. This theory was generally regarded as a liberation from Strauss, in that it seemed to provide a reliable basis for a Life of Jesus derived from the Synoptic Gospels (without, to be sure, the infancy and resurrection stories,[16] which are missing in Mark and Q). This upgrading of the Synoptics was all the more welcome in view of the fact that the Tübingen School had drawn attention to the gnostic background of the Gospel of John, with the result that this Gospel had by and large been eliminated as a historical source.

In research since that time the Fourth Gospel has hardly played an important role in the quest of the historical Jesus. This is true in spite of the fact that Rudolf Bultmann vindicated it theologically over against Schweitzer's own theological depreciation of it. Bultmann also corrected some of the grounds for excessive historical skepticism prevalent in the Johannine research of the nineteenth century by means of his early dating of Gnosticism and hence of the Gospel of John and his assumption of a Miracles Source lying behind the Fourth Gospel. Yet given such corrections,[17] the schol-

[15]*Geschichte*, 149f., *Quest*, 115.
[16]*Geschichte*, 354f., *Quest*, 307f.
[17]Cf. Rudolf Bultmann, "Die Bedeutung der neuerschlossenen mandäischen und manichäischen Quellen für das Verständnis des Johannesevangeliums,"*ZNTW*, XXIV, 1925, 100–46, esp. p. 144: "To formulate the problem as sharply as possible, one could say that we must reckon with the possibility that Johannine Christianity represents an older type than does Synoptic Christianity. Of course this is not said from the point of view of one defending traditionalism. For there can be no doubt but that the Gospel of John as we have it is later than the Synoptics. It both presupposes the literary type of the Gospel created by Mark and shows the influence of specifically Hellenistic ideas. Yet this *is* to say that the emergence and message of Jesus perhaps stood much more closely in connection with the gnostic baptismal movement, in terms of which the Gospel of John is to be understood, than the Synoptic tradition reveals." It has been especially C. H. Dodd who has attempted to vindicate the historical in the Gospel of John. Cf.

arly reconstruction of the message of the historical Jesus still depends on the Synoptics and thus on the Two-Document Hypothesis. The durability of this solution to the Synoptic problem is confirmed by the inadequacy of the attacks upon it that appear from time to time.[18] Nor is the validity of this solution in terms of literary criticism diminished by the invalidity of some of the historical inferences initially drawn from it. The oft-cited historical nearness and the plastic detail of the Marcan presentation were rightly shown by Wrede and Schweitzer to be only a modern reading of the Marcan text. For the literary solution as such was not affected by their discovery that a dogmatic construction was the formative element in the Gospel of Mark. Similarly this literary solution was not shaken by Karl Ludwig Schmidt's recognition[19] that the sequence of events in Mark, previously held to be reliable, is in fact unhistorical—nor by study of the literary *genre* of Q[20] that has tended to invalidate the earlier assumption that Q was free of theological tendency.[21] Such corrections do in part relativize the distinction between the Synoptics and John, but they also define that distinction more exactly and thus validate it in its more modest dimensions. It is precisely in this context that Schweitzer's second either/ or choice is confirmed as a decision made once for all.

Yet Schweitzer did not quite know how to make use of the Two-Document Hypothesis for his own solution. The decision for the priority of Mark had been connected with a modern theological interest he did not share: To produce a psychologically understandable, reasonable life of Jesus. This could be attained only by spir-

---

his *Historical Tradition in the Fourth Gospel*, 1963. Yet both scholars worked out their understandings of Jesus' message on the basis of Synoptic sayings, even though their interpretations were each in its way Johannine.

[18]Cf. William R. Farmer, *The Synoptic Problem: A Critical Analysis*, 1964, and the devastating review by F. W. Beare, *JBL*, LXIV, 1965, 292–97.

[19]*Der Rahmen der Geschichte Jesu*, 1919, second edition 1963.

[20]Cf. my essay "Logoi Sophōn: Zur Gattung der Spruchquelle Q," *Zeit und Geschichte* (Bultmann *Festschrift*), 1964, 77–96, ET "Logoi Sophōn: On the *Gattung* of Q," 1968; and Helmut Koester, "Gnomai Diaphoroi: The Origin and Nature of Diversification in the History of Early Christianity," *HTR*, LVIII, 1965, 279–318, esp. 298–303. Both essays are reprinted in revised form in *Trajectories through Early Christianity*, 1971, first paperback edition 1979, 71–113, 114–57.

[21]Adolf von Harnack, *Beiträge zur Einleitung in das Neue Testament*. II. *Sprüche und Reden Jesu: Die zweite Quelle des Matthäus und Lukas*, 1907, for example, 163, 171, etc., ET *New Testament Studies*. II. *The Sayings of Jesus: The Second Source of St. Matthew and St. Luke*, 1908, 167f., 193ff., 234f., etc.

itualizing away Jesus' eschatological world of thought. Schweitzer saw quite correctly that it had been the advocates of this connection who carried on "the dull and dogged struggle against eschatology down to the end of the century," with the result that "the Marcan hypothesis impeded the quest of the historical Jesus to an almost unbelievable extent."[22] And he conceded: "The small amount of sayings material in Mark does not provide much resistance" to "the possibility of a literary elimination of eschatology."[23] In the Introduction to the sixth German edition this recognition is formulated positively: "The key to understanding is provided by Matthew in the material he supplies beyond what is found in Mark."[24]

When one inquires why Schweitzer did not here appeal to Q, two reasons emerge: The sayings on the imminence of the end that were decisive for Schweitzer occur in the material found only in Matthew; since they are not in Luke, they can hardly be attributed to Q. Furthermore, Schweitzer's argumentation is based on the "connection of the events of Jesus' life." Q does not provide this, since it is largely an unconnected series of individual sayings. If the sequence in Matthew seemed preferable to that of Mark as a basis for the historical connection, the Gospel of Matthew could not be explained as a secondary composition based on working the crucial eschatological sayings into the Marcan framework. For example: The crucial turning point in Jesus' public ministry for Schweitzer is the nonfulfillment of the prediction of the end at Matt. 10.23, resulting in Jesus' withdrawal to the north with the disciples alone. But this key verse is missing from Mark: "The fact which alone makes it possible to understand is missing in this Gospel." But it is also missing from Luke, and hence presumably from Q. Thus the necessity for regarding Matthew not as a secondary compilation from Mark, Q and oral tradition, but as a primary record of the historical sequence. "In the sayings material of Matthew, which one had believed to be able to scatter in at the appropriate place, lie hidden facts, unfulfilled and hence all the more important."[25] Hence Schweitzer preferred to speak vaguely of "the two oldest Synoptics."

[22]*Geschichte*, 168, *Quest*, 134.
[23]*Geschichte*, 248, cf. also 417, 589, *Quest*, 226, cf. also 360; the third reference is not in ET.
[24]*Geschichte*, 36, *Quest*, absent except in the third British edition of 1954, xi.
[25]*Geschichte*, 417f., *Quest*, 360.

In fact, the Introduction to the sixth German edition makes it clear that Schweitzer was not able to use the Two-Document Hypothesis for his own solution.[26] This is all the more awkward in that this hypothesis had been successfully established by his teacher Heinrich Julius Holtzmann as the valid basis for deciding the second either/or. For this reason Schweitzer's solution marks a step backward in terms of the question of the sources. It is no doubt in part for this reason that Schweitzer's own view was not accepted by critical scholarship in the form he gave it. Already Schweitzer's English adviser,[27] F. C. Burkitt, observed in the Preface to the English edition of 1910: "He has his own solution of the problems, and it is not to be expected that English students will endorse the whole of his view of the Gospel history, any more than his German fellow-workers have done."

The third either/or was: "either eschatological or uneschatological." This issue was Schweitzer's major criterion as he presented the history of research from Reimarus to Wrede. Here lies the one-sidedness of the book as well as its most important achievement. He exposed the fact that the quest of the historical Jesus had "spiritualized" Jewish eschatology, that is to say, assimilated it to our modern religious ideals. The result was "that this supposedly historical Jesus is not a purely historical figure, but rather a construction artificially planted into history."[28] The impossibility of such a policy cannot be contested today. Whereas Johannes Weiss carried through a certain "weakening of the eschatological point of view"[29] in the second edition of his epochal work on *Jesus' Proclamation of the Kingdom of God*[30] of 1900, which could easily have misled theology into dismissing the eschatological issue as only a bad dream, Schweitzer posed this issue in his book of 1906 once for all in inescapable fashion. To this extent twentieth-century theology has in him rather than in Weiss its point of departure.

---

[26]*Geschichte*, 36, *Quest*, absent except in the third British edition of 1954, xi. Cf. already *Geschichte*, 441, *Quest* 392, and from the second German edition (not in ET), 550f. In the second German edition (not in ET), 596ff., Schweitzer seeks to interpret Q in his favor, using as his point of departure a remark by Harnack: ". . . traces of a temporal order."

[27]See *Geschichte*, 29 and 585 (neither reference is in ET).

[28]*Geschichte*, 356, *Quest*, 309.

[29]*Geschichte*, 349, *Quest*, 302.

[30]ET (1971) of *Die Predigt Jesu vom Reiche Gottes*, 1892.

Schweitzer appended a fourth either/or, which had pervaded his brilliant research report just as much as did the other three: "One must either be quite skeptical, as was Bruno Bauer, and contest equally all reported facts and connections in Mark; or, if one proposes to build a historical Life of Jesus on Mark, one must recognize the Gospel as a whole as historical, in view of its connections running through the whole material. In the latter case one must then explain why individual reports, such as the feeding of the multitude and the transfiguration, are bathed in supernatural light, and what is the historical basis that underlies them. A separation between the natural and the unnatural in Mark is arbitrary, since for him the supernatural belongs to history."[31] Here Schweitzer is actually debating less with Bruno Bauer, who had long since passed from the stage, than with William Wrede, whose work *The Messianic Secret*[32] was the live alternative to Schweitzer's own sketch of Jesus' life, published at the same time with almost the same title as that of Wrede: *The Messianic and Suffering Secret*.[33] Of course in this debate Schweitzer could hardly build upon Matthew, as he had in the eschatological issue. For as Schweitzer himself recognized, Wrede had convincingly shown "that the view of the Messianic secret no longer had the significance for Matthew that it had for Mark."[34] Hence if the secret is to be regarded as historical, then the Marcan presentation must be shown to be historical.

What view does one take on this debate today? In an essay "On the Question of the Messianic Secret in Mark" Eduard Schweizer summarized the present state of the question: "Already in 1901 Wrede demonstrated that the Messianic secret is an editorial construction by Mark and belongs to the history of dogma, not to Jesus' life. One cannot go back behind that decision."[35] For indeed

---

[31]*Geschichte*, 355, *Quest*, 308.

[32]ET (1971) of *Das Messiasgeheimnis in den Evangelien: Zugleich ein Beitrag zum Verständnis des Markusevangeliums*, 1901, third edition, 1963.

[33]The second fascicle of *Das Abendmahl im Zusammenhang mit dem Leben Jesu und der Geschichte des Urchristentums: Das Messianitäts- und Leidensgeheimnis: Eine Skizze des Lebens Jesu*, 1901, ET (1950) *The Mystery of the Kingdom of God*. Cf. *Geschichte*, Ch. 19–20, *Quest*, Ch. 19: "Thoroughgoing Scepticism and Thoroughgoing Eschatology."

[34]*Messiasgeheimnis*, 153, ET (1971) *The Messianic Secret*, 154. Cf. also *Geschichte*, 417, *Quest*, 359.

[35]"Zur Frage des Messiasgeheimnisses bei Markus," *ZNTW*, LVI, 1965, 1–8; the quotation is from the opening of the essay.

the "unconnectedness" in the Gospel of Mark discovered simultaneously by Wrede and Schweitzer cannot in many cases be derived from Jesus' eschatological consciousness, as Schweitzer proposed; furthermore, his efforts to refute Wrede's explanation based on Mark's editorial tendency are often not convincing.[36] In another context Schweitzer conceded, with regard to the thesis "that the two oldest Synoptics transmit real history," that he himself "goes to the extreme limit and is not even willing to consider such passages as inauthentic that are rejected by the main stream of theology."[37] For this reason one again and again runs across instances in Schweitzer's solution[38] where things are taken as historical which not even conservative criticism so regards today. In fact one cannot "build a historical Life of Jesus on Mark."

It is of course true that Schweitzer wrote at a time when the assumption of inauthenticity served as a convenient way to avoid matters difficult to handle theologically. "But what survives as historical in the Gospels for the main stream of theology, if it considers itself obliged to sacrifice hand and foot and eye because of the offense of pure eschatology?"[39] It is not surprising that Schweitzer expected the final acceptance of the eschatological nature of Jesus' message to strengthen confidence in the historicity of the Gospels. "One can in general say that the progressive recognition of the eschatological nature of Jesus' teaching and action carried with it a progressive justification of the Gospel tradition. A series of sections and speeches that had been endangered because they seemed meaningless from the viewpoint of modern theology, taken as the norm of the tradition, have now been saved."[40] It is true that Wrede had not fully reached the eschatological understanding of Jesus' message, and to this extent Schweitzer was indeed ahead of him. But Schweitzer lacked the perspective of today to see that in substance Wrede did not derive the Messianic secret in Mark from his view of Jesus; Wrede's editorial explanation is not the last stand of the nineteenth century, but rather the first of the twentieth century. He had floundered upon what we today call Redaction Criticism. But Schweitzer

---

[36]*Geschichte*, 403 and Ch. 20, *Quest*, 351 and the criticism of Wrede, 340–350.
[37]*Geschichte*, 493 (not in ET).
[38]*Geschichte*, Ch. 21, *Quest*, 351ff.
[39]*Geschichte*, 275, *Quest*, 265; cf. also *Geschichte*, 589 (not in ET).
[40]*Geschichte*, 292, *Quest*, 286.

uncritically identified the either/or as to whether the Messianic secret in Mark was historical or not with the either/or about eschatology. "There is either the eschatological solution, which then at one stroke elevates the unsoftened, disconnected and contradictory Marcan presentation as such to the status of history; or there is the literary solution, which regards the dogmatic and foreign element as the earliest evangelist's interpolation into the tradition about Jesus and thus eliminates from the historical life of Jesus his Messianic claim as well. *Tertium non datur.*"[41] The third position whose existence Schweitzer denied has subsequently become visible. It is derived from the fact that the two problems, which are of course interrelated, do not condition each other as directly as Schweitzer assumed. Hence his identification of the two had been replaced by their more careful differentiation. It is only by recognizing this that one can understand the apparent paradox in the history of the problem: Wrede was correct on the issue of literary criticism, in deriving the Messianic secret from Marcan theology; Schweitzer was correct on the issue of historical criticism, in affirming the eschatological nature of Jesus' ministry.

C. THE SCHOOL OF THOROUGHGOING ESCHATOLOGY

Schweitzer distinguished between the "Eschatological School" represented by "Johannes Weiss and his followers" on the one hand and his own "Thoroughgoing Eschatology" on the other. "They related eschatology only to Jesus' preaching . . . rather than clarifying, in terms of the newly-won insight, the whole public ministry, the events' connections and lack of connections. . . . It is quite inexplicable that the Eschatological School, given its insight into the eschatology of Jesus' preaching of the reign of God, did not hit upon the thought of the dogmatic element in Jesus' history as well."[42] This was for Schweitzer a crucial omission. "The decision does not lie [in Jesus' teaching], but rather in the investigation of the whole course of Jesus' life."[43] However, the explanation of what seemed inexplicable in Weiss' procedure lies in what Schweitzer himself had recognized to be the basic distinction between Weiss and earlier eschatologists: "Weiss expresses it in a scientifically un-

[41]*Geschichte,* 388, *Quest,* 337.
[42]*Geschichte,* 402, *Quest,* 350f.; cf. also *Geschichte,* 552 (not in ET).
[43]*Geschichte,* 269, *Quest* 257.

assailable way."[44] What Schweitzer felt obliged to add to Weiss on the basis of the assumed historical sequence in "the two oldest Synoptics" is not scientifically unassailable; the New Testament scholarship of the twentieth century, under the influence of Wrede, has been obliged to remove it again. In our time there has been only one serious effort to argue that there is a chronological sequence of individual stories presupposed by Mark. But this attempt, by C. H. Dodd,[45] was soon shown by D. E. Nineham to be untenable.[46]

Nonetheless "Thoroughgoing Eschatology" became a school. For its discoverer and his work were indeed impressive. And the book not only carried through its working hypothesis tenaciously, but it also suggested a series of derivative theses that Schweitzer himself did not work out in detail. For example: "It is high time that, instead of merely asserting Pauline influences in Mark, some proof of the assertion should be given. How would Mark look if it had really come from the hands of a Paulinist?"[47] Hence a young *Privatdozent* at the University of Bern, Martin Werner, aroused by Arthur Drews' book *The Gospel of Mark as a Witness against the Historicity of Jesus*,[48] published in 1923 his study on *The Influence of Pauline Theology in the Gospel of Mark*,[49] "dedicated to Albert Schweitzer in genuine admiration and gratitude," and seeking to

[44]*Geschichte*, 256, *Quest*, 241.

[45]"The Framework of the Gospel Narrative," *ExpT*, XLIII, 1932, 396–400, reprinted in his volume of collected essays, *New Testament Studies*, 1953, 1–11.

[46]"The Order of Events in St. Mark's Gospel: An Examination of Dr. Dodd's Hypothesis," *Studies in the Gospels* (R.H. Lightfoot *Festschrift*), 1955, 223–39. Cf. also above, Ch. 3, Section 1.

[47]*Geschichte*, 353, *Quest*, 306; cf. also *Geschichte*, 384, *Quest*, 333, *Geschichte*, 427, 547, 598f. (all three absent from ET).

[48]*Das Markusevangelium als Zeugnis gegen die Geschichtlichkeit Jesu*, 1921.

[49]*Der Einfluss paulinischer Theologie im Markusevangelium: Eine Studie zur neutestamentlichen Theologie* (BZNTW 1). To be sure, Werner's method of proof consists in showing that the "Pauline" elements in Mark are actually common early Christian traits, which in no way puts in question the derivation of Marcan theology from the kerygma or the Marcan community's theology rather than from the historical Jesus. Willi Marxsen, *Der Evangelist Markus: Studien zur Redaktionsgeschichte des Evangeliums* (FRLANT 67), 1956, second edition, 1959, 83–92, ET *Mark the Evangelist: Studies on the Redaction History of the Gospel*, 1969, 126–138, has at one point narrowed the effect of Werner's monograph, in that he has indicated that the Marcan concept "gospel" may be influenced by Pauline theology. Eduard Schweizer, "Die theologische Leistung des Markus," *EvTh*, XXIV, 1964, 337–55, esp. 346, has also shown that the Pauline and Marcan identification of the gospel with Jesus Christ is to be understood in Mark in terms of the contemporary Deutero-Pauline sense of the gospel as a mystery—an insight that leads us back toward Wrede rather than Schweitzer.

confirm in detail Schweitzer's hypothesis of the non-Pauline character of Mark. And yet this defense on the part of the School of Thoroughgoing Eschatology did not ultimately validate Mark as an objective historical report. The Messianic secret has remained a construct of Marcan theology.

A further outgrowth of Schweitzer's thesis is the recent discussion of the problem of the delay of the *parousia*. Schweitzer himself had noted: "The whole history of 'Christianity' down to the present day, its real inner history, is based on the 'delay of the parousia,' that is, the fact that it did not take place, hence the abandonment of eschatology, and the resultant progressive de-eschatologizing of religion."[50] This relevance of *The Quest of the Historical Jesus* in providing a critical norm for evaluating modern theology was also picked up by Martin Werner in his book of 1924 on *The Ideological Problem in Karl Barth and Albert Schweitzer.*[51] Werner's pupil Fritz Buri followed this up in 1935 with a work on *The Significance of New Testament Eschatology for Recent Protestant Theology: An Attempt to Clarify the Problem of Eschatology and to Achieve a New Understanding of its Real Concern.*[52] In the Preface Buri gave as his point of departure: "Nevertheless theology has kept strangely quiet—I could almost say weirdly quiet—about the thesis proposed for discussion years ago by Albert Schweitzer concerning the delay of the *parousia* and the de-eschatologizing that necessarily results from it."

Theology did not stay quiet for long. For during the second World War, when German language theology was largely limited to Switzerland, there was a sharp debate on this issue between Bern and Basel, between the "free-thinking" and "positive" parties of Swiss Church politics, between Thoroughgoing Eschatology and *Heilsgeschichte.*[53] This tempest in a teapot reached no satisfying so-

---

[50]*Geschichte*, 417, *Quest*, 360.

[51]*Das Weltanschauungsproblem bei Karl Barth und Albert Schweitzer.*

[52]*Die Bedeutung der neutestamentlichen Eschatologie für die neuere protestantische Theologie: Ein Versuch zur Klärung des Problems der Eschatologie und zu einem neuen Verständnis ihres eigentlichen Anliegens.* More recent interpretations of contemporary theology from the viewpoint of thoroughgoing eschatology are Ulrich Neuenschwander, *Protestantische Dogmatik der Gegenwart und das Problem der biblischen Mythologie,* 1949; *Die neue liberale Theologie: Eine Standortbestimmung,* 1953, and Martin Werner, *Der protestantische Weg des Glaubens,* I. *Der Protestantismus als geschichtliches Problem,* 1955; II. *Systematische Darstellung,* 1962.

[53]The debate was instigated by Werner's book, again carrying out a *desideratum* of Schweitzer, on *Die Entstehung des christlichen Dogmas,* 1941, ET (of an abridged

lution until the program of demythologizing that had been proposed by Rudolf Bultmann in Germany as early as 1941 became known after the war and was able in the postwar period to put the delay of the parousia in proper perspective: It was a problem only in the story line of the Jewish apocalypticism used as a vehicle of thought by primitive Christianity, not a substantive problem affecting the existential meaning of Christianity.

The School of Thoroughgoing Eschatology has continued to be active down to recent times, though in terms of ongoing New Testament scholarship it has become increasingly quaint. For their critical stance toward the renewal of the quest of the historical Jesus, one should consult Werner's essay of 1960: "What Does the Historical Personality of Jesus Signify for Us?"[54] This essay has hardly been noticed.

D. THE BROADER IMPACT OF SCHWEITZER'S WORK

An observation by Karl Barth about Schleiermacher fits Albert Schweitzer as well: His significance is less that of founding a School than that of creating an age.[55] When *The Quest of the Historical Jesus* was written, the eschatological orientation of Jesus' and primitive Christianity's message could only bewilder contemporary theology. But for theology after the first World War, which no longer understood itself in terms of cultural optimism, but more nearly apocalyptically (*The Decline of the West*), Schweitzer's discovery provided an orientation for the new understanding of existence. In his essay

text) *The Formation of Christian Dogma: An Historical Study of Its Problem*, 1957. This led to an exchange with the Basel theologian Oscar Cullmann on the theme of the church's hope in the return of Christ, "Die Hoffnung der Kirche auf die Widerkunft Christi," published in the *Verhandlungen des schweizerisch-reformierten Pfarrvereins*, LXXXIII, 1942, 34ff. Buri entered the discussion with his essay "Das Problem der ausgebliebenen Parusie," *SThU*, XVI, 1946, 97ff. Cullmann replied with an essay "Das wahre durch die ausgebliebene Parusie gestellte neutestamentliche Problem," *TZ*, III, 1947, 177–91, promptly followed by Buri's "Replik: Zur Diskussion des Problems der ausgebliebenen Parusie," 422–28, to which Cullmann had the last word, 428–32.
[54]"Was bedeutet für uns die geschichtliche Persönlichkeit Jesu?" in the symposium edited by H. Ristow and K. Matthiae, *Der historische Jesus und der kerygmatische Christus: Beiträge zum Christusverständnis in Forschung und Verkündigung*, 1960, 614–46.
[55]Karl Barth, *Die protestantische Theologie im 19. Jahrhundert*, 379, ET *Protestant Thought: From Rousseau to Ritschl*, 306. Schleiermacher had himself coined this expression, with reference to Friedrich the Great, in an address at the Berlin Academy of Sciences "Über den Begriff des grossen Mannes."

"Between the Times" Friedrich Gogarten characterized this mood of postwar theology as follows:

> It is the fate of our generation that we stand between the times. We never belonged to the time that is today reaching its end. Will we ever belong to the time that will come? And even if we for our part could belong to it, will it come so soon? . . . Space became free for asking about God. Finally! The times fell apart and now time stands still. . . . It is here that the decision must first be made. Until then we can do nothing with all our heart. Until then we stand between the times. This is a terrible human plight. For all that is human collapses and is ruined, all that was and all that is to be. But for that reason we can—if only we grasp the plight in its depths—ask about God.[56]

Even though from the Alpine security of the Canton of Bern such talk might seem only a less-than-candid evasion of the problem of the delay of the *parousia,* Karl Barth for his part was able to find in it a recognition of the Christian understanding of man's situation before God. In the second edition of his *Romans* this eschatological formulation of that understanding received its classic expression: "Christianity that is not wholly and without exception eschatology has wholly and without exception nothing to do with Christ."[57]

To be sure this did not solve the hermeneutical problem posed by eschatology, but only made it inescapable. It was again Barth who carried through the distinction pointing the way for the future:

> As *parables* of "last things" such distant and yet familiar final possibilities could no doubt be quite instructive and edifying, especially if we are unfortunately too callous to sense the prior parables of "last things" that surround us in the past and present without need of migrations of the soul, ice ages, and falling stars. Yet such final possibilities, no matter how real and plainly visible they may be, are *not* "last things" in the sense of 1 Cor. 15 and the New Testament as a whole. Not even if we conceive of them as preliminaries to physical-metaphysical, cosmic-metacosmic transformations and revolutions of a still more incredible kind. Not even if the picture of these obscure final stories is constructed wholly out of material derived from the Bible and perhaps from 1 Cor. 15 itself. All that is

---

[56]"Zwischen den Zeiten," *ChrW,* XXXIV, 1920, 374–78, reprinted in *Anfänge der dialektischen Theologie* II, ed. by Jürgen Moltmann (*Theologische Bücherei, Neudrucke und Berichte aus dem 20. Jahrhundert* 17), 1963, 95–101, especially 95 and 100, ET "Between the Times," in *The Beginnings of Dialectic Theology,* ed. by James M. Robinson, 1968, 277–82.

[57]*Der Römerbrief,* second edition, 1922, 298, ET *The Epistle to the Romans,* 1933, 314.

transitory is only a parable. The fact that the objects of the biblical world of thought belong to what is transitory, that they serve and do not rule, signify rather than proposing to be the reality itself—on this point at least the Bible itself leaves us in no doubt. Final *things* are as such not *final* things, no matter how great and important they may be. The person who would speak of *last* things would speak of the *end* of all things, of their end understood so absolutely, so basically, of a reality so radically superior to all things, that the existence of all things would be wholly *grounded* in it, in it alone. That is, one would speak of their end that is really nothing other than their beginning. And only that person would speak of the history of the end, end-time, who would speak of the *end* of history, the end of time. But again of its end understood so basically, so absolutely, of a reality so radically superior to all occurrence and all temporality, that in speaking of the finitude of history, the finitude of time, one would at the same time speak of that which grounds all time and all that happens in time. History of the end would have to be for such a person synonymous with history of the *beginning;* the limits of time of which one speaks would have to be the limit of any and every time, and thus necessarily the *origin* of time.[58]

Rudolf Bultmann made Barth's insight exegetically more precise:

It seems to me just as certain that in 1 Cor. 15 Paul is talking of such a history of final things, as that he cannot and does not really wish to speak of such a history. That is to say, one cannot get by in 1 Cor. 15 without thoroughgoing criticism as to the consistency of the content (not only occasionally, as Barth does in verse 29 in spite of himself). For however little Paul proclaims such a thing as an "ideology," he, like anyone else, is under the necessity of saying what he says in the terminology of his ideology. And it is not permissible simply to regard the ideological (in this case mythological) elements as "parable" or to eliminate them by twisting their meaning. What Barth concedes for later Christian eschatologists—that they construct out of the biblical material a history of final things that is really not at all ultimately historic, that is, is not history seen from its end— this is true for Paul as well, who derives his material from Jewish or Jewish-gnostic apocalypticism.[59]

Here Dialectic Theology acknowledges Thoroughgoing Eschatology's insistence upon the apocalyptic nature of primitive Christianity. Equally clear is the acknowledgment of the problem of the delay of the *parousia* in primitive Christianity; indeed it is only now

---

[58]Karl Barth, *Die Auferstehung der Toten: Eine akademische Vorlesung über* 1 *Kor.* 15, 1924, 57f., ET *The Resurrection of the Dead,* 1933, 103f.
[59]From Bultmann's review, "Karl Barth, *Die Auferstehung der Toten,*" *TB,* V, 1926, 1–14, reprinted in *GuV,* I, 1933, 38–64, Quotation is from 52.

that the basic monographs on this topic are produced.[60] The Bultmannian School, though rejected by the School of Thoroughgoing Eschatology, has in effect carried the valid aspects of Schweitzer's exegetical work related to eschatology into the mainstream of current scholarship.

The most important advance in carrying through valid though undeveloped insights of Schweitzer has been at the hermeneutical level. The problem that had plagued the study of the mythological was the fallacy Hans Jonas aptly characterized as taking the substitute as ultimate, the language for the content; now it has been exposed as such.[61] The result is that mythological language is understood hermeneutically, as the Mythical School had intended from its very beginning.[62] Schweitzer himself in his final chapter to the

[60]Especially Lucan theology has been made intelligible in these terms by Hans Conzelmann, *Die Mitte der Zeit: Studien zur Theologie des Lukas* (BHT 17), 1954, fifth edition 1964, ET *The Theology of St. Luke*, 1960. This approach was carried through the Synoptics and Acts by Erich Grässer, *Das Problem der Parusieverzögerung in den synoptischen Evangelien und in der Apostelgeschichte* (BZNW 22), 1957, second edition 1960. Cf. for 2 Peter, Ernst Käsemann, "Eine Apologie der urchristlichen Eschatologie," *ZTK*, XLIX, 1952, 272–96, reprinted in *EVB*, I, 1960, 135–57, ET "An Apologia for Primitive Christian Eschatology," *Essays on New Testament Themes* (SBT 41, 1964), 169–95. Such research is all the more valid due to the fact that it does not claim too much. Typical of this precision is Conzelmann's article "Jesus Christus," *RGG*, third edition, III, 1959, 633, ET *Jesus*, 1973, p. 51: "Jesus did not project a system of doctrine. To the contrary, it is striking that the doctrine of God and eschatology, eschatology and ethics, seem at first glance to stand relatively unrelated side by side." Cf. his essay "Zur Methode der Leben-Jesu-Forschung," *Die Frage nach dem historischen Jesus, Beiheft*, 1 to *ZTK*, LVI, 1959, 10, ET "The Method of the Life-of-Jesus Research," *The Historical Jesus and the Kerygmatic Christ: Essays on the New Quest of the Historical Jesus*, ed. by Carl E. Braaten and Roy A. Harrisville, 1964, 65.

[61]"All this derives from an unavoidable fundamental structure of the spirit as such. That it interprets itself in objective formulae and symbols, that it is 'symbolistic,' is the innermost nature of the spirit—and at the same time most dangerous! In order to come to itself, it necessarily takes this detour via the symbol, in whose enticing jungle of problems it tends to lose itself, far from the origin preserved symbolically in it, taking the substitute as ultimate. Only in a long procedure of working back, after an exhausting completion of that detour, is a demythologized *(entmythologisiert)* consciousness able terminologically to approach directly the original phenomena hidden in this camouflage (cf. the long path of the dogma of original sin up to Kierkegaard!)." *Augustin und das paulinische Freiheitsproblem: Eine philosophische Studie zum pelagianischen Streit* (FRLANT 44), 1930, second edition, 1965, 82.

[62]The hermeneutical scope of the Mythical School is not limited to such works as G. L. Bauer's *Entwurf einer Hermeneutik des Alten und Neuen Testaments* of 1799, but rather dominated the whole movement, as Hartlich and Sachs, *Der Mythosbegriff in der modernen Bibelwissenschaft*, emphasize again and again (cf. "Hermeneutik" in their index, 182).

second edition had already proposed such a procedure, although he did not carry it out in detail: "Actually it cannot be a matter of separating between the transitory and the permanent, but only of translating the basic thought of that ideology into our concepts."[63] De-eschatologizing had often functioned as a vestige of the method that eliminated the subject matter along with the temporally limited and offensive forms of expression that nonetheless had preserved that subject matter;[64] now it was brought by demythologizing to its real goal, of liberating the meaning from the language. For demythologizing, as existentialistic interpretation, attempts to comprehend, translate, and thus make accessible to us the understanding of existence coming to expression in the mythological form.[65]

In recent years, now that theological research has achieved at least some impression of the eminent significance of eschatology, a new question is being posed: Does not eschatology, and indeed apocalypticism, involve more in material content than has been assumed thus far? Ernst Käsemann took the initiative in contesting "that the earliest theology" can be adequately grasped "in terms of the theme of existence."[66] For him, however, apocalypticism is not to be found in Jesus, but only in the Church since Easter. "The question of authenticity is of course not irrelevant for the historian, who would like to grasp the center and extension of Jesus' message

[63]*Geschichte*, second German edition, 625 (not in ET). Note the change in tone from the first edition, *Quest*, 401: "It is not given to history to disengage that which is abiding and eternal in the being of Jesus from the historical forms in which it worked itself out, and to introduce it into our world as a living influence. It has toiled in vain at this undertaking."

[64]Cf. the fluctuating position of Fritz Buri, *Die Bedeutung der neutestmentlichen Eschatologie für die neuere protestantische Theologie*, 1935, who in Ch. 8 interprets "de-eschatologizing" as the elimination of the imminent expectation of the end of the world, which belongs "to the essence of New Testament eschatology," 51, whereas in Ch. 16 he interprets the "will to life fulfillment" as the "essential content of eschatology."

[65]For this distinction between elimination and interpretation cf. Rudolf Bultmann, "Neues Testament und Mythologie: Das Problem der Entmythologisierung der neutestamentlichen Verkündigung," which appeared first in 1941 in *Offenbarung und Heilsgeschehen* (BEvTh 7), 27–69 and was reprinted in *Kerygma und Mythos* (TF 1), 1948, 15–53, esp. 25, ET *Kerygma and Myth: A Theological Debate*, 1953, reprinted 1961, 1–44, esp. 12.

[66]"Zum Thema der urchristlichen Apokalyptik," *ZTK*, LIX, 1962, 257–84, esp. 265f., reprinted *EVB*, II, 1964, 105–31, esp. 113, ET "On the Subject of Primitive Christian Apocalyptic," in *New Testament Question of Today*, 1969, pp. 108–137.

as exactly as possible. And it should not be a matter of indifference to the theologian either, who, at least since Albert Schweitzer, has had the problem of apocalypticism thrown up to him, its necessity, significance and limits. Albert Schweitzer and his pupils themselves got in the way of the task they recognized, first by making the whole question into a problem of the quest of the historical Jesus, and then by seeking to explain the earliest history of dogma in terms of the delay of the *parousia*. Both times they ended in a dead end street."[67] It is true that Käsemann has not yet fully succeeded in delimiting Jesus' message from apocalypticism[68] and in formulating what he would like to assert as the material content of apocalypticism that goes beyond Bultmann's existentialistic interpretation.[69] Yet at the same time current theology is undertaking the attempt, in analogy to Ernst Bloch's work on *The Principle of Hope*,[70] to interpret apocalypticism as the prototype for a valid and necessary theology of hope for the future.[71]

In view of the importance generally accorded to Schweitzer's masterpiece, and the role he has played in the world in our century, it is a bit surprising to note how little his own specific theological solution to the problem of the historical Jesus has been followed. The positivistic historiography of his first edition, which replaced the previously assumed contemporaneity of Jesus with a purely an-

---

[67]"Die Anfänge christlicher Theologie," *ZTK*, LVII, 1960, 162–185, esp. 179, reprinted *EVB*, II, 1965, 82–104, esp. 99, ET "The Beginnings of Christian Theology," in *New Testament Questions of Today*, pp. 82–107.

[68]*ZTK*, LVII, 1960, 179f., reprinted *EVB*, II, 100.

[69]For the discussion with Käsemann cf. Gerhard Ebeling, "Der Grund christlicher Theologie," *ZTK*, LVIII, 1961, 227–44; Ernst Fuchs, "Über die Aufgabe einer christlichen Theologie," *ZTK*, LVIII, 1961, 245–67. All three essays are brought together in English translation in *Apocalypticism: Journal For Theology and the Church* 6 (1969): "The Beginnings of Christian Theology," 17–46; "The Ground of Christian Theology," 47–68; "On the Task of a Christian Theology," 69–98. See also Rudolf Bultmann, "Ist die Apokalyptik die Mutter der christlichen Theologie? Eine Auseinandersetzung mit Ernst Käsemann," *Apophoreta* (Haenchen Festschrift, BZNW 30), 1964, 64–69.

[70]*Das Prinzip Hoffnung*, 1954.

[71]Wolfhart Pannenberg, ed., *Offenbarung als Geschichte (KuD, Beiheft* 1, 1961), ET *Revelation as History*, 1968; Pannenberg, *Grundzüge der Christologie*, 1964, ET *Jesus—God and Man*, 1968, 2d ed. 1977; Jürgen Moltmann, *Theologie der Hoffnung: Untersuchungen zur Begründung und zu den Konsequenzen einer christlichen Eschatologie* (BEvTh 38, 1964, 5th ed., 1965), ET *The Theology of Hope: On the Ground and the Implications of a Christian Eschatology*, 1967; Gerhard Sauter, *Zukunft und Verheissung: Das Problem der Zukunft in der gegenwärtigen theologischen und philosophischen Diskussion*, 1965.

tiquarian role for him, fitted well into Schweitzer's own Christ mysticism. For he put in antithetic relationship the "historical Jesus" and the "eternal Jesus."[72] Jesus "passed by our time and returned into his own. . . . Jesus means something to our world because a mighty spiritual force streams forth from him and flowed over our world too. This fact is neither shaken nor solidified by historical knowledge."[73] Thus in debate over the historicity of Jesus in the second edition (chaps. 12–13) Schweitzer came to the conclusion "that religion by its very nature is independent of all history."[74] It is in the context of this theological repudiation of historical research that we are to understand Schweitzer's allusions to "Jesus' spirit," his advocacy of "Jesus mysticism,"[75] his solution to the Pauline problem in terms of *The Mysticism of Paul the Apostle*,[76] and the breakthrough in his own meditation to "reverence for life." Thus in his mystical way he left behind his original point of departure in historical research addressed to the quest of the historical Jesus—just as he replaced his academic position with that of the doctor of Lambarene.

There were trends early in our century congenial to Schweitzer's mysticism and to his rejection of historical research. It was this broader context that provided the cultural cause for the suspension of the quest of the historical Jesus. Yet the precise form this took after World War I was not what one would have anticipated on the basis of the situation just prior to that war. First steps toward neo-idealism matured as—existentialism. The Form-Critical School, in spite of the fact that it was repudiated by the School of Thoroughgoing Eschatology, seemed initially to be carrying through the implications of Schweitzer's mysticism (though in terms of Wrede's research rather than Schweitzer's). But Dialectic Theology thought in terms of the historicness of existence, and not only understood Paul eschatologically rather than mystically, but also accorded a significance to Jesus' historicity denied it by the School of Thoroughgoing Eschatology.[77] Thus there has grown out of Dialectic

[72]*Geschichte*, 367, *Quest*, 321.
[73]*Geschichte*, 620f., *Quest*, 399.
[74]*Geschichte*, 519 (not in ET).
[75]*Geschichte*, 629 (not in ET).
[76]ET (1931) of *Die Mystik des Apostels Paulus*, 1930.
[77]Cf. Frits Buri, "Entmythologisierung oder Entkerygmatisierung der Theologie," *KuM*, II, 1952, 85–101.

Theology a new quest of the historical Jesus, though to be sure in a way quite different from the way Schweitzer would have envisaged it. Schweitzer's emphasis upon the chronological sequence of the Synoptic Gospels is emphatically denied in the quest that has followed upon Form Criticism. And the context of this new research is neither positivistic historicism nor mysticism, but existentialistic interpretation and the new hermeneutic that has grown out of it.

Yet it is indicative of the incisiveness of Schweitzer's thought that he himself transcended the historicism of his original position, making it rather ironic when his good name is appealed to in this sense to criticize the new quest of the historical Jesus.[78] For in the "concluding reflection" of the second edition Schweitzer himself transcended historicism in a nonmystical way by pointing to the "living relationship" present in all understanding and thus pointing to the necessity of a new hermeneutic. It may come as a surprise to those unfamiliar with that edition, never translated into English, that Schweitzer here traced the end of the quest not to the modernizations in the liberal Lives of Jesus, as is usually done in his name, but rather to the shallowness of objective research, a breakdown at the hermeneutical level.[79]

> Our time and our religion . . . found in themselves no equivalents to Jesus' thoughts. For this reason they were not able to translate his ideology out of the thought patterns of Late Judaism into their own insights. They simply lacked resonance. Hence the historical Jesus of necessity remained in large measure foreign to them, not only with regard to the raw material of his conceptualizations, but also in his essence. His ethical radicalism and the directness and power of his way of thinking remained unattainable for them, since they did not think or experience anything comparable. . . . Hence it was the lack of inner congeniality in willing, hoping and longing that rendered

[78]Cf. Oscar Cullmann, "Unzeitgemässe Bemerkungen zum 'historischen Jesus' der Bultmannschule," in the Symposium ed. by Ristow and Matthiae, 1960, 266–80, esp. 267, ET "Out of Season Remarks on the 'Historical Jesus' of the Bultmann School," USQR, XVI, 1961, 131–48, esp. 132.

[79]Schweitzer wrote at a time when hermeneutic had reached its lowest ebb in theological scholarship. One may note Ernst von Dobschütz' appeal in his Rectoral Address of 1922: "What one calls hermeneutic, once the discipline carried on most actively, then criminally neglected for two generations, must be awakened to new life." Vom Auslegen insonderheit des Neuen Testaments (Hallesche Universitätsreden 18), reprinted in his book Vom Auslegen des Neuen Testaments, 1927, 5. Cf. the history of hermeneutic in this period in my essay "Hermeneutic since Barth," The New Hermeneutic (New Frontiers in Theology, 2, 1964), 1–77.

a real knowledge of the historical Jesus and a comprehensive religious relationship to him an impossibility.[80]

To whatever extent such basic deficiencies can be overcome by methodological progress, it is not in terms of claims to "objectivity" surpassing the "subjectivism" of "existentialism," but rather in the hermeneutical reflection initiated precisely by existentialistic interpretation.

Schweitzer was optimistic. "If the signs do not deceive, we are moving toward such a time."[81] In his discussion of the reception that the first edition of his work received, he said: "Thoroughgoing Eschatology can patiently wait for its time to come. . . . Sooner or later the hour will strike. . . ."[82] These formulations call to mind the Preface to Karl Barth's *Romans:* "If I do not deceive myself, this book can do now its own specifically limited service. . . . But should I deceive myself in the happy prospect of a general new seeking and searching after the biblical message, this book has time to wait. Romans itself is also waiting."[83] It was Barth's promise that was first fulfilled. Schweitzer's Preface to the sixth German edition shows that he was hardly able to see in subsequent developments the fulfillment of his own hopes. Yet everyone who reads Schweitzer's book from the present state of research as a participant in the discussion will not fail to sense the affinity between Schweitzer's book and subsequent research, rooted in the depth with which Schweitzer laid hold of the central issues and the breadth of vision found only in the truly great men of an age.

---

[80]*Geschichte,* 624f. (not in ET).
[81]*Geschichte,* 626 (not in ET).
[82]*Geschichte,* 589 (not in ET).
[83]Preface to the first edition of the *Römerbrief,* 1919, vi; ET of the second edition, 2.

IX

JESUS' PARABLES AS GOD HAPPENING

When one speaks of Jesus' parables, one would seem to have shifted attention from the content of Jesus' message to its form. Yet an artist senses that the work of art conveys its message in terms of its form, for form conveys vision, orientation, ultimate concern. Hence the deeper level of a culture's history can be traced in the ongoing metamorphosis of its forms.

> A literature has its history in its forms; hence every real history of literature will be a history of forms.[1]

It has been the fate of Jesus' parables that they were initially preserved by an unartistic tradition which mistook their form for that of allegory—and that their modern study, while rectifying this initial misinformation, has been carried on by the scholar rather than the poet. Among New Testament scholars there have been, however, two who are themselves practicing poets, Ernest Cadman Colwell and Amos N. Wilder, and it is they who have led the way in transcending the dichotomy between matter and form in the interpretation of Jesus' parables.

> His words have the rugged fiber of the cypress tree and the jagged edge of the crosscut saw. . . . [This rigorous element] is not a veneer upon the surface of his message but the natural grain of the wood. It takes its nature from the content of his words.[2]

> There was something in the nature of the case that evoked this rhetoric, something in the nature of the Gospel.[3]

---

[1]Franz Overbeck, "Über die Anfänge der patristischen Literatur," *Historische Zeitschrift,* XLVIII (1882), 417–72; reprinted as a booklet (Darmstadt: Wissenschaftliche Buchgesellschaft, 1954), p. 12.

[2]Ernest Cadman Colwell, *Jesus and the Gospel,* (New York and London: Oxford University Press, 1963), pp. 33, 35.

[3]Amos N. Wilder, *The Language of the Gospel: Early Christian Rhetoric* (New York: Harper & Row, 1964), p. 79.

This insight, obvious and spontaneous for the artist, has been reached also by the laborious efforts of the theologian.

> The procedure of the parables is none other than that of leading the hearer into confrontation with the reality of man's being, in order thereby to make intelligible what is involved in God's coming. One could understand this as a guide to the very nature of theological language.[4]

It is the purpose of the present essay to explicate this recent theological development in the understanding of the parable as such.

A. THE PARABLES AS EXPRESSIONS OF THE TEMPORALITY OF EXISTENCE

The modern study of the parables began in 1888 with the publication of the first volume of Adolf Jülicher's *Die Gleichnisreden Jesu,* in which he carried through his now classical distinction between the parable and the allegory. This distinction holds, irrespective of the kind of parable involved. The parable may merely compare a typical scene, such as a harvest, with another dimension, such as the Kingdom of God. Such a comparison is called a "similitude." But the typical scene may be replaced by the narration of a distinctive story. Such a story may, like the similitude, consist of a comparison, drawing an analogy between two dimensions of reality, such as a story comparing the hiring and paying of day laborers in a vineyard with one's relation to God. In this case one has to do with the "parable" in the narrower sense. Or the story may consist of an example from the same dimension of reality as the point being scored, such as the parable of the Pharisee and the tax collector, illustrating correct religious prayers and attitudes. In this case one has to do with the "illustration," or "exemplary story," a model of right conduct. Regardless of which subdivision may be involved, all parables have as their distinctive characteristic the fact that they are each scoring a single point.

The allegory, on the other hand, tells a story seemingly cast within one dimension of reality, for example, an absentee landowner with sharecroppers in his vineyard. Actually it is disinterested in

[4]Gerhard Ebeling, "Hauptprobleme der protestantischen Theologie in der Gegenwart," *ZTK*, LVIII (1961), 135; ET "The Chief Problems of Protestant Theology in the Present," *Distinctive Protestant and Catholic Themes Reconsidered, Journal for Theology and the Church,* III (1967), 162–63.

that dimension—hence the frequent lack of verisimilitude. Instead, the allegory has in view a "higher" dimension only partly concealed within the metaphorical language. The result is that the story as story is often sacrificed to the interest of scoring points at the "higher" level throughout as the story progresses. The allegory thus invites the reader to search among the minutiae of the narration for still undiscovered "deeper" meanings, whereas the parable invites the hearer to take to heart even more seriously, to get with, the point being scored.

As with the passage of time, Jesus' parables became farther and farther removed from the context of Jesus' life, in which they had originally been quite intelligible, and became more and more associated with Holy Writ, whose allegorical interpretation was in that day rampant, the more the confusion of genres became inescapable. Even prior to Mark, the parable of the sower had succumbed to this fate, with the result that the parable (Mark 4:3–8) was furnished with an allegorical interpretation (v. 14–20). Other parables were simply transformed into allegories: the parable of the dinner (Gospel of Thomas, Saying 54) became the allegory of the great supper (Luke 14:16–24) and the allegory of the marriage feast (Matt. 22:2–10). In the case of the parable of the wicked tenants, the Synoptic examples (Mark 12:1–11, and pars.) were so shot through with allegory that one despaired of reconstructing a parabolic substratum and hence doubted that this parable (or, more exactly, this allegory) went back to Jesus at all,[5] until the parabolic form turned up in the Gospel of Thomas (Saying 65). Thus, because of their form distinct from the allegorizing proclivity of the primitive church, the parables have become the segment of the teachings of Jesus most widely accepted as authentic by scholars today.[6]

This permanence of Jülicher's basic conclusions has kept his book before the scholarly world to such an extent that advances made since then have consisted largely in revising some aspects in which his work was less than definitive. For Jülicher, the point of the parable was a rational principle, the more universal the better, and

---

[5]Werner Georg Kümmel, "Das Gleichnis von den bösen Weingärtnern (Mark 12:1–9)," *Aux Sources de la tradition chrétienne:* Mélanges offerts à M. Maurice Goguel (Neuchâtel and Paris: Delachaux et Niestlé, 1950), pp. 120–31.
[6]*RGG,* 3d ed., III, 1959, col. 643 (Hans Conzelmann).

usually of a moral nature (since Jesus was envisaged by the Victorians as primarily a moralist). Once the eschatological interpretation of Jesus introduced by Johannes Weiss in 1892 and Albert Schweitzer in 1901 had been widely accepted, a reinterpretation of the overarching orientation of the parable's single point from moralism to eschatology was in order. C. H. Dodd conceded the eschatological nature of Jesus' message, at least to the extent of paying lip service to it, by coining, on the basis of Rudolf Otto's *The Kingdom of God and the Son of Man,* the term that has become the standard characterization of Dodd's whole theological position: "realized eschatology."[7] The adjective "realized" was designed to undo all the mischief wrought by the term "eschatology." Israel's future hope had, in Jesus' view, been "realized" in his public ministry, and hence the church's backward look directed at him has his support, upon which the Establishment is properly established. Dodd was the last and most scholarly defender of antidisestablishmentarianism. The Kingdom is here, not near. Jesus' eschatological parables, *The Parables of the Kingdom,* to use Dodd's title, are interpreted in conformity with this de-eschatologized, since already realized, eschatology.

Needless to say, the futuristically eschatological interpretation of Jesus' understanding of the Kingdom was not overcome with one blow, even though scholars tended to concede to Dodd that the Kingdom in Jesus' view was "dawning," "impinging," or in some sense or other operative in advance in his word and deed, even though its ultimate reality was future, beyond an apocalyptic gulf. Ernst Haenchen proposed for this compromise position the German term *sich realisierende Eschatologie,* "eschatology realizing itself," "eschatology being realized," "eschatology that is in the process of

---

[7]C. H. Dodd, *The Parables of the Kingdom* (London: Nisbet, 1935; rev. ed., London: Fontana Books, William Collins Sons, 1961), p. 40, n. 21, refers to Rudolf Otto, *Reich Gottes und Menchensohn* (Munich: Chr. Kaiser, 1934), which has subsequently appeared in English, *The Kingdom of God and the Son of Man,* tr. by Floyd V. Filson and Bertram Lee-Woolf (London: Lutterworth, 1938, rev. ed., 1943, reprinted 1951). Dodd regards Otto's presentation on pp. 51–73 (pp. 47–63 of the ET) as a definitive refutation of Schweitzer's "thoroughgoing eschatology" *(konsequente Eschatologie),* and hence supports Otto's formulation *der Schonanbruch des Reiches Gottes,* "the already dawning of God's reign." This leads Dodd to replace "thoroughgoing" with "realized" (p. 41), thus arriving at his formulation "realized eschatology."

realization." Joachim Jeremias appropriated this designation, and Dodd gave in.[8] Jeremias' standard work, *The Parables of Jesus,* which has gone through six German editions (from 1947 to 1962) and three English editions (from 1954 to 1963), is built upon this mediating position with regard to eschatology in the parables of Jesus.

This solution is satisfying only to the biblicist who is content to find in modern language a close approximation to what he thinks the biblical language meant, without asking further whether this modern language is intelligible, whether it makes conceptual sense. But in this case probing questions of the contemporary theologian can only be met with embarrassed silence: Just how near? How in the future if already here? Which part here and which part near? How valid when the appointed time has passed?

The Bultmannian school of interpretation introduced at this point the view that "Jesus ignores time." Bultmann coined this phrase to summarize approvingly a speech by Conzelmann, whereupon the latter replied:

> I can accept this formulation—in spite of Käsemann's opposition— if the concept of ignoring is understood intentionally, as a positive qualification, in view of the signs which in the moment announce the Kingdom.[9]

This is not a return to Dodd's denial of futuristic eschatology in Jesus' teaching,[10] but rather an effort to interpret temporal aspects

[8]C. H. Dodd, *The Interpretation of the Fourth Gospel* (Cambridge: At the University Press, 1953), p. 447, n. 1, cited by Joachim Jeremias, *The Parables of Jesus* (rev. ed.; London: SCM, and New York: Charles Scribner's Sons, 1963), p.230, n. 3. Jeremias there referred to a letter of June 20, 1944, from Ernst Haenchen, proposing the term he has popularized. Ernst Käsemann, "Das Problem des historischen Jesus," *ZTK,* LI (1954), 151, reprinted in *EVB,* I (1960), 212, characterized Haenchen's position as "die sich von jetzt ab verwirklichende Gottesherrschaft," "eschatology actualizing itself from now on," ET "The Problem of the Historical Jesus," *Essays on New Testament Themes,* Studies in Biblical Theology, 41, (1964), p. 44, "inaugurated eschatology."

[9]Hans Conzelmann, "Gegenwart und Zukunft in der synoptischen Tradition," *ZTK,* LIV (1957), 288, n. 2. ET "Present and Future in the Synoptic Tradition," in *God and Christ: Existence and Providence, Journal for Theology and the Church,* V (1968), 37, n. 42.

[10]This seems to be assumed by Werner Georg Kümmel, "Die Naherwartung in der Verkündigung Jesu," *Zeit und Geschichte: Dankesgabe an Rudolf Bultmann zum 80. Geburtstag* (Tübingen: J. C. B. Mohr [Paul Siebeck], 1964), pp. 31–46, ET "Eschatological Expectation in the Proclamation of Jesus," *The Future of Our Religious Past,* ed. by James M. Robinson (New York, Evanston, San Francisco, London: Harper & Row, 1971), pp. 29–48.

of Jesus' parables in a way more basic and today more intelligible than are the usual chronological formulations—namely, by interpreting them existentialistically, in terms of the temporality of man's being.

> The message . . . produces the decision "now," in the moment in which it is presented in pictorial garb. . . . The reference to God's reign is connected with Jesus' present preaching not only because it is he who composes these parables; this connection belongs to the very substance of what is narrated. This is interpreted correctly only when the interpretation of what is coming and of Jesus' person form a material unity.[11]

In his antithesis to the tradition of attributing a messianic self-consciousness to Jesus, Bultmann had restricted Christology in Jesus' ministry to what is only implicit in Jesus' role as the "sign" of the imminent and already impinging Kingdom.[12] But Conzelmann picked up the positive implication in Bultmann's restriction and proceeded to use Bultmann's concept of Jesus being "in his own person"[13] the last (ultimate, definitive) sign as the basis for an "implicit" or "indirect" Christology.[14]

Already, Ernst Fuchs had proposed a christological interpretation of the parables:

> We must break with the stiff-necked prejudices to the effect that Jesus' parables apply primarily to our relation to God. It seems to me that they apply primarily to our relation to Jesus himself.[15]

This turn of events was welcomed with open arms by Jeremias:

> I can only affirm with lively approval the determination with which Fuchs sees in the parables of the historical Jesus hidden Christological testimonies to himself.[16]

But the way Fuchs applied it was equally promptly rejected by Bultmann:

> The call [to decision] is "simply the echo of the decision that Jesus

---

[11]Conzelmann, *ZTK*, LIV (1957), 288.
[12]Rudolf Bultmann, *Theology of the New Testament*, I, 43.
[13]*Ibid.*, p. 9.
[14]For further documentation of this development, cf. my *Kerygma und historischer Jesus*, 1st ed., p. 24, n. 6; 2d ed., p. 41, n. 77, and pp. 77f.
[15]Ernst Fuchs, "Bemerkungen zur Gleichnisauslegung," *TLZ*, LXXIX (1954), 345–48, reprinted in his *Gesammelte Aufsätze II. Zur Frage nach dem historischen Jesus* (Tübingen: J. C. B. Mohr [Paul Siebeck], 1960), p. 139.
[16]Jeremias, *The Parables of Jesus*, p. 230, n. 1.

himself had made." That may be correct—but why this reflection, which can only arise out of a biographical interest? This then leads to such an absurd consequence as the view that in the parable of the lost sons (Luke 15:11–32) Jesus is not seeking to teach God's grace open to the sinner, but is rather defending his own conduct. To the extent that this can be accurate at all, it is nonetheless no more than the observation of a psychic motif and says nothing about the intention of the parable and the understanding of existence which underlies it.[17]

To be sure, Fuchs's reflection does have something to do with the historical Jesus. Bultmann himself had pointed out that the decisiveness of Jesus' word implies a Christology and that Jesus' word was constitutive of his person. Hence the relation of the parables to the historical Jesus need not be cast in the biographical and psychological context that Bultmann criticizes and that Fuchs's formulations do at times suggest. For Jesus' parables, such as the prodigal son, were not intended to teach general principles, such as "God's grace stands open to the sinner"; rather, they were intended for the concrete situation in which he spoke, his ministry of risking trust in the power of God's grace. Of course, one could deny that this parable was intended primarily to defend his practice, as the secondary context provided by Luke 15:1–2 suggests, and maintain that it is primarily a further instance of that practice.[18]

---

[17]Rudolf Bultmann, *Das Verhältnis der urchristlichen Christusbotschaft zum historischen Jesus* (Sitzungsberichte der Heidelberger Akademie der Wissenschaften, Philosophisch-historische Klasse, Jg. 1960, 3. Abh.; Heidelberg: Carl Winter Universitätsverlag, 1960), p. 19; ET "The Primitive Christian Kerygma and the Historical Jesus," in *The Historical Jesus and the Kergymatic Christ*, ed. by Carl E. Braaten and Roy A. Harrisville (Nashville: Abingdon Press, 1964), p. 32. Bultmann quotes Fuchs' statement from "Die Frage nach dem historischen Jesus," *ZTK*, LIII (1956), 221f., and paraphrases Fuchs' interpretation of the parable from p. 219 of the same essay. This essay is reprinted in Fuchs' *Gesammelte Aufsätze* II, p. 154 and p. 157; ET by Andrew Scobie, *Studies of the Historical Jesus*, Studies in Biblical Theology, 42 (London: SCM Press, Ltd., 1964), pp. 20 and 23.
[18]This is in fact the direction taken by one of Fuchs' pupils, Eberhard Jüngel, *Paulus und Jesus: Eine Untersuchung zur Präzisierung der Frage nach dem Ursprung der Christologie*, Hermeneutische Untersuchungen zur Theologie, 2 (Tübingen: J. C. B. Mohr [Paul Siebeck], 1962), pp. 160f., over against the alternate emphasis on the part of another of Fuchs' pupils, Eta Linnemann, *Gleichnisse Jesu: Einführung und Auslegung* (Göttingen: Vandenhoeck and Ruprecht, 1961, 3d ed., 1964), ET *The Parables of Jesus* (London: S.P.C.K., 1966); American ed., *Jesus of the Parables: Introduction and Exposition* (New York: Harper & Row, 1967), pp. 69, 73. The weakness of Linnemann's position is the admittedly secondary nature of Luke 15:1–2; the weakness of Jüngel's is his neglect of the story about the elder son in its relevance for the situation of the parable. Over against Jülicher, he is right in emphasizing that the parables are not to be seen in the context of intellectual

Yet if the intention of the parable is to interpret the hearer's existence in terms of God's grace, then the understanding of existence
lying behind it is not only to the effect that risking trust in God's
grace is authentic living, but also that in the encounter with Jesus—
specifically with this parable—one's existence gets involved in this
risk. The parable is intended as a language event potentially ad-
mitting the hearer to God's grace, not as a coded presentation of
an abstract understanding of existence.

Some such understanding of language was implicit in Barth's
theology of the Word and Bultmann's kerygmatic theology. But
such an approach to language has come into its own as the new
hermeneutic, which has become the theoretical context for the new
quest much as was the critical-historical method for the original
quest.[19]

B. THE PARABLES AS GOD'S ADVENT IN LANGUAGE

The new hermeneutic, formally launched by Fuchs's *Hermeneutik* in
1954, has shifted its orientation from an "understanding of existence," derived from the Bultmannian interpretation of the earlier
Heidegger, to an understanding of language, derived from the later
Heidegger. This understanding of language is intended as a corrective of the earlier understanding of language primarily oriented to
"ex-pression," the putting into words of one's own subjectivity
(Schleiermacher-Dilthey) or understanding of existence (Bultmann).

---

debate from which a rational judgment is intended to emerge. But the addition
of the story about the elder son to the well-rounded story of the younger son
indicates that the sinner to whom this parable offers grace is not of the "tax-
collector" type, but rather of the "Pharisee" type. Jüngel concedes (p. 163) that
if the parable defends anything, it is in defense of "trust in the power of love,"
which Linnemann in rebuttal accepts (p. 154, n. 26), but as referring to Jesus'
table fellowship.

[19]It is no coincidence that the research oriented to the new quest has thus far
had its focus in the parables, and that the major exegetical activity related to the
new hermeneutic has been directed toward the parables; indeed, the joint concern
for the new quest and the new hermeneutic is responsible for the number of good
recent treatments of the parables. In addition to the German works of Fuchs's
pupils Jüngel and Linnemann mentioned in the preceding note, this convergence
of interests has produced the following American works: Robert W. Funk, *Language, Hermeneutic, and Word of God: The Problem of Language in the New Testament
and Contemporary Theology* (New York: Harper & Row, 1966); Dan Otto Via, Jr.,
The Parables: Their Literary and Existential Dimension (Philadelphia: Fortress Press,
1967); Norman Perrin, *Rediscovering the Teachings of Jesus* (New York: Harper &
Row, 1967).

In the latter case, language was regarded as appropriate when it stayed within the categories of existence. However, it was seen to have a tendency to objectify existential meaning, the model example being the mythologizing of religion in a mythopoetic culture, which necessitated the demythologizing efforts of the interpreter ("existentialistic interpretation"). But now primal language is understood as called forth by being, by world. Such language itself becomes the most concrete manifestation of being or world, in which sense the later Heidegger says that what speaks is not so much man as language itself. Hence the parable is no longer regarded primarily as expressing Jesus' existential understanding, but rather as the bringing into language of world or being (in Jesus' case, the Kingdom of God).

This new understanding of language as the voice of being is the hermeneutical context in which both a further rectification of Jülicher's analysis of the parable and a transcending of the chronological dilemmas of the various eschatological interpretations have been achieved.

For Jülicher, the form of Jesus' message had nothing to do with the message:

> Not in some formal something, but rather in the content, is located the province of God's son.[20]

Hence, the form need not be derived from the content. It was consistent with this view that Jülicher turned to Aristotle rather than to Jesus[21] to supplement his negative definition of the parable (*not* an allegory) with some positive characterization. The "parable" is one type of proof from example that, as a sort of inductive argument, is one of the common kinds of proof. If a comparison draws attention to the similarity between two concepts and permits a rational judgment with regard to the more obscure on the basis of the "analogy" to the more clear, just so the parable compares one set of concepts to another, or, more precisely, compares the judgment contained in the one set to the judgment that should be inferred with regard to the other. The internal relationship or or-

---

[20]Adolf Jülicher, *Die Gleichnisreden Jesu* (2d ed.; Tübingen: J. C. B. Mohr [Paul Siebeck], 1899), I, 117.

[21]It is especially Eberhard Jüngel, *Paulus und Jesus,* pp. 94–102, who has investigated Jülicher's Aristotelianism.

ganization clearly discernible in the one set of concepts clarifies by analogy the relation only dimly sensed in the other set. The relationship of A to B is analogous to and hence clarifying for that of C to D. We have to do with the classical *analogia proportionalitatis* or *analogia relationis*. The proportionateness of the two sets of concepts means that they share one judgment, the *tertium comparationis*, the single point of the parable. Thus the parable is one of the forms of rational argument, making use of the point of a picture to argue for an equivalent point in another dimension of reality. This means that the parable has a "picture half" (the language of the parable) and a "material half" (the "higher" or "spiritual" dimension, for example, the Kingdom of God). The hermeneutical method for the interpretation of any parable consists simply in setting up this structure and transferring the point of the picture to the higher subject matter. Of course, having seen the point, one could dispense with the picture, and argue the point without the illustration. The parabolic form is ultimately irrelevant.

This understanding of the parable as a form of rational argument antedated by more than a generation the focus upon symbolic language introduced by Ernst Cassirer's *Philosophy of Symbolic Forms* (1923–1929), and hence seems in retrospect all too rationalistic. This is even more the case in view of the understanding of language inherent in the new hermeneutic. For, somewhat like the understanding of language as "performatory" in the English tradition, the new hermeneutic has sought to overcome the dichotomy between act and word by appeal to language as meaningful happening. This understanding of language focuses attention not upon the conceptual information communicated, but rather upon "communication" in the sacramental meaning of the term: communion or participation. Its interest is in what happens when language takes place, the happening it calls forth.

The parable, instead of being structured in terms of two set "halves" sharing a common point, is ordered in such a way as to get in gear with the hearer, engage one in the movement of the story, and release one at its end back into one's own situation in such a way that the parable happens to the situation. But for the parable to be such an event, to expose the truth of the situation, to show up the situation as it truly is, it must be so ordered that the hearer is caught up into the story along with one's situation. Hence the story makes a concession to the hearer—the prodigal son *is* as immoral as a sinner, *is* as unpatriotic as a tax collector, his older brother *is* as worthy as a Pharisee—ensuring thereby that the hearer will get with it. This *captatio benevolentiae* thus gets the parable as language event moving, ensuring that when the parable releases the hearer back into one's own situation, one will see it as what the parable interpreted it to be, and hence have to reappraise it in view of the parable's claim to have exposed its true being. The concession of some truth to the hearer's view of one's situation ensures that the hearer will concede the realism of the speaker's grasp of that situation and hence consider seriously the parable's naming of its true being.[22]

This development of the new hermeneutic's understanding of language has left its trail in the history of modern theological vocabulary, in the shift from "saving history" (von Hofmann-Cullmann) to "saving event" (Bultmann), and then to "language event" (Fuchs) and "word event" (Ebeling).[23] For the Christian message has to do with a particularly acute instance of the convergence of factuality and meaningfulness, in that, to use Bultmann's formulation, a historical occurrence is at the same time the eschatological event. This eschatological meaningfulness that comes with, indeed comes as, the language of the parables, there to happen in Jesus' factuality, is what was lost on the chronological debate about futuristic eschatology, realized eschatology, and eschatology realizing itself. The material role of the language itself in the actualizing of God's reign was overlooked. Hence it is in terms of this bit of unfinished business that the new hermeneutic's contribution to the study of the parables is to be seen.

[22]Eta Linnemann, *Gleichnisse Jesu,* 1st ed., p. 35, designates this kinetic structure of the parable as *Verschränkung,* which *Jesus of the Parables,* p. 27, renders as "interlocking." The term could also be translated: "intertwining," "interlacing." The hearer's assessment of one's situation is "interwoven" into the parable to such an extent that one becomes involved. Since the parable is not an allegory, one's assessment of one's situation is not directly present, but is only refracted in the parable. Hence caution is in order in drawing inferences from the parable about one's situation or in identifying traits or personages of the parable with "equivalents" in one's situation. The parable addresses the hearer's situation as something comparable to, though distinct from, the parable's own story.

[23]Cf. *The New Hermeneutic,* ed. by James M. Robinson and John B. Cobb, Jr., New Frontiers in Theology, Vol. 2 (Harper & Row, 1964), p. 57, for the details of the development.

Bultmann had laid the groundwork for the new advance, in his understanding of futurity as possibility. In view of the irreversibility of time, the past is immutably fixed, even though the understanding of the past is an ongoing process where the past continues to act in ever-changing ways, in which sense one can say that even the past has a future. On the other hand, the future is not immutably fixed, but is open; it is not a given, to that extent not yet reality, but is contingent, full of possibilities. The future impinges on the present as such possibilities, which the present transforms into reality or discards into unreality in choosing among them. Even the past can have such futurity impinging upon the present, in that the past provides possibilities for understanding existence and thus offers a future that can by decision be actualized. It is in this sense that Bultmann, while regarding Christian existence as dehistoricized eschatological existence, can yet regard this existence lived out of the future as consisting constitutively in encounter with Jesus. While being a person of the historical past, Jesus is also an eschatological figure opening up a future as a possibility actualizable in present decision.

It was Ernst Fuchs who developed this Bultmannian interpretation of the future, as the dimension of possible understandings of existence, into an understanding of language as the possible, which grants reality truth.

> Language helps reality to its truth. In faith's view it is the possible that helps the real [come] linguistically to its truth and thus expresses itself as itself, i.e. as what is becoming.[24]

For reality is not meaningless, not a conglomerate of brute facts. Rather, reality is caught in a web of possible meanings, given with the cultural configuration in which it is experienced as real. Reality can receive new meaning as the language world in terms of which it is experienced changes. Thus, just as Bultmann understood the future as the dimension of possibilities from which one's present reality is derived by the decision constituting one's existence, just so Fuchs understands these possibilities as various language worlds, which, from anything other than a purely relativistic point of view, cannot be all equally valid (or, ultimately, equally meaningless). To be sure, the criterion as to which possibility is the truth of

---

[24]Ernst Fuchs, *Hermeneutik* (Bad Cannstadt: R. Müllerschön, 1954), p. 211.

reality is no longer formulated simply in terms of man's being ("existence"), with the definition of authentic and inauthentic derived from existentialism; rather, evaluation is in terms of the fact that language itself is hermeneutical, called forth to reach understanding and agreement, is itself the medium of rapport and mutual participation, hence in its true nature the language of love. On this basis, true language is the proper being of reality; that is to say, true language is the way in which reality should be. Ultimately, reality is admitted into its truth by the language of love. Of course language is historic, sharing in the finitude of man and the ambiguity of his existence; hence, reality is always in varying degrees distorted or depersonalized, which becomes evident in the current technological depersonalizing of man. But something more wholesome can also happen in language, as it is called forth by a differing world (not to be confused with otherworldliness) and grants reality a new being, in which its true nature as love becomes audible. It is this language event which is both the saving event and God's word—God's happening and God happening.

In this way, Fuchs modulated Bultmann's understanding of the future as the dimension of possibilities impinging upon the present (with the eschatological future presenting the possibility of authentic existence), into language as reality's possibility, with the language of love as reality's true possibility. Bultmann had already interpreted the nearness of the Kingdom nonchronologically as the inescapability of the ultimate. Indeed, the otherwise conflicting sayings of Jesus about there being signs and not being signs before the end converge when one recognizes that all confront the hearer inescapably with God now, in the encounter with Jesus' word.[25] Thus the understanding of language as that which presents the possibilities from which reality is actualized identifies in Jesus' language itself the locus of God's reign—not in the present as a reality, nor as an apocalyptic reality near or far, but as the structuring of reality that reveals it as immediate to God, God's "creation." God's reign is not the Establishment, but its truth to which it is to be reformed. Nor is God's reign some mythical reality, but rather the truth of real reality. Put still more abstractly, God's reign is the true being of all that is, all the beings' true "world." It is Jesus'

[25]Cf. Conzelmann, *ZTK*, LIV (1957), 287f.

language that gave reality that orientation; it is in his language that God's reign is inescapable, as invitation and challenge, grace and judgment. Between the presumption of the Establishment that identifies reality with God and the fanaticism of otherworldliness that separates reality from God—the Scylla and Charybdis between which the chronological debates about the nearness of the Kingdom oscillated—lies the event of Jesus' language in which God's reign happens as reality's true possibility. /

Language thus serves to mark what Heidegger abstractly called the ontological difference, the distinction but not separation between things and the orientation they have, between things and their being. He reproached the West for the forgetfulness of being in that various beings had been taken for being itself, with the result that one was not even aware of what had been lost from sight, namely, being itself. There is the same structural problem with regard to the possible and the real, the future and the present. The possible is not to be simply identified with the real, even when one possibility has been actualized and thus becomes reality. For the reality thus actualized is not irrevocably the actualization of that possibility, but, as a given, can be cast in quite another dimension by language that obscures its original possibility. That possibility, if wholly identified with its actualization, loses the contingency of freedom and thus the constitutive characteristic of the possible. Similarly, the future presents itself for decision and thus calls forth the present, only to become fixed as past and lose the structure of futurity. This is why, from a purely formal point of view, the Establishment is not eschatological existence, why idolatry is the built-in proclivity of *homo religiosus*.

The parable is singularly suited to mark this "ontological" difference distinguishing worship from idolatry, and hence to serve as a model for the new understanding of language with respect to Jesus' teaching. For the parable, rooted in the comparison, speaks a language that cannot be simply merged with the reality whose truth it is intended to make audible; accordingly the possibility proposed by language cannot be simply identified with and hence obscured by that reality. In a true comparison the retention of the analogous language preserves distinction while preventing separation. God's reign is analogous to the situation with regard to a fisherman's net, but the Kingdom of God is not to be identified with the visible church.

The advantage of parabolic language over mythological language is much like its advantage over allegory. Myth, like allegory, identifies rather than compares, and hence invites, especially in a post-mythopoetic age such as ours, an absolutizing of the symbol rather than its relativizing (cf. Tillich's "Protestant principle"), or a rejecting of the myth because it is identified with the no longer real medium into which it objectifies its meaning. The parable has a further advantage over the myth: It stays within the dimensions of the personal, instead of undergoing the myth's *metabasis eis allo genos* inherent in the expressing of personal meaning in cosmic objectifications. Although the parable includes nature in its scope, it is the nature involved in man's history—his crops and fields, his fishing—whereas the pseudoscientific speculations of myth interpret man's history in quite different, often cosmic categories. Both have to be decoded, but the myth has in addition to be transposed if indeed it intends the same concreteness as does the parable. Nowhere is the union of form and matter with regard to Jesus' parables more evident and more important than in the analogy between the down-to-earth dimensions of the stories and the concrete involvement they intend. There is no doubt also a converging of form and matter with regard to myth, in that it flourishes most where its message has to do with speculations distant from concrete involvement, as in Gnosticism. Both language forms are preconceptual, pictorial, primal, poetic; but of the two, it is the parable that has the grit and pith, the ruggedness of what Jesus had to say.

BLEND INTO THE ROCK!
Back! Into the Stone
Whence you were hewn
Resume its grain—
Granite-rough, rugged!
Stand Steadfast in the Stone!
—*Ernest Cadman Colwell*

INDEX OF AUTHORS

Index of Authors

Index of Authors

INDEX OF REFERENCES
TO BIBLICAL, RABBINICAL,
AND EARLY CHRISTIAN LITERATURE